The Nature of the Journey

A Trail Guide for Companioning Your Person on the End-of-Life Journey

TRACY L. CHALMERS

Pownal Street Press
Charlottetown

pownal street press

www.pownalstreetpress.com

www.endwell.ca

Cataloging data available from Library and Archives Canada · ISBN 978-1-998129-44-7 · E-book ISBN 978-1-998129-50-8

Edited by Mo Duffy · Copyedited by Alison Strumberger · Designed by Jordan Beaulieu · Type set in Garamond

Pownal Street Press gratefully acknowledges Mi'kma'ki, the ancestral and unceded territory of the Mi'kmaq First Nation on whose land our office is located.

Printed and bound in Canada by Friesens.

1 2 3 4 5 25 26 27 28 29

I am deeply grateful to those who have welcomed me on their journeys.
You have given me armfuls of insights—you have been my greatest teachers.
I am honoured to hold your love stories of life, death, and grief—
wisdom about the nature of the journey.

—*T.L.C.*

Table of Contents

Author's Note

When I was in Grade 5, my best friend's brother died of leukemia. And while death came so close, my world and my homelife with my parents and two brothers was strangely unchanged. I went to school the next day and continued with my activities without missing a beat. There was no talk of death or the fallout of grief, he just vanished. This distancing—this lack of knowing—left me to imagine what had happened. Where was he now? Was he okay? Were his parents okay, and moreover, were *we* okay? I held my grief in secret; the door of my room closed, surrounded by red and white heart-patterned wallpaper. This combination of fear, vulnerability, and unwitnessed grief created a storm of confusion in ten-year-old me—a storm that lasted over a decade.

Just before I turned 20, I volunteered at the local hospital. During my first shift, I was assigned to work in the palliative care ward. I was terrified. My job was to push a rattling cart down the hospital hallways and refresh the water in the patients' flower vases and discard the rotting bouquets. I was surprised with what I discovered. Those rooms, spaces that I had imagined being full of horrible things—unbearable sights, sounds, and smells—were almost always filled with tender moments; expressions of love, forgiveness, and gratitude; sacred silence, hands nestled in hands, and hearts broken open. There was a softening and a falling away of the stuff that doesn't matter, and a revelation of the stuff that does—the relationships of the patients with those closest to them. The limitation of time seemed to cause priorities to present themselves allowing what mattered most to rise to the surface. Surpassingly, these rooms were full of different expressions of giving and receiving love.

From that moment, I became dedicated to helping others understand the nature of gentle dying, and the beauty and healing that so often exists alongside the loss and pain at the end of life. Offering a more balanced narrative, one that is more rooted in love than in fear, has been the guiding force behind all that I do.

How to Use This Guide

This guide is about how to show up for your person within the context of your one-of-a-kind relationship. With death on the horizon, increased presence will support you and your person. Surrendering to the guidance of your tender heart will keep you on course as you follow the lead of your person in the wilderness of their dying time. The heart has wisdom that the mind cannot always understand. Inviting your person to find connection, awareness, meaning, pleasure, and presence will support them to travel a little lighter.

TRAIL KEY

Expected Changes on the End-of-Life Journey

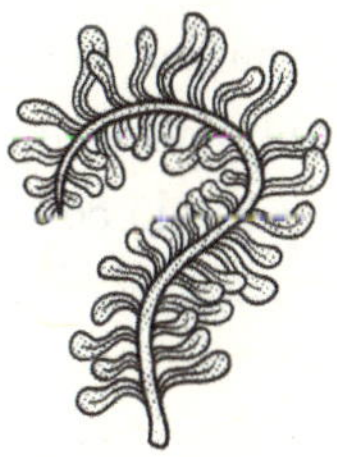

I Wonder . . .

CAMPP: A Sensory invitation for Connection, Awareness, Meaning, Pleasure, and Presence

Grounding Practices for Companions

Stories from the Trail

Why a Trail Guide?

This book is written as a trail guide for the end-of-life journey. It helps you become familiar with the terrain and invites you to support your person along the way. Many of the physical, psychological, social, and spiritual changes you may encounter are marked, much like the bright trail markers nailed to the trees, helping you stay present, less surprised, and more prepared.

Along the way you will find invitations for sensory connection for you and your person, as well as nature-based rituals to nourish and sustain you both as you journey. Serving well asks you to slow down, tune in, and listen with your whole self.

Being trusted to walk alongside someone on their end-of-life journey also brings us closer to this great mystery. It offers insight into the nature of the journey by familiarizing us with the route. The terrain is often rough, and most of the time—with the extended dying that we see more frequently today—death comes after a series of losses. By sharing stories of those who have already travelled this path, the signposts and suggestions in this guide are intended to provide comfort and connection as you make your way.

> "The universe is made of stories, not of atoms."
>
> —Muriel Rukeyser

STORIES FROM THE TRAIL

My friend, Linda

Being well in any relationship starts with listening. When we listen with our whole selves, we step into presence. From this place of presence, it becomes effortless to honour others and ourselves, naturally. When we listen to understand, and offer the most fitting compassionate action, we can skillfully companion each other in life and in death. We do this by softening, by being as open as we can in any given moment to giving and receiving love, whatever form it takes within our unique relationships.

This is not always easy to do. Our hearts are not designed to be open and tender all of the time, but having an awareness of your heart sense—you can start by simply placing a hand on your chest—will serve you well. This guide is about how to companion your person wisely and wholeheartedly on the end-of-life journey.

This book was inspired by own dear friend, Linda. Let me tell you about her.

Linda and I have taken turns guiding each other over the years. She was a rational thinker, wired to find logical sequencing, analyzing everything. She was a born engineer. Linda lived from the left side of her brain—very different from the right side, which I inhabit most of the time. My approach to life is more creative and intuitive. Despite our differences, or perhaps because of them, we deeply admired and trusted each other, and we enjoyed a blossoming, harmonious friendship founded on respect.

Linda suggested I write this guide. She felt so strongly that I share what I have learned from companioning the dying. She began calling herself my book coach and led me from the birth of this project all the way through to the last chapter. The project then came to a halt just before I wrote the final chapter because Linda died. The story of her dying time became the last chapter—a different ending than the one we'd anticipated. When she first suggested I write this guide, Linda was in her early fifties, vibrant and full of life.

Linda and I first met when she generously offered her project management superpowers to lead myself and a handful of others to create some policy around the emerging role of end-of-life doula. She was drawn to this project because she had just published her first book to support Canadians in estate planning. Her book was an act of service, fuelled by the desire to help more Canadians understand the importance of having a will.

Linda helped us write the scope of practice and the body of knowledge for the role of end-of-life doula, which was just at its infancy as an emerging role in health care. She encouraged us to come up with a metaphor for the role, and together we decided that the most fitting archetype was that of a guide. Doulas are familiar with the end-of-life journey. They come alongside the dying and their people to offer practical, emotional, and spiritual support. With Linda's support we created the foundation for the End-of-Life Doula Association of Canada. Looking back, the beginning of our friendship was serendipitous, since Linda and I would go on to guide each other on various journeys in the years to follow.

Initially, I considered Linda as my smartest friend. She had more letters after her name than *in* her name and her career successes were endless. However, over the course of our friendship I began to think of her the most considerate person I have known. Linda was a beloved partner, sister, aunt, friend, neighbour, and mentor. She regularly gave away her books on estate planning with the hope that they would help others.

Our friendship deepened during the pandemic. One day I received a call from Linda; she was sobbing as she revealed that her younger brother had just received a life-limiting diagnosis. He lived across the country with his wife and two young children. He began treatments as the family struggled to keep up with all the changes. Desperate to connect with her brother, Linda asked me to help his family navigate this challenging time, and I agreed to serve as his virtual doula. When Linda reached out to her brother to offer my services, however, he declined. His response brought Linda to her knees: "I don't need a doula. I need a sister."

My friend was in crisis. Linda didn't know where to start. How could she show up for him? Linda was someone who knew so much about so many things, yet at this precious intersection of life and death, she found herself at the trailhead with no map, not sure what to bring, and terrified about where she was going. It was time for Linda to step up and to trust. Taking her brother's lead, we worked together to prepare for the journey to companion her sibling.

Due to the COVID-19 restrictions at the time, Linda was unable to travel across the country to be with her brother, so we focused on how she could offer support from a distance. We discussed the waypoints on the end-of-life journey—common physical, emotional, spiritual, and social changes that are expected—and soon, Linda learned what to know, what to expect, and how to show up for him as his disease progressed.

This clarity was comforting to Linda, and it enabled her to be more present with her brother, allowing her to meet him in the moments with more intention. Less than a year later, Linda's brother died at home.

Linda wisely took time to tend to her broken heart. We met weekly to discuss her journey with her brother, the heartache of losing him, and the deep healing and comfort that came with knowing she companioned him right up until the end. She was grateful for her experience and felt so strongly that everyone should be equipped with simple strategies for creating connection on the end-of-life journey, which inspired us to begin envisioning this trail guide. We met at her home regularly over the next two years, with her partner, their cats, and their dog coming in and out of the living room. Linda served the best coffee, or soup, or popcorn, and occasionally gave me goodie bags to take home to my boys. Her generosity was always overflowing.

A few months into the book project, Linda revealed to me that she too was living with a life-limiting illness. The news shocked me—she was young and healthy. She loved her whiteboard and spreadsheets and was an expert problem-solver, so it was fitting that she applied her pragmatic organizational skills to her health predicament. I have often wondered if the motivation for her to help me with this project was twofold—to encourage others to demystify normal dying for the benefit of others on the journey, and for her to access doula support in a way that was comfortable for her, with her taking the lead as project manager.

At the beginning of writing this book Linda sent me logical and detail-oriented prompts. Her engineering brain craved information. Her desire to understand the end-of-life journey instigated writing prompts such as "Why do we die?" and "Who has escaped death?"—questions that were overwhelming for me to even begin to answer. I now understand that they reflected her yearning and searching for answers and understanding as she faced her own death. After I became aware of her diagnosis, our weekly sessions were complex to navigate. I was constantly checking in to make sure that I was sharing information in an appropriate manner, and sensitive to her placement of being on the journey. Perhaps her way of being in the world, thriving in the realm of data and commanding this book project, was the most fitting way for her to be supported in her dying.

Linda did not want to die. She fought hard and she did all that she could to stay alive. She pursued chemotherapy, radiation, and surgery. She would often call the hospital and demand that her appointments be fast tracked. She assembled a team of specialists to support her in finding a solution to her death. She hired a nutritionist to create a customized diet and a researcher to look into cutting edge treatment strategies for her disease, and she pursued experimental clinical trial opportunities. Her efforts were valiant, but her health continued to deteriorate, and her imminent death became an unavoidable reality.

In the last few months of her life Linda continued to guide me not only in the writing of this book, but also into the actual wilderness. As I companioned her on her end-of-life journey, she literally set the course to help me find my way through the wilderness for an upcoming hiking trip. A longtime friend and I had planned to hike the West Coast Trail, a wild week-long adventure along the rugged west coast of Vancouver Island. Being a tech gadget junkie, Linda was excited to let me borrow her Garmin device. Her engineer brain was fuelled by clear and specific directions. She enthusiastically programmed the waypoints on the digital map to help orient us on our journey. This handheld GPS allowed us to navigate to our campsites each day and send texts to our people by way of satellites.

Linda had always hoped to do the West Coast Trail but at this point it was clear that she would never get the chance. One sunny autumn afternoon on the trail, my friend and I stared out at the Pacific Ocean and felt inspired to honour our friend. In silence, we wrote Linda's name in the sand just below the tideline. We framed her name with an enormous heart made of bull kelp. We knew that her time was nearing the end and this act symbolized that Linda was with us on our journey in spirit. Over the next six days, from her home, Linda kept track of us as we found our way along the gnarly coastline. It was an incredible adventure.

When we returned, I did my best to do the same for Linda. Just as she had marked waypoints to orient us on our hike, I highlighted the expected landmarks of the end-of-life journey as her health continued to decline. These trail markers served to reassure Linda that she was on course. She wanted to know the purpose for interventions and the details of what was going to happen. Feeling validated and understood made it a little easier for her to keep up with the losses as they rolled in.

I supported her partner, family, and friends by sharing much of the ideas I will share in this guide. I invited them to dream into creative ways to support Linda to find connection, awareness, meaning, pleasure, and presence. I explained how this companionship would hold Linda, how it would support her; it would safeguard her from feeling lost and alone in the wilderness of her dying.

Bodyfulness

This guide will highlight opportunities that have the potential to create moments of connection, awareness, meaning, pleasure, and presence. The senses are portals to the present moment. The here-and-now is void of the regret of the past or the worry of the future. Our senses serve as gateways to being fully present in our bodies and thereby to experience bodyfulness, the embodied version of mindfulness.

As a result of our personal life experiences, we each have a unique relationship to our body. For some, the idea of bodyfulness may be accepted without question; for others it may be confusing. Our relationships to our bodies are influenced by cultural factors and personal experiences. If the idea of being more present in your body brings discomfort, you are not alone. Start where you are, even if it is just with a little bit more awareness. Honour what feels right to you.

Through the body, life is available to us all, right up until the last moment. This book celebrates how life simply unfolds when we are truly in the moment, which we can achieve by being in a close relationship with the world through the senses.

> "You are here.
> Be where your feet are."
>
> —Unkown

Agency

This guide is written to honour the autonomy of your person. Gently guiding your person to bring attention to their senses can encourage an authentic experience, welcoming what is true in the moment. It is so important to meet your person where they are, allowing them to engage or not, and offering open suggestions—all is welcome, and everything as an invitation.

> "If I'm going to die, the best way to prepare
> Is to quiet my mind and open my heart.
> If I'm going to live, the best way to prepare
> Is to quiet my mind and open my heart."
>
> —Ram Dass

Part One: The Inner Landscape

Introduction

The basis of this guide is simple. It is about sharing maps of the end-of-life journey and wondering together about the mystery inherent in dying. It invites you to slow down and listen to your person. Really listen. It is a reminder to follow their lead and consider the senses as inspiration to offer invitations that inspire connection, awareness, meaning, pleasure, and presence (CAMPP). A life-limiting diagnosis often creates an artificial separation between the world of those living and the world of those dying. This isolation from life and from others makes dying difficult. This guide is written to reduce this separation through supporting connection.

At some point in our lives, most of us will experience an extended dying process, a side effect of modern medical advancements. This anticipated dying is very different from sudden death. With a life-limiting diagnosis there is a gradual loss of bodily function that ends, in time, with death. As organs gradually fail, there is often a long period of time in which you will journey together with others. During this time, we can look to sight, smell, taste, touch, and hearing and find opportunities to create CAMPP.

Sensory experiences are always immediate, as opposed to experiences that require story-based thinking. Stories can entangle us with the past or future, removing us from the here and now; however, when we attend to the senses, we begin to live in the present moment, which helps us focus on life and leads us to the direct experience of being alive. Focusing on life is the foundation of palliative care.

In this guide, we will take a deeper look at the nature of the end-of-life journey as we explore how to show up for your person. May what follows on these pages support you to feel resourced so that you feel prepared in your role as companion.

Why "Your Person"

In this guide, "your person" is used when referring to the dying, as opposed to the commonly used term "loved one." This term recognizes the varying degrees of intimacy in relationships. Human connections are complicated, and attachment, trust, and the ways in which care is offered vary. These qualities impact how you will companion the dying, and this guide recognizes that "showing up" looks different for everybody.

As you read through these pages, take the information that feels supportive to you and your situation and simply skip the sections that do not apply. Honouring your unique relationship and boundaries by being clear about what is okay with you and what is not okay with you is essential to care for yourself and your person appropriately.

This guide has been written with the caregiver in mind. Companioning the dying can be overwhelming, and the experience of loss impacts cognitive functioning, which can make reading challenging. The trail notes used throughout this guide take into consideration this decreased capacity for attention. In these sections you will find trail markers highlighting expected physical, emotional, social, and spiritual changes that are common on the end-of-life journey. These sign-posts will serve to reassure you that what you are experiencing is normal and expected. You will also find trail notes to support you in the role as companion. These heart connection practices are sensory based embodiment practices that invite you to connect with your body—the place where your head and the heart meet. There are also boxes for sensory invitations to inspire CAMPP with your person. Stories about the nature of the journey will also be shared—with the hopes that they inspire you to look to the senses as gateways for compassionate action. Lastly, you will find trail notes that invite you to wonder with prompts; not knowing has been shown to be good for us. In this state of not knowing, curiosity and engagement with the world arise and experiences become intimate and acutely alive.

CAMPP: CONNECTION, AWARENESS, MEANING, PLEASURE, PRESENCE

Camp as refuge: Pausing for connection, awareness, meaning, pleasure, and presence (CAMPP)

If you are someone who enjoys spending time in the outdoors you will likely relate to the idea of camp as a refuge, a place to pause, or somewhere to take in the journey. When we hiked the West Coast Trail, I remember how my body instantly relaxed and a sense of comfort arose as we arrived at camp each night. I recall the feeling of relief after taking off the heavy pack at the end of a strenuous day, the relief of unlacing my hiking boots and slipping my swollen feet out, allowing them to expand and find their full form again, my aching legs and tender shoulders about to get a break. Setting up the tent created a refuge. The warmth of a crackling fire, cozy clothes, the full body satisfaction of resting after a big journey allowed me to take pause, reflect and take in the place, gaze at the stars, smell the ocean, and taste a warm meal. This pause offered the space to reflect on where we had been, where we were in that moment, and where we were headed, a recalibration that led to more awareness of the present.

In this guide, you will see the acronym CAMPP used often. As mentioned earlier, these letters stand for the concepts of connection, awareness, meaning, pleasure, and presence, and they are designed to inspire you and your person to create sensorial experiences. They are also offered to you, the companion, as a little respite along the journey—a little pause and stop and catch your breath, to notice life that is still available, and to nudge you to make the most of your moments. Supporting engagement in this way increases wellbeing by focusing on life that is here and now. Taking opportunities to intentionally offer your person moments of pause and inviting them to become present will deliver them to their lives that are right here, right now.

Connection

Creating connection has been shown to allow those on the end-of-life journey to travel with more ease. The illusion of separation makes life, including death, harder than it needs to be. From the moment we're born, we begin to experience separation, and with it, the longing for comfort, reassurance, and belonging. When we engage in sensory experiences with intention, we find the opportunity to come into presence with what is real and we begin to reconnect. This sense of connection helps to ease fear and soften the experience of dying. Whether it's through nurturing relationships, cultural or spiritual beliefs, time in nature, or the power of music, connection reminds us that we are not alone. Nature especially offers a mirror of our belonging, providing what we need to survive and gently guiding us back to the truth—that we are part of everything. In this remembering, the journey becomes more bearable, more meaningful, and more whole.

Awareness

Awareness is the first act of love. It begins with the courage to truly see—this person, this moment, and yourself—as they are, without the filter of desires, memories, or assumptions. While it can feel simpler to rush into helping, to act before witnessing, awareness asks something deeper of us—it asks us to pause and look with clear, compassionate eyes.

When you companion your person at the end of life, awareness means noticing the subtle language of their body, the unspoken needs, the tender shifts in energy and emotion. It also means observing your own heart—your hopes, fears, impulses to fix or control—and naming them honestly. In doing so, you create a space where love can take root, free of self-seeking and pretence.

This kind of presence is not passive. It is alive, responsive, and sometimes uncomfortable. Awareness will draw you forward into action when it is needed and restrain you when stepping back is the kinder approach. It may soften you into gentleness or call you to be firm and clear. It dissolves the hard shell around the heart so that your care becomes attuned rather than habitual.

To be aware is to let the present moment enter your senses and touch your heart. It is to witness suffering, beauty, and all that arises without clinging or turning away. From this place, love, freedom, and serenity emerge, not because you strive to create them, but because you have met reality with your full attention. In awareness, your vision becomes clear and your heart-wisdom facilitates connection. This is the quiet power that allows you to companion another with dignity, humility, and grace.

Meaning

Meaning in life is an essential psychological need, and at the end of life, it often rises gently to the surface. As companions, we can support this by offering simple sensory invitations, like playing a familiar song, feeling a moment of sunlight on the face, or tasting a favourite food. The senses can awaken memories, evoke stories, and reconnect a person to what has mattered most. In this way, meaning is not forced but gently revealed, since it is already woven through a life lived. When we invite sensory engagement, we help the dying remember who they are, what they've loved, and how deeply they've belonged. This can offer comfort, deepen connection, and bring a quiet sense of wellbeing as the journey nears its close.

Pleasure

Pleasure has a sacred place on the end-of-life journey. A warm blanket, the scent of cookies in the oven, the sound of waves—these simple sensory moments can spark comfort, connection, and even joy. Why not invite more of that in, just because? When we slow down and become curious about our bodies, we begin to trust the quiet messages that surface from within. By tuning in to what feels good, what soothes or stirs, the opportunity to honour life's sweetness arises, even as it nears its end.

Presence

Our senses are portals into the present moment, anchoring us in the life that is happening now. Though it may sound abstract, it is very real. What do you see, hear, feel, smell, or taste in this very moment? When we pause and gently direct our attention to the body, we are immediately rooted in the now, without the regret of the past or the worry of the future. As companions to the dying, inviting this kind of sensory awareness—through breath, touch, sound, taste, or scent—can open a gateway to presence.

Chapter 1

You Are Here

Dear Reader,

You are here. This placement is often marked by a big colourful star on the map, allowing you to see where you have been and where you are headed. Because our dominant culture does not support engagement with dying very well, the end-of-life journey is often a place where so many feel alone and unequipped even though it is a place most people will eventually find themselves. If you feel as though you have not planned or prepared enough to be on this adventure, you are not alone.

This journey you are companioning your person on will likely be full of surprises. The maps available are a best guess but your person's route will unfold step by step. It may be steep and gnarly or flat and long. The trail may have unexpected twists and turns, weather may kick up, signposts may disappear. Despite the maps we have, the journey is wild and it is impossible to anticipate exactly what lies ahead.

At times you will likely feel overwhelmed and unsure of where you are. There may be days when it seems like you can't even feel the ground beneath you, a sense of being swept away by uncertainty and change. Wherever you find yourself, know that you are not alone. This is the nature of the journey.

Don't forget to look up—doing so may remind you that you are as vast and open as the sky. Feeling the sun on your face may help you remember that your heart is as naturally warm. Perhaps noticing nature inside and out will support you in remembering that you belong and you are enough.

I hope this guide will support you on your way, and that these maps and signposts offer reassurance. As on any trek, it is important to support yourself in ways that are right for you. I will remind you often to check in with your dear body and listen to what it is asking for so it can be nourished and carry you as far as your person goes. I have included some invitations to offer your person along the way, to keep the focus on CAMPP. This will likely sustain you both.

I have been honoured to travel this journey with many and I am holding their stories with reverence. I am sharing some of these stories with you in the hopes that you can find inspiration and understanding and become a little more familiar with the terrain. May these stories reassure you that you are not alone, and that whatever you are experiencing is normal—maybe you will see things in a different way. May you feel more trust as you follow the lead of your heart, and may these stories help you to stop and notice the changes around you.

This guide is based on the understanding that we need each other. Your ability to companion your person will be sustainable if you remember that we are designed to live and die with the help of others. Once you can lean out for support, you will be more aware that you already have what it takes to companion your person. You may need many reminders of this… I will suggest you pause on the trail, take a seat under the shade of a tree, and just breathe. I wonder what you will notice? What your heart will reveal?

So here you are here, two human beings on the edge of the mystery, opening to your truth together.

Wishing you heart-centered travels,
Tracy

What Complicates End of Life?

This chapter serves as the big star on the trail map that orients you, the traveller, to their placement in relation to the trails that lie ahead. We will explore where we are and how we got here, where the end-of-life journey can seem like a complicated place. We will also consider how to die well, and what it means to be a companion for the dying.

So here you are, reacquainting yourself with all of life, which includes death, so that you can show up for your person on their end-of-life journey. Getting to know death by scouting the trails in advance also supports you in your own dying time, however far down the track that may be.

The stories I share in this book come through the lens of this over culture and are woven with privilege. I live in an affluent city in a developed country, where most folks can access supportive palliative care that addresses physical, social, emotional, and spiritual needs. As wonderful as this sounds, this care is manufactured, offered by (almost always) deeply caring trained professionals who work in institutions that are run in the private sector This care is not equitably distributed. Affluent communities have more, and where I live the hospice is a newer standalone building with a lush garden. Residents are cared for by many who tenderly offer comfort by way of music, delicious food, yoga, meditation, peer walking groups, and choirs. Just a short drive away you will find areas where social determinants of health such as income and race, and systemic inequalities restrict access to health care, and it can even be challenging for many to afford nutritional food to sustain good health.

Culturally, we were better acquainted with dying in the past. Knowledge of death was held by the people, and it was transmitted from one generation to the next. The cultural aversion to death that we face today was not a barrier, and there was no college course or book to buy to learn about death. We had a healthier relationship to dying—it happened in the home and was familiar. We understood the journey and we knew how to offer comfort and care. Because we knew death, it wasn't as scary as it is today. The cultures that continue to support this intimacy with death often embrace death as part of life; they are cultures that are rich with rituals that carry the dying and their caregivers when the end is in sight. Death is a community affair that honours that we need each other.

In this industrialized culture, however, we have come very far away from this intimacy with end of life. We are constantly being guided away from the fundamental truth of life—that all living beings die. Death continues to be something to be avoided, a sign of failure, or something that happens when things have gone wrong. Our dominant culture holds progress, growth, and eternal youth as its ideals, and it does not accept loss as having a purpose. A person's natural decline is seen as something to "solve" and great effort is made to avoid the ultimatums of aging and death.

We distance ourselves so much from the inevitable, that even when death arrives on our doorstep, the most common cultural response is to rush through the discomfort—so everyone can return to normal as quickly as possible.

An army of forces consistently reinforce the message that it is best to avoid death. From the medicalization of death that tucks our dying people away from us behind closed doors, to our death-phobic culture that has distanced us from the dying, to the media that distorts the narratives about what dying looks like, it is no wonder that death has become more complicated than it needs to be. In addition, we are a secular society that lacks much of the meaning-making, support, guidance, and community that Indigenous cultures and traditional organized religion once offered. When communities are reminded of the nature of dying and are inspired to care for those on the end-of-life journey, the forces that influence the mainstream dysfunctional relationship with death are quelled.

Healthcare hasn't always played the leading role in dying, as it does today. In the past, when dying happened within the context of the home, and people were cared for by families, the culture of death was less charged. Even as we have benefitted from advancements in modern medicine at the end of life, the interventions are often excessive and driven by a focus on the quantity of time over the quality. Additionally, medical involvement usually replaces the care from those closest to the dying. The roles of families and communities have largely receded as death and dying have become unfamiliar facets of life. Today, with the buckling healthcare system, families and friends are being called to provide most of the support as death nears. Those closest to the dying are thereby finding themselves in unfamiliar roles, often at a time when grief is heightened, which results in a sense of unpreparedness and overwhelm.

In the past, when people were more familiar with the changes that occur physically, emotionally, and spiritually, folks would learn how to care for and provide comfort to their dying. As little as two generations ago it was normal for most children to have seen a dead body, while today death tends to happen behind closed doors, most often in institutions such as hospitals, hospices, long-term care facilities or nursing homes, outsourced by paid workers. We have lost valuable wisdom about how to show up for each other at the end of life. When care is outsourced, it is common for those on the receiving end to feel like a burden. Those on the end-of-life journey often lose social roles when placed in strange environments, leading to an increased feeling of isolation and even a sense of being dehumanized.

Modern-Day Death

Many hold a "doctor knows best" attitude, so people don't always feel empowered to ask for what they need. Information empowers individuals, so ask any questions that will support you to step in and show up. What do you want to know?

Dr. Kathryn Mannix, a palliative care physician and author of *With the End in Mind*, draws an intriguing comparison between birth and death. She states that in pregnancy, we know the nine-month period ends in an anticipated outcome of birth. Watching someone die is similar; there are progressive stages that people pass through when they die naturally with little intervention. Mannix asserts that normal birth is likely more uncomfortable than normal dying, and yet people tend to associate dying with pain and indignity which, in her opinion, is rarely the case. Mannix believes that when we are truthful and share information about the process of dying with others—simple things about what is to be expected—it allows everyone involved to hold a little less fear and settle into the experience.

The development of this "modern-day death" is partially due to our increasingly secular society. While many still find guidance in established spiritual traditions that have long helped us make sense of death, the way we navigate the end-of-life journey today has shifted. Traditional organized religions guided us with knowledge about how to die. Religion provided end-of-life care, community, rituals, and ceremony for the dying. Without this support, the dying and their families are left to navigate death alone, without supportive rites of passage. There is a trend toward personalizing dying by creating universal rituals to navigate the end-of-life journey, but many are left untethered, lacking meaning-making and maps on how to proceed on an inner level in a way that acknowledges the emotional and spiritual changes inherent in dying.

Today, dominant culture is fast paced. This skipping-along-the-surface way of being has created a lot of disconnection. Many humans today are distanced from themselves, from each other, and from our naturalized way of being. Many people today live without a sense of their placement in community. This is a big shift from our recent past, when people were much more connected, often staying in the same town and even living with multiple generations in the same home. With neighbours to lean on, people gathered often and took care of each other in life and in death. Humans, like all living beings, were never designed to live in isolation. Many of our relationships are merely acquaintances. We have connected to technology and distanced ourselves from each other. Modern-day culture places a lot of worth on self-reliance, being praised for our resilience, independence, and individualism; however, dying is a social event. Dying calls for collectivism, leaning out on each other—being held in a web of support makes dying less hard.

Folks often say that we live in a death-denying culture. That may sound fairly accurate, however Stephen Jenkinson, a farmer, activist, teacher, musician, and author, disagrees. He suggests that to deny something, we must engage with it long enough to choose not to interact. Jenkinson asserts that our modern-day culture does not engage with death. He calls it instead a death-phobic culture, where the dominant culture is so terrified of dying that we turn our backs and run in the opposite direction. This phobia magnifies fear, which causes unnecessary suffering for everyone. Jenkinson goes on to say that it would benefit us greatly if we befriended death, if we welcomed it in. I wonder what it would feel like to get familiar with death. I wonder how dying would be different if we asked what it is that death is here to teach us, before it comes and knocks on our door.

This guide has been written for you—family, friends, and community members—to feel prepared and supported in the role of companion to the dying. It acknowledges your placement as the most important member of the palliative care team. It's time to shift from complete reliance on the buckling systems, professionals, and protocols of individualism to the support of family, friends, and community members. We are all being called to reconnect fully with the human experience, to seek understanding of what natural dying looks like and to develop the language to talk about death. With this information the confidence to support our dying naturally arises. These simple interventions to walk alongside and to find moments of CAMPP have the potential to empower those who feel called to support their people by focusing on life that is here until the moment it is not. This is a place to start.

Navigate the end-of-life journey with more ease

It can be helpful to understand what it takes to make one's way with ease in advance of your travels, as you consider companioning your person and preparing for your own end-of-life journey when the time comes. Here are some considerations to support you to travel with more comfort.

This concept is deeply personal and complex. A person's worldview, including cultural, spiritual, and personal beliefs, shapes how they will meet death. But at its heart, dying well is about living well. It reminds us that death is not separate from life; it is part of it. When we tend to the quality of our living, we naturally contribute to the quality of our dying. For the most part, people die as they have lived. This is not a fatalistic view; there is always room for change and healing, even up to the final breath. But death comes when it comes.

As a companion, it's important to understand this. Your role will be more difficult if you carry the burden of unrealistic expectations—either for yourself or for the person you're supporting. Death is messy. It involves human beings in all their complexity, entangled in relationships, emotions, regrets, grief, and to-do lists that will never be finished. The notion of a "good death" or "bad death" can be limiting and may cause unnecessary guilt or a sense of failure if the process doesn't unfold perfectly. Let go of perfection. Instead, aim to support a death that is fitting—unique and deeply personal. Dying is a one-size-fits-one experience.

Pack Light

As with any meaningful journey, the end of life is easier when we pack light. If unexamined, a lifetime of grief, regret, or unfinished business can weigh heavily on the heart. Taking time to look back—to acknowledge the whole journey—can be deeply supportive. A life review is a powerful practice. By recalling memories, revisiting love, offering forgiveness, and looking back with a soft gaze, your person may begin to make peace with their life, one memory at a time. In this way, the past is not left behind but gently woven into the present. Reminiscing about joy, facing losses, and speaking regrets aloud can help lighten the emotional load. Forgiveness and self-compassion, especially near the end, can diminish sorrow and make room for the lightness of acceptance.

Forgiveness is life-renewing. It gently closes loops of unfinished business—not by condoning harm, but by softening harm's hold on the heart. With grace, it shines a light on pain, and in doing so, offers freedom. While death will release us from our physical bodies, the inner work of releasing what we've carried—resentment, shame, self-blame—can allow us to travel more lightly. We can put down the heavy burden of self-loathing and, instead, hold gratitude for the people and moments that shaped us. Self-compassion reminds us that we are, and always have been, enough.

Gratitude is a powerful companion. It grounds us in presence and connects us to life energy, even as life begins to fade. When we engage the senses—notice the warmth of a blanket, the beauty of a bird's song, the taste of something sweet—we can awaken gratitude. This helps balance the difficulty that may arise when death is near. Gratitude is a practice and a choice. It helps us appreciate what is, rather than resist what is not. It turns our gaze toward what matters most and softens our attachment to material things, status, or control. As companions, we can invite others to notice what is still remarkable, still beautiful. In doing so, we align with what is true in us, and true in the nature of the journey itself.

Acceptance

Acceptance of death offers a sense of peace, allowing people to focus on what matters most with the time they have left. But arriving at acceptance is not as simple as it sounds. We all know, intellectually, that we are going to die, though many of us don't all *live* as though we know it. Death competency, defined as a person's ability to identify, explore, and work through one's own death anxiety, influences how we live and directly impacts how we support others in their dying. In a culture that often views death as the ultimate failure, coming to terms with our mortality is a radical act.

After my weekly hospice shift on Mondays, I often call my mom on the drive home. When I walk through the door, I hug my kids and my husband a little tighter. The presence of death—of people nearing the end of their lives—lingers. If I see a sunset, or hear birdsong, I think of the people I visited earlier that day. They may never again experience these simple moments that are so easy to take for granted. This weekly reminder of impermanence is a gift. It inspires me to slow down and be more present in my life. Being with the dying reminds me that I too will die one day, and it nudges me to inhabit the moments more fully.

Reflecting on impermanence can be a gentle and accessible place to begin cultivating death competency. Simply look around. No matter where you are right now, I promise you will see countless examples: the flowers in the vase beginning to wilt, the tear in the couch cover, the rambunctious dog that was a puppy last summer, the night slowly giving way to morning. Everything is changing. Even we are changing—thought by thought, breath by breath. We have around 80,000 thoughts a day that come and go, a powerful reminder of impermanence that suggests that in a way, "the old me" has already died. The cells in our bodies die constantly and every five to seven years we are biologically an entirely new organism. These "small deaths" are powerful teachers. If we can learn to soften around them, they may help us loosen our grip on the bigger fear that surrounds physical death. Because when we come to truly understand that nothing endures but change, we may begin to shift from the dread of dying into the wonder of living.

Practical Planning

Phobias and anxiety around death often prevent people from planning for their own final days. Even those who reach out to me for support with end-of-life planning frequently begin the process, only to tuck the papers away for another day. Planning for difficult scenarios such as incapacity and what you want done with your body after death confirms, in real terms, that you will not always be in control. It asks you to acknowledge, directly, that your death is not just possible, but inevitable. Intellectually, we all know this. Yet somehow, many of us carry on as if it won't happen to us.

It may be helpful for you to think of this practical planning as a process rather than a checklist to be tackled all at once. It's not just paperwork—it's a series of conversations, reflections, and choices. When approached this way, planning becomes a meaningful practice that can help people die well. The process of contemplating what makes your life worth living, identifying your guiding values, and considering your wishes for future care not only offers clarity, but it also makes things less hard on you and your friends and family when the time comes.

Practical planning often begins with simple, everyday conversations. I recall a moment when I was sitting on the couch watching a show with my adult son, and there was a scene set in a long-term care facility. He turned to me and asked what I thought about living in a place like that. That opened a nourishing, spontaneous conversation about life, incapacity, and care; and my beliefs, values, and hopes. It wasn't planned but it was meaningful. That ordinary moment became an opening to reflect on impermanence and to communicate what matters most to me.

Of course, there are formalities too. The legal requirements of end-of-life planning vary depending on where you live, but the core elements are relevant to everyone. Incapacity planning involves appointing people to make decisions on your behalf if you are no longer able to do so. A healthcare representative can speak to your medical care and treatment preferences. An appointed attorney can make legal and financial decisions on your behalf. Creating a will and deciding on a method for disposition (what you want done with your body after death) are the foundational elements of end-of-life planning.

This kind of planning is a gift—to you, to your people, and to your care team. While recording these wishes in writing is best practice it is the conversations about those wishes that matter most. Talk to those closest to you about what makes your life worth living, what values guide your decisions, and your hopes for future care. These conversations may feel daunting, yet more often than not they are deeply life-affirming. They invite connection, offer peace of mind, and bring clarity in uncertain times. A past client of mine even described the process as "fun"—and truly, it can be. These conversations and documents help ensure that your wishes are upheld and that your people will feel supported if ever called to speak or act on your behalf.

Autonomy

Self-determination is often considered a key element of dying well. This involves having control over decisions related to healthcare treatments, the type of end-of-life care one receives, and the preferred place of death—ensuring that a person's core values are recognized right up until the very end. At a time when so much may feel out of one's control, the ability to make these decisions can offer a sense of agency and empowerment.

Today many people have the legal and practical ability to shape how, when, and where they choose to die. Assisted dying is a legal end-of-life option in many countries around the world. In Canada, this practice is referred to as medical assistance in dying, or MAID, and an increasing number of people are choosing to die on their own terms.

However, the value placed on autonomy at the end of life is shaped by culture. While Western cultures often prioritize individual choice and self-determination, this is not a universal perspective. In some cultural traditions, decision making is a collective process with families guiding end-of-life choices on behalf of their people. In such contexts deferring to the wisdom and care of the family can itself be considered an essential part of dying well. We will return to the role of culture in shaping the dying experience in Chapter 9.

Full-Circle Relationships

Completing relationships is a common longing for those on the end-of-life journey. While the idea may feel overwhelming at first, expressions of forgiveness, gratitude, love, and farewell can bring a sense of peace. Later in this guide you will find prompts to help support these conversations, should they feel right. Of course, not every relationship lends itself to this kind of completion, and that's okay. But if one feels called to express what is asking to be said, however difficult, it can be a powerful opportunity for healing. Turning toward gratitude and love in this time can support both the dying and their companions to travel light.

Dying is a social experience. For many, dying well includes being surrounded by others. Companionship can offer comfort, presence, and a sense of meaning. What gives life, including death, its deepest significance is rarely our achievements or possessions, but rather the relationships we hold close.

At the same time, it is important to follow the lead of the dying. Some people become more private or introspective as death nears, while others may long for connection but find themselves isolated due to circumstance. In these cases, it can be helpful create a web of support around them to ease the journey.

Comfort

Of course, comfort is considered as an essential element of dying well, but what does this mean? Comfort is personal. It arises when we attend to the whole person—their physical, emotional, social, and spiritual needs. This is precisely why end-of-life care is best approached as a shared responsibility. A compassionate circle may include including family and friends, medical professionals, spiritual care advisors, and members of the broader community, each playing a role in supporting the emerging needs of the dying person.

Pain at the end of life is not just physical. It has emotional and social components that include experiences of grief, regret, isolation, and estrangement. These invisible burdens can become heavier as the end draws near and carrying them alone can be exhausting. Grief can be lightened by exploring losses and sharing experiences with trusted others who act as witnesses. Regrets, when acknowledged and spoken aloud, may lose their grip. Sometimes, simply being heard is enough to soften what once felt sharp. Attending to this inner terrain is profoundly personal—and essential to the experience of comfort.

For many, dying well also includes spiritual comfort. This might involve religious rituals, prayer, or simply being reminded that there is something greater than the self, something more to being human than a sensory experience. Spiritual support can ease the suffering that arises when people feel burdened by their failures, when they carry unwitnessed grief, fear what lies beyond, or feel disconnected from something larger than themselves.

The relief that spiritual practices can bring is often surprising. For some, comfort is found in faith and practices of a specific religion—prayer, sacred texts, community, rituals, or visits from a spiritual advisor. For others, spiritual grounding comes through meaning-making relationships with people and pets, time in nature, music, or being of service. Reflecting on one's legacy may also offer comfort—a reminder that while the body may not endure, those left behind will be the keepers of one's life story—remembering meaningful moments, perhaps even setting a place at the table for special family gatherings. It can soothe the spirit to know that they will, in some way, remain part of the community after they are gone.

As death approaches, it becomes apparent that the world we move through is made not only of matter, but of heart, mind and spirit. We will explore these dimensions of spirituality in Chapter 10, The Gateway of Wisdom.

I WONDER . . .

What is a somatic practice?

Somatic practices are approaches that focus on the body and its sensations to promote healing and wellbeing. The word "somatic" comes from the Greek word "soma," meaning "body." Somatic practices involve becoming more aware of sensations in the body, as a way to address stress or emotional challenges. By paying attention to how emotions and experiences are held in the body, people can be guided to find balance and healing. I wonder what you are noticing in your body in this moment. Is your body asking for anything? Do you sense tension in your body? Can you bring your awareness to that area and let go a little? Is your body asking for a stretch? A sip of water? Movement? A hug?

STORIES FROM THE TRAIL

Echoes of a life

Recently I supported a woman who was planning to have a medical assistance in dying (MAID) provision. She was 95 years old and ready to die. Her quality of life was deteriorating due to shortness of breath, and even with supplemental oxygen she would tire easily. Simply keeping up with daily tasks left her exhausted and in need of a rest. Even though she was ready to die, she expressed that she had some "inner work" to complete.

We met for a handful of sessions. She shared that she was not religious, so we began by exploring where she found meaning. She naturally began to share memories and revisit the past. During our sessions she would tell stories about her life, starting with her childhood and up until the present. These stories brought up many warm and wonderful memories that would steal her away for a moment or two. She would smile, eyes twinkling, the past brought into the present moment. Grief and regret also surfaced as she reviewed her life. She would pause with a look of concern on her face and then speak. She unpacked some of life's heavier moments. Together we acknowledged them, and then she would move along to the next memory. We did not fixate or pick away at the grief or regrets; instead, when they surfaced, we sat there together as she remembered and they lightened with her awareness. My role was simply as witness.

Often, the most effective intervention for spiritual pain is acknowledging the presence of the suffering with another who can simply listen with empathy. Most of the time, there is no need to fix or help in any way. The medicine is being there completely, offering your whole self—to be completely present and listen, really listen. This requires us to push beyond the natural tendency to turn away or try to avoid, to push down or fix the situation to avoid uncomfortable feelings. This gentle and spacious human-to-human connection allowed her to be relieved of some of the weight from the past and celebrate the people, places, and things that made up the most meaningful moments in her life. We have evolved to need each other—this is how we travel a little lighter.

Honest Communication

As the end-of-life journey unfolds, the inner landscape can shift quickly and often. It's a time marked by uncertainty and vulnerability, both of which can serve as opportunities for deepened intimacy. In the midst of change, communication becomes more that just exchanging words; it becomes a lifeline, a way of staying connected, of making meaning together, and of navigating the unknown together.

A life-limiting diagnosis impacts everyone in the family-and-friend constellation. Because each relationship is unique, honest communication will look different in every situation. Still, doing your best to engage in authentic conversations can deepen connection, offer comfort to the dying person by affirming they are not alone, and help ensure that their preferences are respected. You may feel called to share your own needs, fears, and hopes; to ask questions; or to gently explore what remains uncertain or unsaid.

Slowing down and leading with your heart—especially when things feel tender—can help you both be sincere and clear; do your best to keep the communication open and current by honouring what arises as things change from moment to moment. Honest communication is not about saying things perfectly. Take a breath. Speak as clearly as you can. If your words tumble out awkwardly or don't feel quite right, it's okay to pause, acknowledge that, and begin again. On the end-of-life journey, honest communication isn't a single moment—it is a series of conversations unfolding along the way.

STORIES FROM THE TRAIL

Building community one conversation at a time

Interdisciplinary artist Angela Fama has made it a large part of her life's work to support people to engage in honest conversations about death. She understands first-hand the importance of these courageous conversations. She believes that facing the fear we hold about dying can lead to more connection to ourselves, each other, and all of life. Angela is convinced that having end-of-life discussions benefit those who are willing to participate.

After a tragic car accident near her thirtieth birthday, Angela suffered a severe brain injury. She was in a coma and found herself face-to-face with death. When she was able to communicate verbally, she wanted to talk about death with her people, but she found that those closest to her were unable to meet her in these conversations. Not being able to talk to those closest to her left Angela feeling isolated, making her difficult situation even more challenging.

Angela understood that her people were doing the best they could. She knew her community cared, and through this experience learned that the inability to navigate these conversations is a much larger societal issue. Angela revealed that after her accident, she would see death whenever she opened her eyes. This experience was "freezing" her. Perhaps due to how unhappy or upended she seemed at the time, it was as though those around her were trying to make her happier, rather than talk to her directly about what her experience of being so close to death was really like. She has learned since then, through practice, that talking about death is a skill. She said to me once, "I had a need that I didn't know how to fulfill for myself, as I'd had no previous experience with talking about death so directly."

To this day, she holds much compassion and gratitude for those who supported her at that time. She speaks of a couple that "just simply showed up" and how the three of them bonded through action rather than words. In that time, Angela recalls deep appreciation for the "bodies that weren't leaving me." Her community showed up, offering food, time, and rides to appointments. She recalls how these compassionate actions held her at that time even when they weren't able to talk about death. "How could we?" she says tenderly. "We were all just shown how incredibly fragile it is, and we didn't really know how." She understands now that her people, including herself, did not have the words, ability, or the culturally taught narratives to fall back on in order to engage in conversations about death. Thinking back to that time, Angela says, "We might have even talked about it, just not to the amount that I needed. I felt very alone in my need to talk about death, no matter how unskilled my approach may have been at the time. Death and the conversations that surround it can be messy; part of the skills needed for these conversations is an ability to hold space for that messiness."

After a long recovery, Angela set her sights on doing what she could to help change culture by supporting people to become more comfortable through "co-creating new narratives" in the act of "normalizing talking about death." To facilitate this, she created the Death Conversation Game, a deck of cards each with a provocative prompt about death. She now dedicates much of her time sharing the game and facilitating accessible conversations in community. Angela hosts in-person and virtual Death Conversation Game events, changing the culture around death one conversation at a time. Through the Death Conversation Game, and her advocacy around facilitating conversations and inviting folks to speak more openly, she has expanded her dream community. Through her experience, Angela has come to believe that even unknowingly, part of us often avoids death to focus on the path in front of us—survival. Our reconsideration of death often happens in the future, when people believe they will have more capacity. Since her accident, Angela has been tending to herself and her community, creating the resources for patients and caregivers that she was yearning for, then. It is her hope that she can support others in similar situations, to feel less isolation—and more connection.

STORIES FROM THE TRAIL

When the couch became sacred: A movie, a moment, a conversation that changed everything

I supported a woman who was caring for her husband as he died at home. They had been married 50 years and nurtured a very intimate connection over the years. They loved conversation and enjoyed spending lots of time together; despite this, they had never had a conversation about end-of-life care. Even in his dying time, they were yet to discuss his end-of-life wishes, and the fact that she didn't even know if he wanted to be buried or cremated was causing her great worry.

When we first met, her primary concern was how to start the conversation about death. We talked about some prompts to consider and opportunities for starting the discussion. When we met the following week, she shared that it hadn't gone so well. Looking defeated, she admitted that she just couldn't find the right words. I held space for her disappointment and worry and assured her that resistance to talk about death was normal.

We met a couple of weeks later and she showed up with a big smile and a look of relief on her face. She shared that a few nights before, she and her husband were watching a movie together, and one of the characters was facing death. As the two sat side by side on the couch she turned to him and gently asked what he would want in that situation. A connecting conversation followed, and he shared his hopes and fears. She felt liberated finally knowing his wishes.

The movie and that moment on the couch when the two of them were relaxed and connected was an opening. As the weeks went on, they were able to have more conversations about his hopes, fears, and goals as he approached his death. These conversations about what mattered most to them lessened the fear and anxiety and brought them closer. Somehow it often seems too early until it is too late to have these important conversations with the people you love.

Legacy

Legacy refers to the lasting impact a person leaves behind—tangible or intangible—after they die. This can include memories and values, life stories, wisdom, family traditions, cultural practices, or teachings shared with others. Acts of love, service, or generosity that shaped the lives of others are examples of legacy; others may be personal belongings or creations such as letters, art, recipes, or recorded stories remembered. Some folks create intentional statements of beliefs and hopes for future generations by way of ethical wills.

Legacy is not just about what is left when one dies; rather, it is created by how one lives—the meaning they create and the connections they nurture with others. A legacy project can be supportive by offering a distraction and a focus on life. In addition to honouring relationships, legacy work can celebrate personal achievements or share meaningful objects that bring comfort and connection.

Legacy might include sharing wisdom, memories, or things that have personal significance. It can capture achievements that highlight meaningful work, faith, personal values, or passions, and can range from compiling one's favourite recipes to working to protect nature. A simple yet powerful way to begin is by asking your person, "What are you most proud of?" This can invite reflection and help someone consider how they hope to be remembered.

Dying well is personal, and it is supported by moving towards acceptance of death as a natural part of life, and by engaging in open-hearted conversations. As companions we can approach the end-of-life journey with respectful curiosity and care. Though often tender and courageous, making space to express forgiveness, gratitude, and love can help both the dying and their people live and die with greater ease. In doing so we make the most of the moments.

> "Time is the only currency you spend without knowing your balance. Use it wisely."
>
> —Unknown

Each year, I lead a year-long book study of Stephen Levine's *A Year to Live: How to Live This Year as if It Were Your Last.* Anyone is welcome to join. As a group, we engage in practices that support us to both live well and, when the time comes, to die well. At our monthly meeting, we explore life, including death, through discussion, contemplation, and meditation. Levine generously offers guidance to soften the belly when feeling anxious, coaches us on how to relate to fear rather than to run from it, nudges us to practice self-forgiveness and forgiveness of others, offers permission to celebrate life through a life review, shares inspiration to increase mindfulness, and provides tools to keep our hearts open even when they feel constricting. Together, we wonder about what happens to the body and soul after death. All these practices support death competency, which can be thought of as the capability of the individual to deal with death, as well as the skills, beliefs, and attitudes that one might use or develop while navigating the end-of-life journey. The term also encapsulates our beliefs and attitudes about these capabilities.

> "Being death competent does not necessarily mean that a person does not experience death anxiety—feeling anxious about death is a natural part of being human. It is possible for us to feel anxious about dealing with death and dying whilst also being highly competent at doing so—it all depends on our awareness and the steps we take to self-development."
>
> —Dr. Emma Clare, founder of The Center for Death Competency Development

Death competency is about being aware of and managing your own relationship with death and dying. In my experience, this benefits relationships and brings attention to the wonder of living. Befriending death is an affirmation of life.

Death competency increases our ability to support others on the end-of-life journey as we explore and work to overcome our own death anxiety. As a companion, increasing your intimacy with death will serve you well, and will allow you to show up with less fear as you support your person.

GROUNDING PRACTICES

A slow and gentle start

Take a moment to begin your day with intention. Tune into your own needs and offer yourself a small act of kindness. This simple gesture can help you to meet the day more grounded and resourced, better able to respond to situations rather than react.

If you are seeking inspiration, read something that uplifts you. Do you feel the need to slow down and reflect? Offer yourself permission to pause—catch up to all that is unfolding around and within you. Brew your favourite tea and sit quietly.

Is your body holding tension? A few gentle stretches and deep breaths may help you soften and release what you cannot control.

What are you noticing?

The Life–Death Continuum

It is important that we explore how to support the dying now so that in the future, we can regain a whole-life view of the life–death continuum. The factors that have distanced us from death, including the medicalization of death, the dispersal of families, women pursuing jobs outside of the home, and the outsourcing of care, have all contributed to dying becoming shrouded in mystery, but together we can start to reintegrate this knowledge into our lives. Honouring death is not the opposite of life, but part of life.

Feeling prepared to companion someone on the end-of-life journey is valuable and profoundly meaningful. Do what you can to get reacquainted with natural dying by familiarizing yourself with the skills and knowledge around how to support people on the end-of-life journey practically and spiritually; this will enable you to show up when you are called on to companion. Being more familiar with the nature of the journey will make it more likely that you will be equipped to show up for your people when they lean on you for support.

Alternatively, the fear that results from the unnatural distancing from death often prevents folks from being there in supportive ways for each other at a time when we need each other the most. This can often lead to those on the end-of-life journey feeling abandoned. It can also often result in those left behind feeling empty, disconnected, and full of regret for missed opportunities and things left unsaid. This unnatural separation from a natural part of life is often transmitted to the next generation, preventing them from embracing all of life. The cost of turning away from death and dying is enormous. The COVID-19 pandemic was a stark reminder that how we die matters, not only to the dying but to those left behind.

The stories shared of people dying alone during the COVID-19 pandemic have highlighted that the consequences of family and friends being withheld at the end of life are enormous. Trauma is a natural reaction to a deeply upsetting event that overwhelms an individual's ability to cope. It causes feelings of helplessness, and it can diminish one's sense of self. Ultimately, trauma can impair our capacity to feel a full range of emotions and experiences. Based on my practice and what happened in hospices and care homes during the pandemic, when many friends and family of the dying were physically prevented from entering institutions due to the COVID-19 protocols, there was great fear of not knowing what to do—which served as a barrier to showing up for the dying, here in Canada and also around the world.

Now is the time to get reacquainted with what to expect on the journey, and to remember, honestly, that we are enough. It is so hopeful to see community end-of-life care blossoming, and to reinstill that we already have what it takes to walk alongside the dying. It is only natural to familiarize ourselves with the full human experience from birth to death.

It is you, the family, friends, and community members of the person living with a life-limiting illness, who are being summoned to remember. While every situation is different, most of the care on the end-of-life journey is provided by those closest to the dying, unless your person is in a care facility. Some have a lot of people, and are held by a sturdy web of support, connected through life with people who are equipped to provide end-of-life care. Some live more privately and have fewer social connections. In these cases, caregivers may need to create a support system to facilitate emerging needs, including inviting others into the circle of care. It is not only okay but recommended that we all lean out on others for assistance when we are feeling overwhelmed. This is the way humans were designed to live, and when the time comes, to die.

In the global North, there is an unprecedented shift in demographics upon us as the number of people over 65 is about to load enormous pressure on our already overburdened healthcare systems. We are being summoned to look at new ways to support the dying, and we are all qualified to step up and provide this simple compassionate care. Understanding what to expect and how to provide comfort is a start. Being creative and inviting your person to find CAMPP by meeting them where they are makes dying less hard. Then, they not only feel less isolated, but they are also encouraged to remain focused—on life in the present moment. We already have the tools to show up in this way, we just need to remember.

Contemplating death is a radical and courageous act. Even in other cultures, where the concept of death is woven into life and folks live more communally, supporting each other offering ritual through all final transitions, death anxiety continues to persist. Of course it does! Many people express that they no longer want to be afraid of death, but it is unlikely that humans will ever be completely comfortable with the idea of existing outside of our physical bodies. A certain amount of worry about death is normal as fear naturally comes with the unknown, and there is a lot we don't know about dying. Reducing our distress around death is something that is best done collectively, and culturally. By simply sharing information about "normal" dying, stories about this natural experience and suggestions on how to show up, we can replace a great deal of that fear with heart-centered presence, which is love in action.

The Wonders—and Drawbacks—of Modern Medicine

As effective as modern medicine is at increasing our lifespan, it often serves to distance us from death. In the science of modern medicine, human beings are often treated as patients, rather than participants in their healing. With the need to provide medical care at scale, reducing people to their symptom management can quickly become the focus, often without the capacity or cohesion to address the whole person. (This systemic issue is no way a reflection of the outstanding individuals who work in modern-day medical services, most of whom continually work to bridge the gap.)

There has been a shift around cultural storytelling in the last century, where most of our stories around end of life have become medical-based narratives. In these, the body is reduced to its smallest parts—be it organ-based, tissue-based, or molecular—and there is a reliance on the experts in those areas who are ultimately responsible for our survival. To be sure, this approach has saved countless lives. And medical advancements that support the holistic experience of dying have successfully managed to find ways to control most physical pain at end of life, reducing suffering for so many on the end-of-life journey. Modern medicine deserves a deep bow when it comes to managing physical pain. It has been proven that physical pain at end of life can be effectively controlled, for the most part, with medical interventions. In a study conducted on palliative cancer and AIDS patients, it was found that 85–95 percent of physical pain can be controlled by medication or therapy. These are impressive statistics to be sure.

However, this lopsided focus on the medical side of dying can be dissociative and disempowering for those living with a life-limiting illness, as it creates the sense that they need to be separated from their community to heal, as well as from an inner sense of self. This is where increasing knowledge about the whole process of dying—the social, emotional, physical, and spiritual aspects—from one to many individual community members can be complementary. It is not about replacing the medical care team, it is about honouring dying for what it is—a complex, psychosocial, community process that is often best facilitated with the support of many, in both medical and non-medical settings.

With this awareness, we have the opportunity to choose to hold different narratives about death, ones that honour our human nature. We can choose stories that celebrate community care and person-centered narratives that are enhanced by medical care. What if more of us held stories that focus on the specific needs of the dying being tended to by friends, family, and community, offering personalized care rooted in what matters most to the dying? Remembering our human nature and honouring that we need each other throughout our lives, including our deaths, will support us as we companion the dying.

You are the medicine

Showing up with your presence and imagination can greatly increase comfort. The medical care team has many tools to decrease physical pain on the end-of-life journey, such as interventions like medication, surgery, and chemotherapy. But pain is complex.

British Hospice pioneer Dame Cicely Saunders created a lot of awareness around the concept of "total pain." Saunders guides us to consider the psychological, social, and spiritual needs of the dying as well and the physical. We all have the superpowers of listening, creativity, and taking a heart-centred approach. If we are present, and we increase our capacity to navigate the complexity of death—to not turn away from the suffering—we can show up as supportive companions. Dying people commonly yearn for touch, communication, and love. Interventions such as simply sitting, listening deeply, and holding hands are incredibly effective. You, as one of those closest to the dying, are the most qualified to offer these comforting acts. In a sense you are the medicine.

This is where palliative care comes in; this is where you come in. Palliative care is a misunderstood field. Essentially, palliative care is a type of care that can be given in homes, health centres, and hospices, and people are often connected with palliative care teams after a life-limiting diagnosis. The support available varies from region to region. The palliative care team consists of a vast array of professionals and volunteers, ranging from doctors, spiritual care advisors, social workers, doulas, nurses, music therapists, care aids, pet therapists, and most importantly, you and other friends and family members that support the dying.

The aim of palliative care is to relieve physical, psychosocial, and spiritual distress. When this is offered effectively, palliative care has been proven to increase wellbeing, increase choice, reduce medical treatments and hospital visits, reduce the stress and burden on the family, and even lengthen life by 25 percent. Appropriate palliative care focuses on living a full life, right up until the last moment. Showing up in this way by attending to the whole person is how we most effectively support the dying.

> "Palliative Care providers usually recognize that most people are not as afraid of dying as they are of being abandoned. The worst thing we can do is abandon someone who is hurting. Attitudes which promote death rather than affirm life are the ultimate abandonment."
>
> —Dame Cicely Saunders

Taking Saunders' cue, we can continue to consider what other scholars believe contributes to the experience of suffering as to how to show up and support the dying. Suffering her been defined as "a sense of impending disintegration experienced by a person." This is relevant to aging and dying for many today who express a sense of diminishment of roles, identity, and sense of being in the world. The felt loss of meaning and purpose has been described as the basis of human suffering. These perspectives support the notion that you are perfectly positioned as a non-medical care provider to offer comfort by complementing the medical care team and guide your person to find CAMPP through showing up, listening, and using informed imagination moment to moment.

As our current systems are buckling under pressure, the call to step up and support our own is urgent, even with a healthcare system full of well-intentioned, deeply caring humans that most likely entered the field with the hope of providing comfort at every opportunity. It is heartbreaking to consider that because of our over-burdened system, the individuals in it are often prevented from receiving the best quality care. In a recent webinar that I attended, acclaimed palliative care physician and author Dr. Kathryn Mannix stated that her dream after retirement was to become a hospice volunteer. She expressed that she yearned to simply sit at the bedside and companion the dying at their pace, something she revealed was a rare experience in her role as a busy palliative care physician.

Collectivism at the end of life: The importance of shared care

An all-hands-on-deck approach is needed to do dying better. Family, chosen family, friends, neighbours, and colleagues are being summoned to simply to get reacquainted with dying and remember how to offer comfort. Perhaps by answering this call we will create the compassionate communities that so many of us yearn to belong to. We all benefit when the full human experience from birth to death is honoured.

At Vancouver's Douglas College, I facilitate a class on death and dying. Every month, I see the class fill with people answering this call to service. I constantly hear participants express frustration with our distancing from death, often enrolling in the course because of a yearning to familiarize themselves with the process. How strange it is that we need a college class to learn how to do something that is as natural and universal as dying. Often participants share personal stories of missed opportunities at the end of life, and they want to learn different ways to meet death in the future. Other stories are full of inspiration and wonder, and others still are tales of gentle dying experiences. These stories serve to remind us that death—this experience that we are encouraged to fear and avoid—isn't completely horrible, and alongside the enormous sense of grief, companioning the dying can often offer incredibly tender moments of beauty, laughter, connection, and love.

People often seek support for their dying person on the end-of-life journey. Each person has unique needs and thus the amount of support required can depend on the individual who is available to assist with care, and access to the available systems in place to offer care. These factors vary from person to person, community to community. Some families (without qualifiers) are small and can benefit from building out the web of support around the dying person by inviting others to join in the care circle. In other families where the web of support is sturdy, and people are available to come together and support the journey, simply encouraging individuals to step up and provide care where needed is the goal. There is often a tragic disconnect between folks who really want to show up for their people but just don't know how, caused by a lack of confidence and unfamiliarity with the end-of-life journey, and this inaction can cause great regret.

We research and contemplate how to prepare for our retirement, how to plant a garden, and how to sail a boat, yet we often turn away from how we want our dying time to play out. How strange, since it is the one thing that is guaranteed. I wonder why we don't engage with the full human experience with more curiosity. Why is it not more commonplace to learn how to die well? Sadly, when it comes to the end-of-life journey, people often find themselves half-way up a mountain in the middle of a blizzard wearing flip flops and a t-shirt, when overwhelm takes over. It doesn't have to be this way. A little more understanding, a little more communication, a little more planning, and a little more reaching out to those around us can greatly support the journey. By simply acknowledging that we are going to die and sharing basic information and stories about end of life, we can get to know death a little better and prepare for the journey and travel with more ease.

GROUNDING PRACTICES

Dying as a practice of heart wisdom and collective belonging

Place your hand on your heart. Feel your heart anytime you want a reminder of the softness inside.

For most of us who spend much of our lives fixated on productivity and performance it takes resistance and effort to slow down and meet the present moment with awareness. It may take many reminders to do so, but dropping from the busyness in your head and into your soft heart will support you to act from a place of service. Your person will feel this shift; it is a softer and more spacious way of being that will comfort, allowing you to meet them where they are from moment to moment, allowing you to respond appropriately to their needs and preferences as they arise.

Companioning the dying is not about doing it right or getting it wrong; it is about increasing the awareness of your heart. Can you feel it? The softness of your heart? This is a subtle sensation that may not be available at first but over time, with awareness, your ability to attune to your heart sense will develop. With attention to your heart and the intention of serving from this place as best as you can from moment to moment, while honouring your humanness with loads of self-compassion, your journey will require less effort.

What if you turned to your heart as a compass? I wonder if the way of the heart is the natural antidote to needing to be perfect, resilient, and always in a rush. Can this heart awareness serve to dampen privilege? What if this heart attunement helped to foster a culture of kindness and mutual aid? It's worth a try. A hand on your heart—a seemingly small action that may have the ability to support you in this world as you companion your person on the end-of-life journey.

GROUNDING PRACTICES

Step outside, come inside

Consider taking some time for yourself to get outside, even if it is just outside your front door. Breathe. Just normal breathing. There is always the sky, a tree, a bird…

Take some time to check in with your senses. What do you see? What are you hearing? Does this place have a smell? A taste? What sensations do you feel? What are you noticing?

STORIES FROM THE TRAIL

The gentle generosity of listening

I am reminded of being with a very frail woman as she was coming to the end of her journey. Sitting beside her bed, she turned and looked over at me with large sunken eyes. "I don't know how to do this," she whispered.

"Of course you don't," I replied. We sat for a while in silence. "None of us really do until we have done it." I gently reassured her that those around her would be there with her, step by step. She lowered her gaze and we sat and wondered about dying together without saying a word.

My offerings were simple: the gifts of validation of her experience, and space for her fear to be held—to allow her to feel seen and heard and in that way, to not feel so alone. My heart ached as I met her in the moment. These simple yet challenging offerings are generous gifts. This is how we can companion others in their dying time.

GROUNDING PRACTICES

With these hands: A ritual for companions

Here is a simple ritual. The everyday action of handwashing—infused with intention—will support you as companion. This ritual will also encourage you to release whatever it is that you no longer wish to carry.

When preparing to visit your person, wash your hands with intention. This enables you to be more present, which will help to communicate to your person that they are not alone. You can do this ritual in your car using hand sanitizer, or you can visit a bathroom and use soap and water. This ritual is about slowing down and bringing mind and body together—if only for a moment.

1. Slowly pump or squeeze the soap or sanitizer into your hands.
2. Notice the sensations in your hands as you rub your palms together.
3. Focus on each finger, one by one.
4. Massage your thumbs.
5. What do you smell? What sensations arise? Perhaps you are aware of the slipperiness of the soap, the coldness of the hand sanitizer, or the warmth of the water as you rinse the soap from your hands.
6. Bring your presence to this moment. Just this moment. Notice your living body in this moment.

Take a breath. This pause will offer the space for you to set your intention. How do you want to show up for your person? You can add some personal words of comfort that support you: a prayer, an affirmation, or simply whatever offering comes to mind. You can also expand your prayer, affirmation, or thoughts to your person, to the people nearby, perhaps to those that work in the hospital or care home and even beyond. Just take a moment here. Pause and be intentional before you meet your person.

Take another breath.

This pause will support you to be with whatever feelings arise within you and within others during your time together. You may feel at ease or you may find yourself full of worry. Just meet whatever is arising with your spacious awareness. This will help you stay grounded and present. This will support you to be with your person, even in the company of big feelings such as fear, worry, and regret. Be gentle with yourself and know that as humans it is in our nature to make mistakes—perfection is the enemy of connection. Accepting this reality can support you to be more present, which will naturally support you and your person.

When you leave, wash your hands again, following the same steps above. The intention of this washing is to cleanse yourself of that which you want to release, or perhaps to support you to integrate the experiences you shared. Bring your awareness again so that you are fully present with yourself. Even if your experience was upsetting, it can be honoured by this hand washing ritual. Again, notice the physical sensations that arise as you pause and mindfully wash your hands. What is arising in you? Honour what happened during the visit and cleanse yourself of what is asking to be released so that it feels less intense. This simple action with intention may support you to be with the unknown, and bolsters your capacity to bear witness, increasing the chances for compassionate action to arise naturally.

Chapter 2

The Journey Begins: Diagnosis

Embarking on the end-of-life journey often feels surreal. Looking back, you may not even be able to recall the start of the journey. Your person has been given a life-limiting diagnosis. Your known reality, all expected order—life as you know it—vanishes in an instant.

This great loss of felt safety from what is known and expected, of life before a diagnosis, instantly creates a grief response. Grief is a natural response to losing someone or something we love. Grief is commonly associated with death loss; however, it is much more than that. When faced with a life-limiting diagnosis, the fear of losing everything important becomes a reality. These real or imagined losses, be they physical abilities or core aspects of identity or emotional safety, can all bring about a grief response. Grief can feel confusing and overwhelming, especially if you don't know you are experiencing it or how it manifests. Naming and recognizing grief at the start of the journey can help you and those around you feel less disoriented.

EXPECTED CHANGES ON THE JOURNEY

Grief storms and human nature: Compassionate companioning in crisis

When your person is given a life-limiting diagnosis, it can feel like the ground has vanished beneath your feet. This news will affect everyone who cares about your person differently and each person will look to their unique coping mechanisms. Personality traits can become more pronounced in a crisis, so you can surely expect the characteristics of those around you to intensify.

The period following a diagnosis is a liminal space, caught between the familiarity of life that once was and the uncertainty of the future. The loss of this known reality creates the complex and often misunderstood experience of grief. The best way to support those around you who are grieving is to listen deeply, take the time do your best to connect with their experience, and feel with them. Offer empathy to communicate that you see them, you hear them, and you are there for them. This is not always easy when you are grieving too, but making the effort to understand and normalize these new feelings will increase compassion and support for everyone involved. Similarity, leaning out on trusted others who are empathic listeners will support you in your journey as companion.

GROUNDING PRACTICES

The grief before goodbye: A companion's reflection on anticipatory loss

As with any long journey, it is best to do what you can to take it slow and steady. Obviously external circumstances may make this challenging. Feeling the feelings that arise from anticipatory grief will make the experience less difficult. If you can express these feelings to trusted others, even better. You do not have to carry your sorrow alone. If you are able, then leaning out on trusted others as you companion your person will make you feel less burdened and you will travel lighter. We need each other. It's okay to feel like you can't face grief head on; it's okay to feel your grief in small doses. The best way to do grief is your way. This honouring of your anticipatory grief will support you in going the distance as a companion.

It takes time to adjust to this "new normal" and only you will know what you need from moment to moment. This grief experience can evoke physical, emotional, somatic, and behavioural responses. You may feel forgetful, consumed with worry about the future, have trouble sleeping, feel angry at the world, or all of the above. Know that your reactions are normal. Something enormous is happening, and your life is about to change forever.

Elizabeth Causton, a retired social worker who has worked supporting people for over 40 years, brilliantly explains how families and friends are affected by a life limiting illness diagnosis in her essay "The Dance," excerpted below. The metaphor she draws in this piece helps to normalize the effect of a crisis on the family and friend system.

> "The idea of a family dance is not new, but it works particularly well as an image that reminds us of the importance of paying attention to boundaries. The image can also be used to describe the sense of continuity of the family dance, which has evolved over generations. It reminds us that every family dance has its own history and that every step taken on the family dance floor has a reason in the context of that shared history. So, when one member of the family either sits down or lies down on the dance floor because of terminal illness, the dance may look quite clumsy as the family tries to modify their routine to accommodate the changes, but the new steps are not random. They too, have meaning in the context of what has gone on before. Still, as we watch families struggle with a difficult dance, to music that always gets faster and louder in a crisis, we may be tempted to get onto their dance floor to try and teach them a new dance, with steps from the dance that we are most familiar with—our own. Of course, this rarely works, for the obvious reason that our dance steps do not have a history or a reason in the context of another family's particular dance."
>
> —Elizabeth Causton, from "The Dance"

This metaphor beautifully captures the changes within the family and friend system that can be observed on the end-of-life journey. Sharing this metaphor helps folks to recognize that amidst the chaos, there is order. When people can consider how individual family members have responded to crises in the past, they can predict what to expect in the future. Reflecting on unique personalities within families by highlighting strengths, weaknesses, and challenges can diffuse tension and make this highly charged time seem much less unpredictable.

Adding to the dance, your person's life-limiting diagnosis may erode their sense of autonomy, individuality, and social identity. Frequently, the loss of one's sense of self goes unnoticed by others. While your person may display physical changes, such as being restricted to a wheelchair or a bed, oftentimes their appearance can remain unchanged. The loss of one's identity is also cause for a grief response, one that can become complicated if it goes unacknowledged. These feelings add to the confusion and isolation, and a sense of powerlessness arises when one's sense of identity and social roles are taken without permission, sparking a struggle to maintain control. This may result in your person seeming uncooperative or challenging. Of course there is a struggle to find a foothold on the trail, because so much is being lost. Keep showing up, follow the lead of your person, and listen. This may not feel like enough, but it is generous and good, and it is the medicine most people in struggle are looking for. Trust that you are enough.

EXPECTED CHANGES ON THE JOURNEY

The steps we know: The family dance

We are all wired differently. As the comparison to a dance suggests, we all move, sway, and step in our own way. The rhythm that each person finds on the dance floor in relation to everyone else there is not random. Notice predictable patterns and honour your family's unique dance; this will help you understand that even though the situation may feel chaotic, the dance is progressing as expected. Sharing this information with your family may offer comfort to all on the dance floor.

What does your family dance look like? How have your family and friends responded to crises in the past?

Seeking New Knowledge

The tides are shifting, and community end-of-life care is on the rise. Many are seeking this precious knowledge about the social, emotional, and physical changes at end of life. More and more people are understanding the importance of becoming familiar with the end-of-life journey and the importance of having conversations about death.

It helps to understand where you are and where you are going. Often knowledge gaps between clear understandings of the trajectory of the specific disease can amplify feelings of overwhelm. Each life-limiting illness has a beginning, middle, late stage, and end. When individuals understand the trajectory of a disease, it makes dying more manageable. This information can often be provided by the care team; if it isn't offered, ask. Knowing what lies ahead can support a sense of control for the family care team and invite more presence and understanding.

An experienced palliative care nurse shared that before she leaves the room, she always asks patients and families if they need any more information to understand the dying experience. In her busy role in a buckling system, this is a generous act. In her experience, the answer to this question is always a resounding "Yes!" Our healthcare system is overburdened, and staff are often overworked and overwhelmed, unable to meet the needs of those receiving care. Regrettably, dying often feels messy and complicated in part due to the lack of time to share sufficient information.

In the liminal space after a diagnosis, life can feel like it is spinning out of control. Change is constant and it can be hard to keep up. It is completely normal to feel overwhelmed. We can benefit from increased death literacy, sharing information about what we know about dying, but we can't grasp it all. The end-of-life journey is filled with mystery, and much about dying is unknown. In this space, we are called to surrender to the unknown and wonder.

I WONDER . . .

Companioning: What is your intention?

As you set out on this journey take a moment to consider the expectations you are holding. Are they realistic? If they are not, you will be frustrated and disappointed regardless of your efforts. You are not superhuman. You are not here to tidy everything up or to make everything okay. You are not expected to neatly package the experience and adorn it with a big bow. There is no such thing as a shiny "good" death. Life and death are wild and unpredictable—this is what we know. Consider setting your intention to be present for your person on this challenging trail and find moments to offer invitations for connection. Let go and trust that your person will engage in a way that is right for them, either accepting, modifying, or declining your invitations. Journeying with this intention is a realistic goal to support the wellbeing of all.

GROUNDING PRACTICES

Writing practice

A client once shared that she googled "anxious about my person dying" and found a website that suggested writing to the following five prompts:

1. Make a list of all your concerns.
2. Identify what you've already lost.
3. Practice mindfulness.
4. Learn about death and dying.
5. Talk about your fear with others.

She wrote to the first two prompts and emailed them to me for witnessing.

Over the course of her dad's end-of-life journey we had ongoing conversations around mindfulness and education about death and dying, and she expressed fears as they surfaced. I listened. This practice offered a sense of calm and clarity to her situation, perhaps it may support you too.

What to Say When You Don't Know What to Say

Perhaps rather than considering what to say, it would serve us well to begin by exploring a different question: *How can we begin to listen more deeply?* When people are in crisis and they reach out for support, most of the time they are simply wanting to be heard. Listening is love and it is the medicine most of us are looking for. It is a blessing to have even just one person who offers their presence and generously listens. This sounds simple enough and yet it can be a challenge for many of us, in an overstimulating world where we are so often guided to move towards comfort, distraction, or numbing the pain. Hearing someone express fear, worry, pain, sadness, and uncertainty is uncomfortable, so we often offer responses in an attempt to diffuse these strong feelings or distract the person in distress rather than to simply listen.

People often don't know what to say. That's because there really is nothing you can say to take away fear and worry. Instead, we must turn our gaze from fixing and helping to companioning—to feeling with and wondering with your person. Keep showing up, despite the discomfort. Being there with your heart first in service will create connection, and connection makes things a little easier.

Once feelings are acknowledged, validated, and normalized—once your person feels truly seen and heard—you may choose to gently explore the situation further with open-ended questions. From this grounded place of presence, and by taking their lead, you can wonder together. This shared curiosity may open the door to practices, resources, people, or insights that offer comfort. But it's important to remember that meaningful connection does not always require a solution. Sometimes, simply being with what is—without rushing to fix—can be the most powerful balm of all.

Your person may have a lot of questions about meaning and purpose. They will likely feel doubt, regret, uncertainty, and sadness. In these conversations there are often no answers; this is where you can offer the gifts of listening, holding space, and companioning. As your person expresses what they are holding, do your best to keep breathing and lead with your heart.

Approaching end-of-life conversations can feel daunting. Regrettably, the dying, their people, and even medical professionals often sidestep the subject of death altogether. This may leave those living with a terminal diagnosis feeling isolated, resentful, and hurt. Avoiding the subject may even lead to inappropriate medical interventions. The absence of honest conversations kills connection by separating the dying from their people and distancing them from the truth of what is really happening.

It's amazing that in our modern world, communication skills can be so lacking. Meaningful conversations require space to develop, allowing what is asking to be said to surface when the time is right. Instead, we often direct and hurry conversations, forcing our words to make a point or to soothe our own unease. As discomfort arises, especially in the face of suffering, the urge to help can become a reflex—to fix, advise, analyze, or steer the conversation away from pain. These impulses often come from a place of love, but also from our own fears: fear of not knowing what to say, fear of saying the wrong thing, fear of the truth itself. Control becomes a subtle strategy to manage that fear, to regain footing in the unfamiliar terrain of someone else's vulnerability. We may not realize we're trying just as much to make ourselves feel better as we are trying to ease another's pain. But true presence asks us to stay, to soften into the discomfort rather than override it. In time, the depth of connection will reinforce the generous offering that most of us are yearning for: to simply be heard, without judgement or agenda.

GROUNDING PRACTICES

Choosing connection

Do you usually find yourself trying to fix, advise, or gather more information instead of responding to suffering with empathy?

Empathy creates connection and it is the response that offers the most support when people are in crisis. Before we can offer empathy, we need to deeply listen—to be fully present with the other person and feel with them. It's in this space of listening that empathy naturally arises. Once we have attuned to their experience, we can offer empathic statements. Here are some examples:

- I am here to listen.
- You are going through a lot.
- Take your time. There is no rush. I will be here as long as you need.
- I'm listening.
- I don't know how this feels, and I wish things were easier. Know that I am here to listen.

It is important to use language that feels natural to you. Do any of these empathic responses help you to increase connection?

GROUNDING PRACTICES

Weaving together self-care and shared care

Is there something important that you feel called to share with your family and friends? Perhaps you're carrying a worry, holding important information, or even keeping a secret that wants to be spoken aloud. Consider planning an activity you enjoy doing together—something that feels natural and nourishing. Sharing everyday moments can shift the focus from the heaviness of illness or companioning, back to the rhythms of life.

If you are facing a decision alone, ask yourself: "Can I bring my wondering to those I trust?" Naming your questions out loud can invite support and connection in ways that holding them silently cannot. Can you share your questioning with your family and friends so they can offer you support?

GROUNDING PRACTICES

Finding your way into the conversation

Consider using "I" statements, such as "I am noticing…" or "if I understand correctly, what you are saying is…" instead of jumping in with direct questions.

If starting a conversation feels difficult, look for natural openings in day-to-day life—a shared moment while watching a movie or reading a book can gently open up a dialogue. These moments of connection can make it easier to begin. It may help to keep the following in mind:

- Don't speak—listen with respectful curiosity to understand.
- Speak from your heart—let the words arise from your heart first, then your head.
- Speak honestly—be yourself, be natural and relaxed, and lead with your heart.
- Speak clearly—use plain words and make sure that we are understood.
- Speak often—not just one conversation or two, but conversations that are ongoing.
- Offer empathy—offer simple statements communicating that you see and hear your person.

How to Engage in Conversation with Your Person

When initiating a conversation with your person, let them take the lead. You can begin by asking for permission, with a statement such as, "Do you want to talk about how you're feeling?" Starting here honours agency and is a very differently approach than abruptly asking your person how they are doing. This gentle conversation starter is less intrusive and gives your person the choice to respond. Autonomy is so important on the end-of-life journey. Your person may or may not welcome reflection. From time to time, it is normal to just want to keep things light and avoid heavy conversation, so try to pick and choose times when you feel your person might be ready for the conversation.

Holding space for your person to express what is alive in them is a generous act. Often people wonder if they will make their person upset by opening these conversations; it is when we don't acknowledge what others are going through that people feel abandoned. This can lead to feelings of isolation, as if they have to carry the weight of their worries on their own. When we communicate to others that they are truly seen and heard, the journey becomes lighter—not just for them, but for everyone. There is strength in being witnessed, and comfort in knowing you are walking this path together.

> *"It's just as important for you to hear yourself speak your stories as it is for others to hear you speak them."*
>
> *—Tommy Orange*

CAMPP: CONNECTION, AWARENESS, MEANING, PLEASURE, PRESENCE

Releasing the weight: Speaking regrets and travelling lighter

Offering invitations for your person to find connection, awareness, meaning, pleasure, and presence is not always about feeling comfortable. Regrets are not only heavy, but they also often have a sharp edge. Yet they can also draw us closer to what matters most. They remind us that while death can feel frightening, it is often the unlived parts of life that stir the deepest sorrow. For this reason, as a companion you are called to hold space.

So many regrets are not about what we did, but about what we left undone—the words left unsaid, the love we withheld, the moments we postponed while waiting for a more perfect time. As a companion, you can support your person in travelling light by gently opening a space where regrets can be spoken without shame or defence. If it feels right, it may be fitting to ask questions such as:

- Are there things you wish you had done differently?
- Are there people you hoped to love more openly?
- What feels unfinished or unspoken?

Holding space for these truths requires courage and compassion. It is not about fixing or erasing the past, but about allowing regrets to be named, witnessed, and honoured. Often, simply telling the story of what we wish we had done can soften the ache and lighten the load we carry. It can reconnect us to meaning, to love, and to the preciousness of the time that remains.

It may be comforting to reassure your person that regrets are only visible in hindsight. Every choice was made with the knowledge and capacity that they had in that moment. Offering this perspective can ease self-blame.

This honesty becomes a kind of medicine. Speaking regrets aloud is an act of truth telling. It can help your person feel less alone on the journey and affirm that even now, there is time to be present, to share love, and to be comforted by awareness and connection.

GROUNDING PRACTICES

Guided by heart wisdom: The art of compassionate communication

In conversation, many thoughts and emotions will come up while you are listening to your person. Simply notice what you are thinking and feeling, and without judging yourself, bring your attention back to your person.

Not knowing what to say is okay. Being honest about this and naming the unease are supportive gestures. A generous amount of tenderness and self-compassion is required when we courageously step in to support the dying. Know that it is normal to have a reflexive desire to fix the situation in an attempt to minimize the discomfort. In addition to fixing, it is common to respond to discomfort by advising, one-upping the situation, or minimizing what another is feeling.

When we settle in and offer to provide a container for whatever others are experiencing, we invite the wholeness of the complexity to be witnessed. This is how we facilitate wellbeing. Even when it gets really hard—when you feel your heart breaking—keep showing up. Trust that your companionship will help relieve the suffering.

If your person doesn't want to talk or share, follow their lead. Keep showing up and continue to meet them where they are. Instead of forcing a big conversation, consider doing what you enjoy doing together. Work on a puzzle, tune in to a podcast, or watch your favourite show. Continue to let your person know that you are there with an ear to listen and a shoulder to lean on, honouring their privacy, timing, and process.

It's not about just having one conversation; rather, the goal is to have an ongoing dialogue that allows for stepping in and stepping out, a dance of sorts. Know that when you take your person's cues it is normal for them to not to want to talk about death all the time. If your person diverts the subject from dying, respect this and consider circling back to the conversation another day. Don't forget to keep the focus on life—continue to reminisce about the past, engage in pleasurable activities, and talk about upcoming events.

The end-of-life journey is wild, unknown territory, so there is no perfect thing to say or one way to show up. We will all experience life, including death, in our own unique way. Let your heart wisdom guide you and keep showing up. Again, self-compassion is an essential quality of an effective companion. This means that you accept your humanness and understand that you are likely to stumble. It is about doing what you can to stay curious and continue to understand how you can best support your person. It is about being gentle with yourself and giving yourself the benefit of the doubt. It is about letting go of worry and regret about how you have responded in the past and trusting that as you get to know yourself better and finetune your communication skills, you are able to show up differently.

When Things Go Wrong

If you hear unsupportive words slip out of your mouth, simply acknowledge your misstep and respond with a statement such as "Hm, that didn't come out quite right. What I meant to say was…" Even as I facilitate the course on how to show up and what to say to the dying, I often say things unintentionally that minimize the experience of those I am attempting to comfort. If you are feeling provoked, or worried you may say something that causes harm, or you can't find the right words to offer support, simply listen. What is most important is that you continue to be there and challenge yourself to find balance on this bumpy terrain. Communication is a skill, and we get better through awareness and practice. It has been proven that this tender-hearted act of being vulnerable and feeling with another is deeply supportive.

As difficult as it might be, resist your urge to fix the situation. This will be ineffective because nothing is broken. It is natural for your person to express fear, sorrow, regret, or anger, or to withdraw and express nothing at all. This is grief, the natural human response to loss. There really is no need for a response or even to fully understand what another is expressing. If you habitually respond by attempting to solve problems, you are not alone. This is how most of us respond when we react to people seeking comfort. The adjustment is to be made on your end, not theirs.

We are wired to feel with those closest to us; our brains have mirror neurons which copy the emotional and physical experiences of others and reproduce them inside our own bodies. These neurons allow us to be empathic. When we attempt to resolve the discomfort in others, it is often motivated by a desire to stop the distress we are feeling. Furthermore, the grief of others may intensify our own grief, causing our own losses to be activated, motivating us to resolve our uneasiness. Unfortunately, when we attempt to fix instead of listen, it doesn't relieve suffering; rather, it pushes the pain deeper into the body. The only way to release uncomfortable emotions is for people to have space for feelings to surface, trust enough to share, and feel witnessed. With expression, we can be supported to face our own pain, which allows it to be set free.

Heart wisdom is nurtured by slowing down. Take the time to listen to your body and acknowledge your experience as a companion on the end-of-life journey. This will support you to show up resourced and soft-hearted. By being humble and honest, you can model vulnerability and communicate from your heart, encouraging your person to do the same.

Don't forget to be normal! The best way to approach what to say is to be sincere and be yourself. Greet your person the way you always have and continue to chat about what's happening in your life. This communicates to your person that they are still a part of the living. You do not have to be an expert on all of the mysteries of life and death to have a conversation with your person about their experience of the end-of-life journey—you simply need to be present, authentic, open, and non-judgmental. Listening deeply to them and offering validation that highlights connection and love are generous offerings.

Showing up, taking your person's lead and respecting their pace will open up the space for sharing. The end goal of communication is to communicate that *you are right there with them.* Often simple empathic statements such as "Wow" or "That sounds really difficult" are all it takes to let your person know you are there. It is important that these empathic responses be heartfelt and feel natural. Use ordinary, everyday language that is comfortable to you. Often, the most powerful responses don't involve any words; gestures such as a hand on the shoulder, a hug, or shared silence are sometimes the most effective way for our hearts to speak. These nonverbal responses are generous and can communicate a depth of care beyond words.

> "Things are far too serious for us to lose our sense of humor!"
>
> —Terry Patten

GROUNDING PRACTICES

Giggles and grace: How humour heals

Humour is healing, and it has physical and emotional benefits. Consider spending more time with the people in your life who make you laugh. Watch funny movies and listen to comedy that makes you giggle. Recall fun and funny times. Can you remember a time when you laughed uncontrollably? Simply closing your eyes and recalling the laughter of someone close to you can bring great relief.

GROUNDING PRACTICES

Releasing what is not yours to hold

As simple as it sounds, holding space for your person to share their experience is not easy. Witnessing others in pain is often the most difficult thing that we are called to do. Staying present to another's pain takes effort. It may be supportive to honour your energetic boundaries by reminding yourself that this is happening to your person, not you. With awareness you can feel deeply and maintain your sense of self. It may be supportive to push the soles of your feet into the ground and imagine what is not yours to carry moving through you and out of the bottoms of your feet and into the earth to absorb the energy. This ritual may support you to stay present, feel deeply, and release what is not yours to hold.

Often when others express anger or the desire to withdraw, it can be confusing. Understand that your person is going through a lot, and anger and withdrawal are common responses to loss. It is not easy to witness these strong responses, but do your best to meet this discomfort heart-first and try to not take it personally. Just like any other emotion, anger just wants to be seen and heard. When given to opportunity for expression it decays—its energy is diffused. As with any unpleasant emotion, witnessing anger can be so uncomfortable, but understanding that it is simply a signal that your person's needs are not being met may support you to respond from a place of compassion.

If your person withdraws or doesn't feel ready to share their experience, that's okay. Let them know you are there for them and then follow their lead. You may not know when they'll reach for support, but your steady presence will let them know it's safe to do so, whenever they're ready.

Shifting the focus from responding to listening is a practice. In our society, we are often taught an overly active model of listening. We learn that listening is a responsive process, one in which we are guided to add to the conversation, as opposed to simply offering space for your person to be witnessed, without distraction, minimizing, or disagreement. With awareness you can quiet your internal commentary. When you notice your mind swirling with questions such as "What would I do in that situation? How does that make me feel? How can I fix this situation? What experiences can I share that are similar?", you can choose to journey from the business of your head and into your heart, enter the moment, place your feet on the ground, and simply listen.

I WONDER . . .

How do you communicate? A compassionate path to deeper connection

Listening is a skill that we can all work on and with awareness we can finetune our communication style. Think about how you converse with others:

- Do you listen with presence and respectful curiosity?
- Do you ask open-ended questions that encourage people to share?
- Do you give ample time for others to answer?
- Are you comfortable with silence?

Be gentle with yourself. In our culture, there is very little guidance around how to listen and how to navigate courageous conversations. Each day is a new beginning.

When showing up this way, there is often an exchange. There is vulnerability and intimacy when we share authentically. It may be hard at first for us 21st-century humans to understand that *being something* is what is called for rather than *doing something*. Seeing and hearing those navigating end of life and offering our truest presence is the most potent medicine available.

> "Here's why I will be a good person. Because I listen. I cannot speak so I listen very well. I never interrupt; I never deflect the course of the conversation with a comment of my own. People, if you pay attention to them, change the direction of one another's conversations constantly. It's like having a passenger in your car who suddenly grabs the steering wheel and turns you down a side street."
>
> —Garth Stein, The Art of Racing in the Rain

CAMPP: CONNECTION, AWARENESS, MEANING, PLEASURE, PRESENCE

Saying goodbye

If it feels appropriate, gently let your person know that you understand they are dying. As the end nears, it can be deeply supportive to say goodbye and offer reassurance. Let them know they will be missed, and that those who love them will carry on and be okay. Simple, clear statements such as “It’s okay to let go,” and “You are not alone,” can offer profound comfort. This kind of compassionate reassurance is a gift—one that can ease the transition for both the dying and those who remain.

GROUNDING PRACTICES

Finding steadiness within

If you are experiencing fear or deep grief it may be supportive to find your center. You can hold your centre. Try putting both hands over your center, which is just below your ribcage, above your belly button, and feeling like you're holding your core. Here, you can give yourself strength. Here, you can give yourself support.

This gesture can be really helpful, especially if the emotions you are feeling are in your core—take the time to hold yourself here.

A Changing Role

> "It's about identifying with being rather than doing. The doctors and nurses are doing. You can just be. Just be love—a loving rock, loving awareness."
>
> —Ram Dass

As your person approaches death, change happens quickly. Priorities often shift and what once seemed important may begin to fade. Each time you engage with your person, imagine that you are meeting them for the first time, without expectation or judgment. Gently let go of who they used to be, and instead meet them where they are in this moment. Take your person's lead—they can do and say no wrong. Even if you are consumed with worry about your person's declining abilities or loss of independence, try to stay grounded in compassion. Changes in their cognition, a fading sense of hope, or the loss of shared future dreams can shake your sense of stability and security, but this is just the beginning of your grief process. It is common to grieve someone before they die, as changes in their identity—as well as shifts in your own—redefine your relationship.

Anticipatory grief is not just about accepting the future death, but also about the many losses that occur as an illness progresses. Feelings associated with other deaths that have impacted you in the past are likely to bubble up. Grief is messy but each time it is felt, it is also an opportunity for growth and healing. Consider intentionally taking the time to be with any big emotions that arise. There is great value in holding space for yourself as you would for a dear friend, to do your best to listen and be guided to how to best care for yourself. By tending to your grief, simply by acknowledging it and expressing it in whatever way feels right for you, you will feel more grounded and be more available to companion your person as their illness progresses. It is all about slowing down, attuning to yourself, and responding to the feelings and needs in the moment.

In addition to responding to anticipatory grief, you may find yourself burdened by doubt, wondering if you are making the right decisions or fearing that you're somehow disappointing or angering your person. You may be holding on to feelings of guilt for not doing enough, or grappling with discomfort over making choices your person doesn't agree with, even when those decisions come from a place of love and good intention. Resentments arising from the caregiving role are common. This stress is often compounded with intense anxiety and deep worry about your person's physical and emotional safety. This is a lot to hold. If you are feeling stretched too thin, consider leaning out for support. Dying is a communal experience—we are not designed to do this alone.

How Can I Show Up and Comfort the Dying?

People often approach the role of companioning their person by diving in headfirst. There is so much to do and so many pragmatic aspects of care to manage, that it's easy to overlook the importance of being intentional about how to show up. It is much easier *to do* than *to be*—often the distractions of "getting stuff done" can feel like a welcome relief rather than the quiet work of sitting down, slowing down, and companioning. However, if you are intentional, you can choose to show up with an open heart, to be grounded, empathic, and vulnerable. You can serve as a witness, guiding your person to find connection, awareness, meaning, pleasure, and presence. It is about expressing love, whatever that looks like in your unique relationship. The ideal way to show up for others is with a mix of both head and heart.

> *"Companioning is the art of bringing comfort to another by becoming familiar with her story (experiences and needs). Of course this may well involve tears and sorrow and tends to involve a give and take of story. I tell you my story and you tell me yours. It is a sharing in a deep and profound way."*
>
> —*Dr. Alan Wolfelt,* The Handbook for Companioning the Mourner: Eleven Essential Principles

GROUNDING PRACTICES

Walk through it

Walking is one of the simplest and most supportive ways to call on your head and your heart and regulate your nervous system. As you move, your eyes naturally scan your surroundings side to side. These bilateral eye movements engage both hemispheres of your brain: the left, which supports logic and decision-making, and the right, which helps you connect with and process emotion. This whole-brain activation can support you in navigating life with more clarity and calm when things get hard.

Consider taking a walk with intention before a courageous conversation, when you feel frayed, when the weight of grief feels heavy, or anytime you need a little more space to think and feel. You don't have to figure everything out; just begin by taking a step.

GROUNDING PRACTICES

One breath to be here

A one-breath meditation is a simple way to support you to feel calmer and more grounded. You can look to this accessible ritual whenever you feel contracted. You can take a sip of space and ventilate the situation with one breath. This practice can guide you to the present moment with more steadiness by returning you to your body:

- Inhale—*I am separating for a moment the experiencing I am in, and I am coming back to my body.*
- Pause
- Exhale—*With this out breath, I am returning to the space I am in.*

I WONDER . . .

Be where your feet are

Do you have practices that support you in feeling grounded? Tools that bring you out of your head and back into your body and the present moment?

Do you have practices that support you in feeling grounded? Tools that bring you out of your head and back into your body and the present moment? Be where your feet are. Notice the solid ground beneath you, the steadiness it offers. Sometimes simply pausing to breathe, to feel the earth holding you, can shift your whole perspective. When the mind races ahead or loops back to the past, your body is an anchor, always inviting you to return to now.

Trust Your Inner Guide

Consider being as present in your body as feels right for you. You can look to your senses—your ever present companions—to guide you to listen with your whole being, listening to your person as well as yourself. This "whole body" listening can support you to understand a lot more, and can allow you to offer all of yourself to serve your person more completely.

Some call this listening with intuition. Listening this way can allow you to tap into your inner guidance system. The key to opening this intuitive pathway is learning to listen to your body, which is communication with you all the time. Due to our fast-paced culture that values ideas over feelings, we are rarely encouraged to seek this inner guidance; many of us are distanced from our natural wisdom. Examples of physical intuition may include being guided to stretch or move your body a certain way, or the experience of having a strong gut feeling about something. The more you attune to yourself by way of your body, and listen with all your senses, the more effortlessly you will be guided to show up in just the right way.

GROUNDING PRACTICES

Rooted in rest

When overwhelm sets in, the first thing we often neglect is loving care for our own dear bodies. But without tending to yourself, the journey becomes harder—for you and those you support. You may need frequent reminders that caring for yourself is not selfish. Sustaining your ability to serve begins with preserving your own wellbeing.

Taking a break allows you to return with greater presence. You can only love and care for others to the extent that you love and care for yourself. Caregiving can be a long journey, and so it is vital to pause, breathe, and refuel along the way. Only you can truly know what you need from moment to moment. This requires regular check-ins and the gentle awareness that your needs may shift over time. Tending to yourself is best done often, throughout the day in small steady ways, as opposed to waiting to feel overwhelmed and completely depleted. May the list on the following page offer you some inspiration on how to nourish your dear self—body, mind, and spirit.

GROUNDING PRACTICES

The wheel of self-care

We are complex beings so it's important to take a holistic approach to self-care. Each of us has unique preferences and needs, which means the practices that nourish and support us will look different. May the suggestions below offer you inspiration. Consider weaving one small act from the following categories into your self-care routine. Tending to your wellbeing in this way allows you to show up in service with your whole self.

Physical

- Nourish yourself with balanced meals, even if they are small.
- Move your body (bike, dance, swim, yoga) or go for a walk.
- Spend time in nature.
- Sit in the sun.
- Take a nap.
- Drink plenty of water.
- Get a massage.
- Rest and sleep.
- Focus on your breath.
- Wear something soft.
- Garden or put your hands in the earth.
- Consider complementary therapies (like reiki or energy work).

Emotional

- Find ways to be supported with your grief experience.
- Creatively express your emotions (draw, paint, sing, or cook a new meal).
- Make a gratitude list.
- Find quiet time to be alone (even a few minutes).
- Plan time away from care on a regular basis.
- Meet with a support group or counsellor.

Social

- Stay connected with your favourite activities (time in nature, sports, hobbies, going for lunch).
- Cuddle with pets.
- Call a friend.
- Ask for support from family and friends.

Spiritual

- Stay connected to a faith community or spend time in a nurturing place (beach, sacred place, nature).
- Look up.
- Pray.
- Meditate.
- Reflect on your beliefs and what is most important or meaningful to you now.
- Listen to music.
- Keep the focus on life by being with your favourite people and doing your favourite things.

Inspirational

- Listen to your preferred music.
- Disconnect from electronic devices.
- Go on an adventure.
- Read an inspiring or light book.
- Watch a movie.
- Meditate, or use your personal stress reduction exercises.
- Journal, paint, or make art.

"I want to do more of ______________. I can do ______________ for myself more often."

Finding balance can be challenging. It can feel overwhelming to think about caring for yourself while you are caring for your person. You may have additional tasks and responsibilities over and above your usual roles. The practical aspects of companioning such as organizing caregivers, picking up prescriptions, driving to appointments, giving medications, and keeping the care team up to date takes a lot of energy. You may find it supportive to plan breaks and activities that you enjoy into the day to support you in finding balance.

You may also find that you are overwhelmed at times by conflicting thoughts and feelings about your role as companion. You can feel grateful to be able to care for your person but could also feel anger or resentment about the added responsibilities. You may feel physically and emotionally exhausted, unsure of how much longer you can sustain the tender care you want to offer your person. Of course you feel overwhelmed and worried. The future is uncertain. Now is the time to lean out on family, friends, and community services such as home support agencies, cleaners, meal delivery services, and other support programs available in your community.

I WONDER . . .

Receiving is part of the journey: Leaning out on others

- How can you care for yourself while caring for your person?
- What three things would be most helpful to you at this time?
- Think about ways your family, friends, or neighbours could support you (help with errands, practical jobs, or offering a break from caregiving).
- What would a little rest or break look like to you right now?

GROUNDING PRACTICES

Nourishing your body to stay grounded

One of the simplest ways to stay grounded is to nourish your body with protein. Eating protein helps keep your energy stable and your mind clear, so that you can show up more fully. Eating a handful of nuts, a slice of cheese, or some veggies and hummus can make a big difference in how you feel and how present you can be.

What Is a Companion To the Dying?

A companion to the dying is a person who walks alongside. A companion is led. Companioning is rooted in service. It is not about directing. Companioning is about accepting, normalizing, and validating the experience. It is about surrendering to the unpredictability of the journey. The role requires humility, equanimity, and intuition.

Humility in the face of mystery is required to manage the frustration we often feel when we think we are supposed to know it all and be in control. We're not. On the end-of-life journey we are only one part of the whole unfolding. The quality of humility in a companion will support healthy expectations that honour that we are enough, and guide us to just do what we can, without feeling the situation has to have a certain predicted outcome.

Equanimity refers to mental calmness, composure, and evenness of temper, especially when in a difficult situation. This may be easier for some than others. Equanimity can be strengthened by meditation, whether that is an in-depth practice or as simple as a long exhale. Awareness of the importance of equanimity and reflection on what practices work for you will support you in your role as companion.

Companions are intuitive and have the ability to understand something without conscious reasoning. Allow yourself to receive guidance from your deeper self and a greater source. Intuition invites us to embrace what may not be fully understood by our rational mind, to become more open to the mystery of life and death. You can think of intuition as a kind of knowing that bypasses our conscious mind, a knowing that is informed by our senses and our consciousness. It is an understanding that precedes reasoning, logic, or inference. Intuition is a spontaneous sureness that is different from rational deduction. This is available to all of us, as we can increase our intuitive nature with awareness. In this culture of meeting most things headfirst with our mind, the heart-first role of companioning is a radical act. It's about feeling first, being open to all possibilities, and then calling on the mind.

To companion well, you don't have to agree with your person but you must know their hopes so you can be congruent with their needs. For this, consistent communication is required. Companioning is most powerful when guided by heart wisdom, as it enhances the ability to truly attune to others. Attunement is defined as the ability to be aware of and respond to another person's needs and is a key part of emotional attachment and trust. It is literally the process of making something harmonious or bringing it into tune.

What softens your heart? What makes it close up in defence? Our hearts were not designed to be open all the time, but over time, this heart-centered awareness will make it easier to access your heart sense when you want to. All relationships will benefit from this attunement, but it is especially fitting for times of change, and there is so much change on the end-of-life journey.

It is normal for there to be dissonance along the end-of-life journey. Conflicts within families are more common than not, and it's rare for everyone to be in full alignment without any differing perspectives. It's possible that your person may not agree with the treatment plan. As a companion, it is not your role get everyone to agree—this impossible task will likely result in frustration and exhaustion. Instead, do what you can to soften your heart and listen. This will diffuse the situation and create space for understanding.

Thankfully we have other members of the palliative care team who can put their heads together and address the medical issues and the things that can be changed, such as pain management, diagnosis, prognosis, and offering insights into expected patterns. Even these more practical, head-centred conversations benefit from a heart-forward approach.

GROUNDING PRACTICES

From mind to heart: Grounding practices for presence

Do you have ways to bring yourself back to center when you are feeling frayed? Connecting with the natural world may offer support such as going for a walk, gardening, or being barefoot on the earth. Perhaps you enjoy breath work, a deep exhale, or a specific breathing pattern. Do you benefit from yoga, journaling, running, swimming, martial arts, cooking, knitting, praying, dancing, spending time with family, friends or pets, listening to music, making a cup of tea, soaking in a bath with epsom salts, or simply just looking up?

Cultivating a grounded, calm presence, this resonance will expand outward and affect all that you do for your person.

Even if we know showing up in this way is deeply supportive, we may need consistent reminders of the power or presence. The simple compassionate action of seeing and hearing your person is often what is missing from end-of-life care. Lean in. Showing up as a grounded, calm, non-judgmental presence that just by being, reassures your person that they are not alone.

The Five Roots of Practice

1. Show up grounded and heart centered.

Identify any practices that help you feel grounded and connected you to your heart and use them intentionally before you spend time with your person. If you feel activated when you are with your person, do what you can to find your centre and ground yourself in the moment so you can stay present despite the discomfort.

What you do before you show up to comfort your person is important. Dying is a time of great change. This can be destabilizing, so it is essential to be grounded. Feeling calm and centred enables change to happen with more ease. There are endless ways to cultivate a grounded calm presence and finding the practice that is best suited to you is important.

2. Follow the lead of the dying and honour their autonomy.

Your person is at the center of this journey now. Whenever possible allow them to lead the conversation and make their own choices. Showing up in this way reflects a deep respect for your person's values, beliefs, and ability to decide what matters most to them.

Your person is the most important person now. Autonomy is vital at this stage. Supporting autonomy means honouring their independence and empowering them to express themselves and guide their own care.

Even as you are affected by the experience of companioning, do your best to have an awareness of your own activations. When you feel evoked, take note and remind yourself that this is not happening to you. Maybe you have had a similar experience or grief that hasn't been tended to that may present itself; simply notice what is happening. Although it may take restraint, do your best to tend to your emotions on your own time. Breathe and stay rooted in why you are there, and what you are generously providing. This is not to say you can't share how you are being touched; rather, it is about supporting your person first and doing what you can to stay present to their needs.

3. Focus on life.

Life is there until the very last moment, and it is supportive to focus on life, not in a death-denying way, but with life-affirming intention. When we lose this focus, we abandon the dying. Can we find creative ways to highlight life that is here, now? Offering favourite foods and drinks, rest, loving touch, and casual conversation about simple things in life, all shift focus away from the realm of death and back into the wonder of the living world.

4. Empower those closest to the dying to provide care.

It is most supportive to empower those closest to the dying to step in and provide care, as they are the most fitting and qualified to do so. They know the personal preferences, the small comforts, and the unique needs of their person in ways no one else can. The intimacy of their relationship allows for a deeper level of comfort and support, something individuals offering support who are not as close, can only help facilitate. While we can model care and come alongside them, in this situation our role is to create space for connection, encouraging them to step in fully, offering the most meaningful presence.

5. Lean out for support.

Caring for the dying asks for collective support. Consider bringing in other people to bolster the web of support around your person. It is essential that you lean out on others as well; this will help you to express the complex emotions that are inherent in companioning the dying, and also to address your own wellbeing.

Remember that holding space for big emotions for others can be challenging at the best of times, and it's impossible to do well if you aren't resourced. You are undoubtedly experiencing a lot of grief if you are companioning your person who is dying. Leaning out on your closest people or a mental health professional is a healthy way to express and tend to your grief. Have an awareness of the emotional weight you carry—of what is yours to hold and what you can let go of.

Show up the way you always have with your person. Greet your person with a smile and a cheerful demeanor. It may be challenging for others to show up in this way, making your smiles all the more important. Humour is not only okay—it is powerful medicine. Remember that your person is the same person they were before their diagnosis. Affirming this by how you engage with them is a way of honouring.

Being there for your person requires you to be expansive. It's normal to feel a wide range of emotions—grief and joy can exist side by side. Your person most likely wants you there, just as you are. This moment calls for you to be spacious enough to hold the discomfort, the sadness, and the lightness. Do your best to show up as the person you've always been in this relationship. Be natural. Don't hold back your happiness—let it be part of the love you bring.

It is so important that we offer people what they truly need, as opposed to what we feel compelled to give. Being a companion is about slowing down in order to give your person the time and space to keep pace with all of the changes that arise at the end of life. It's about making room for each ending, and for each beginning. This is how we can travel alongside others with grace.

Setting Expectations

One unrealistic expectation that companions to the dying may want to reflect on is the belief that a life-limiting diagnosis will change a person's fundamental nature. Personality traits are often amplified on the end-of-life journey. If your person has lived as a quiet, gentle soul, they may become even more quiet and gentle. If they have been demanding, they may become more so. It is helpful to be aware of this pattern of behaviour, as it will help to inform your expectations and meet your person where they are.

Your motivation to companion someone at the end of life may be more sustainable if you release the expectation of receiving anything in return. Caring deeply for someone who is dying is not easy. Recognizing this may encourage you to lean out for support, making it more likely that you will be able to continue showing up. This is wild terrain—doing your best to stay present, to honour of the uniqueness of your person, and to remain open to whatever arises will serve both of you well.

GROUNDING PRACTICES

Companioning the dying: A practice of love and letting go

Dear companions, do your best to try not to fix anything or to lead your person in a particular direction. Be aware of your own fears of death and your attachment to the dying person, and refrain from wishing things were other than they are. This will support you to be still, relaxed, straight forward, genuine, and present. This will support trust. Take some time stop, be present, and remember why things are as they are. You can always come back to this list to remind yourself of this practice:

- Listen.
- Be present.
- Be humble.
- Be with each moment.
- Accept and honour that we are designed to die, and have confidence in the natural process.
- Don't lose your sense of humour.
- Expect nothing and be ready for everything.
- Do your best to relate to your fears and not from them.
- Follow the lead of the dying.
- Lead with your heart.

It is normal to feel lost on the end-of-life journey. Death is wild and each journey is unique. We can start by simply naming this and accepting, perhaps even embracing the mystery. There are so many questions that simply can't be answered, and yet in some ways, dying is surprisingly predictable.

So what can you expect? Stories of natural dying consistently demonstrate that the psychosocial changes at the end of life tend to follow a foreseeable pattern. Anticipated landmarks have been identified that can normalize the emotional and social changes that the dying commonly experience. Understanding these touch points can empower you to support your person as they begin to release social roles, such as saying goodbye to acquaintances, and gradually turn inward in preparation for death.

As our human bodies are designed to die, most often the natural changes that present as one moves towards death are foreseeable as well. There are anticipated stages that the physical body moves through, and being aware of these changes can normalize the seemingly random experience and reassure the dying and their people that what is happening is expected—dying is often much gentler than people expect. Sharing this information with those closest to the dying is important as it allows all involved to be more present to what is happening and to appropriately embrace what time is remaining.

As the end approaches, physical, spiritual, and emotional changes often accelerate, creating the sense that everything is happening at once. Since dying often happens behind closed doors, most people are unaware of what normal dying looks like, and this can create fear. When we become aware of the predictable stages of dying, the end-of-life experience becomes easier.

Many people find relief when they know what to expect. However, if your person has dementia, they will not follow the predictable patterns outlined in this section. Those living with dementia, might start to sleep more, eat and drink less, and have little interest in the outside world years in advance of their death. When they have difficulty or become unable to swallow, the dying process begins. At this stage, you may oberserve signs of approaching death similar to those seen in other diseases and old age.

As disease evolves, challenges, fears, and anxieties may arise; however, for some this journey can also be filled with extraordinary and wonder-filled moments. The body, mind, and soul are all involved in this profound transition. When people understand that what they are experiencing is normal and expected, they are more likely to be able to be present to the life that remains.

Helping Young People Navigate Death

It is essential that families talk with young ones about the death, and even invite them to take part in the decision-making process when appropriate. Excluding children from the process can leave them feeling powerless. Open, honest conversations about options are essential. Reading books about grief and pet loss to children can provide a gentle way for parents and children to talk about the concept of death together. I love idea of an adult or parent sitting down with a child, snuggling under a blanket on the couch, and sharing a simple yet profound picture book about death. These books offer not only gentle guidance to help children understand death and grief, but also serve as simple, meaningful reminders for the adults reading them. There are countless children's books about death and grief; the local library is a great place to explore age appropriate reads.

Parents often wonder if a child should be allowed to be present during death and see the body after. Begin by asking the child what they feel comfortable with—this step is often overlooked. If the parent or child decides not to be present during the final moments, they can still spend time with their person afterward and say goodbye. Seeing their person after they have died can help provide a sense of closure for both children and parents.

EXPECTED CHANGES ON THE JOURNEY

The inner terrain of letting go

In *Awake at the Bedside: Contemplative teachings on palliative and end-of-life care*, Dr. Ira Byock lists predictable tasks that guide people to complete or close their personal lives. These tasks are emotional, relational, and spiritual in nature. Byock acknowledges that the process is somewhat orderly, and for most people, the sense of completion of these tasks is rewarding.

The developmental landmarks and tasks listed start outward and progressively work inward. Allow your person to take the lead as this is not about checking off boxes and directing your person; it is about having an awareness of expected waypoints so you can notice opportunities for healing.

Byock outlines key landmarks and associated task work on the end-of-life journey. The first landmark is a sense of completion with worldly affairs, where the task work involves transferring fiscal, legal, and formal social responsibilities. The next landmark is a sense of completion in relationships with community, where the task work includes closing multiple social relationships across various spheres like employment, commerce, and community organizations.

The sense of meaning about one's life is another important landmark, with the task work of reviewing life through storytelling and transmitting knowledge and wisdom. This is followed by experiencing self-love, which requires self-acknowledgement and self-forgiveness. In relation to others, the task work involves accepting one's worthiness of love. A sense of completion in relationships with family and friends comes next, with tasks that involve reconciliation, full communication, and closure in important relationships. This includes expressing regret, forgiveness, gratitude, affection, and saying goodbye.

As individuals come to accept the finality of life, they work through the emotional pain of existential loss and acknowledge the personal tragedy dying represents. Emotional withdrawal from worldly affairs and connection to enduring constructs become part of the process, along with the acceptance of dependency. The landmark of a new sense of self or personhood beyond personal loss follows, requiring task work that develops self-awareness in the present. Another landmark involves finding meaning in life more generally, which involves entering a state of awe, recognizing transcendent realms, and becoming comfortable with chaos.

The final landmark is surrender to the transcendent and the unknown, where the task work involves letting go. At this stage, the doer and the task are one, with the ego largely dissipated, with only the will to surrender remaining. These stages and their accompanying task work illustrate the complex emotional and existential journey individuals undergo at the end of life.

Beyond these pragmatic tasks of closing down a life and completing relationships, people may explore and perhaps achieve a sense of meaning, and maybe even a connection to something greater than themselves, such as God, nature, family, or community.

These developmental landmarks help to guide individuals to transition from experiencing a sense of meaninglessness to a sense of wholeness. As a companion, recognizing these landmarks can support you to encourage your person to complete the task work where possible—all the while remembering that this is not a checklist for a good death; what matters most is that your person has the freedom to act according to what is most fitting to them. This is the art of companioning, calling for deep listening, patience, trust, and releasing expectations. If your person is open to being supported to complete some or all of these tasks, this may assist your person to let go of the things that become less relevant to their current life situation. When your person feels that nothing more needs to be done, a natural letting go can occur. Byock believes that completion increases the chance of a peaceful, even transcendent, death.

Another helpful way to understand the end-of-life journey is by learning about the changes that occur in the physical body. Knowing what to expect can offer reassurance and allow for more presence. In the past, this knowledge was often passed down through personal caregiving in our in homes and communities. Today, it can still be invaluable in supporting both the person who is dying and their companions.

EXPECTED CHANGES ON THE JOURNEY

Waypoints toward the end

There are common physical, emotional, and spiritual changes that are often experienced as one approaches death:

- **Sleeping more** – Your person will have less energy, and they may spend most of the day sleeping or resting. They may appear to be uncommunicative and at times difficult to wake. This is a result of changes in metabolism of the body and brain. At this time, simply being present, offering gentle touch with consent, and speaking from your heart can offer comfort.
- **Eating and drinking less** – As the body slows down it requires less energy, so your person doesn't need to eat or drink as much as before. The digestive system becomes unable to process food or fluids. Your person may begin to refuse food or drink, causing weight loss. Forcing food at this stage can make your person uncomfortable. You can offer popsicles, ice chips, ice cream, or smoothies, but be aware of your person's ability to swallow. If dehydration is causing dry mouth and lips you can use a moisturized swab or a water-soluble lubricant to moisten.
- **Little interest in the outside world** – Your person will become weak and fatigued, making it exhausting to concentrate and socialize. Withdrawing like this is part of letting go. Reassure your person that it is okay to rest and let them know that it is okay not to respond when you speak.
- **A burst of energy** – Near the end, your person may have a sudden burst of alert behavior; they may say what needs to be said, they may sit up or get out of bed, or request a big feast, only to later return to a state of decline. This is referred to as "terminal lucidity" and it is often a sign that death is imminent.
- **Breathing changes** – Your person's breathing may become noisy, rattly, irregular, and laboured. You may hear Cheyne–Stokes breathing, a cyclical breathing pattern characterized by periods of apnea (no breathing) followed by shallow, rapid breathing that gradually increases in depth and rate before returning to apnea.
- **Bladder and bowel changes** – As the body's systems slow down, your person may have trouble emptying their bladder. A catheter may be inserted into the bladder

to drain urine. Medicines may be prescribed for constipation. As the person eats and drinks less, they will produce less urine and feces. Loss of bladder and bowel control sometimes happens in the last stages of the dying process.

- **Disorientation and confusion** – Your person may seem confused about time, place, and the identity of people present, even close friends and family. Sometimes the care team will be able to identify causes of confusion that can be resolved, but often this is just a natural part of the dying process. Introduce yourself by name before speaking. Use a soft clear tone and simple language when communicating.
- **Increased restlessness** – In the days leading up to death your person may begin squirming, twitching, groaning, fidgeting, or calling out. They may become increasingly restless and even make repetitive motions such as pulling at their clothing or bed linen. Your person may become frustrated, irritable, and angry. Terminal agitation is often the result of metabolic changes and a decrease in circulation to the brain. Know that this is common and that there is no need to restrain these motions. If you believe your person is in pain, or experiencing shortness of breath, talk to the care team. These symptoms are common and not necessarily uncomfortable for the dying person. Consider how to comfort your person. You can offer reassurance in a calm, quiet voice, read or play their favourite music, or offer a gentle hand or foot massage.
- **Cool skin and colour changes** – As circulation slows down, your person's arms and legs may become cold or hot, or their skin colour may change. This is a natural consequence of circulation changing to support the central organs. Varying temperatures can also be caused by the brain sending unclear messages to the body. If your person appears cold, keep them warm; if they feel warm or remove their covers or clothing, consider using a light sheet or crack open a window.

Note: If mucus builds up in the throat, breathing can create a gurgling sound as air moves past. We unconsciously swallow these secretions all the time but as your person enters reduced states of consciousness this reflex ceases. Know that your person is breathing just fine, and this mucus build up does not affect oxygen levels. Hearing this rattle can be distressing, often making it challenging for friends and family to be relaxed and present at the bedside. Understand that your person is unaware of what is happening at this stage. Dr. Kathryn Mannix offers a powerful reframe. She insists that this change in breathing is a sign of safety—that your person is so deeply unconscious, they are safe.

There are medications available that can be administered to reduce secretions; however, side effects can often complicate the process.

Sometimes there is a moaning sound on exhaling. This is not due to discomfort; rather, it is air passing over relaxed vocal cords. You can speak to the care team about repositioning your person, perhaps elevating the head or turning them to one side, but this is not necessary—again, this is a normal part of dying. You can offer comfort by sitting with your person and offering gentle and reassuring words.

EXPECTED CHANGES ON THE JOURNEY

A perfect design

When the body begins to change as death nears, ketones are produced, and this is a good thing. Ketones suppress appetite; they are created alongside dynorphins due to the breakdown of proteins. These dynorphins are a type of endogenous opiate that is six-to-ten times more potent than morphine and provides an analgesic and anesthetic action. The body is designed to be born, to grow, and to die when the time comes.

CAMPP: CONNECTION, AWARENESS, MEANING, PLEASURE, PRESENCE

Mirrored breathing: Breathing better together

If breathing changes, becoming erratic or laboured, you can consider co-breathing with your person. Begin by slowing down—really take your time to match your breathing to theirs. When you are breathing together, you can invite your person to inhale with awareness, with a focus on filling the lungs just a little more. Your steady breathing can support them to take more controlled breaths. You can make an *aaaaahhhh* sound when breathing out to encourage a long, smooth exhale. Mirrored breathing may offer comfort while communicating connection and care.

I WONDER . . .

Beyond the quiet ideal

Do you have expectations about the requirements of a good death? There is often an assumption that a quiet, calm, clean death—one without fuss—is more spiritual. We consider noise, confusion, and mess to be less desirable, but binaries don't apply to humans, they only apply to computers. And the experience of living and dying is messy. Quiet isn't good and noisy isn't bad.

Noisy and messy are natural as the body begins to shut down. Restlessness is expected in one of the greatest transitions we are called to make, one involving the body, mind, and spirit. Dying is a human experience—of course folks can get angry, sob, and vomit. This is just part of normal dying.

As a companion, do your best to be there, leaning on the medical care team when appropriate. At the end of life you are not only providing care but also cooperating with the body's processes to offer comfort and healing.

Keep in mind that this information on some of the expected physical changes is offered to help you understand the natural processes of the body as it approaches death, but each person's journey is unique. Not all of the signs occur; there may be different normal changes, or these changes may occur in a different order.

It is supportive to tend to the physical body in a way that allows the inevitable to unfold peacefully. Ask the care team for more information if you are feeling uncertain. You can directly ask, "What does this illness look like over time?" Understanding what to expect helps both you and your person to make informed decisions with the time that remains.

EXPECTED CHANGES ON THE JOURNEY

The pace of letting go

The rate of change at the end of life can often hint at what is to be expected. If changes happen month to month, life expectancy is likely months. If changes occur week to week, life expectancy is often weeks. If changes are apparent from day to day, it's often days. When they're hour to hour, death is most likely imminent. Look for trends. These changes over time can give you a sense of how quickly or slowly an illness is progressing. When we know what to look for it allows both you and your person to remain present, listening, and following the body's natural wisdom.

STORIES FROM THE TRAIL

Not dead yet: A declaration of life

I was honoured to companion a neighbour on his end-of-life journey. His family was the center of his universe, he was a generous community member and colleague, and on weekends he was a talented musician and played in a band. At 50, he was living with cancer. He was not one to draw attention to himself so in the year or so leading up to his death, he surprised many when he wore an understated black hoodie with "NOT DEAD YET" printed in large white letters on the back: his declaration. He wore that hoodie when he was admitted to hospice and right up until the last few days of his life. He was alive and he let everyone know.

For some, the act of wearing this hoodie may have seemed like playful nod to Monty Python's memorable skit, for others this may have been imagined to simply be poor judgement brought on by his relentless brain tumour, but I like to think that he was simply reminding others that life exists until the moment it doesn't. So often we treat people living with a life-limiting diagnosis as if they were the disease, or only a transparent version of their former selves. People are alive right up until the last breath so treat them accordingly.

Being an embodied companion—being present in the body as well as in the mind—will serve you well. When we direct awareness from the business of our heads and into our physical bodies, we can access natural wisdom. Bodyfulness celebrates the senses and honours autonomy and natural intelligence. It touches on what it means to be a relational being. Your person's body is asking for care, and by slowing down and tuning into this awareness we can listen with all of our senses.

So how does a connection to our bodies through the senses lead us to contentment? Many of us living in this busy modern world do not often focus our attention on the sensory experience of the body, and when we do, it can be surprising how powerful this attunement can be. When we engage with the world through our senses instead of through our minds—our thoughts and judgments—we can directly experience and know life through our bodies. In return, we can let the world know us as well.

It is through attuning to your own body and gently facilitating sensorial experiences for others that you can invite your person into possible encounters with wholeness. It is through the senses that your person can be reminded of their life force and connection to this world, and participation in the direct experience of life—the universal nature of our being.

> We are all beginners—every death is unique. If you have seen one death, you have seen one death. There are no experts here.

GROUNDING PRACTICES

Finding calm, one sense at a time

Consider the gateways of sight, hearing, smell, taste, and touch. What makes you feel at peace? Perhaps it is listening to your favourite song or soaking in a warm bath. Choose one grounding practice for each of the five senses.

CAMPP: CONNECTION, AWARENESS, MEANING, PLEASURE, PRESENCE

Butterfly hug

You can offer a comforting practice to your person through a soothing butterfly hug. Guide your person to cross their arms (as if they were giving themselves a hug) and invite them to alternately tap the left and right upper arm. Breathe and gently tap for a minute or two.

The Sea of Fears

> "We are afraid of fear, which gives it great power."
>
> —Ram Dass, Walking Each Other Home

"The anticipation of pleasure is pleasure itself." I would often say this to my kids as the presents rested wrapped, adorned with glossy bows, under the Christmas tree for most of December. The same can be said for fear: the anticipation of fear is fear itself.

We may wish for fearlessness in the face of death, but fear is a natural response to facing the unknown. No one can tell you what it is going to be like, making dying the most solitary thing we are going to do. As a companion, you may be lucky enough to get a little more intimate with death. You may have a front-row seat, allowing you to get to know death a little better.

With the acceptance that we are afraid to die, we can turn our attention to what matters—how we meet that fear. Exploring the sea of fears with another takes courage. Taking a long exhale and trusting in the potency of holding space will support you. Do your best to simply be with what your person is expressing and resist the need to solve for anything. There is a way to support your person to be less frightened. You can invite them to become aware of their fear. You can support them in noticing the felt experience of fear and just be there for them to share their fears when and if they choose to.

EXPECTED CHANGES ON THE JOURNEY

Companioning your person through fear

Here are some fears—both universal and specific—of the dying:

- Struggling to breathe
- Being on a ventilator
- Losing your hair
- Becoming ugly
- Being in pain
- Becoming incontinent of urine or stool
- Being weak or dependent on people
- Losing freedom, independence, or ability to make decisions
- Having no privacy—everything gets revealed
- Getting an autopsy
- Getting needles
- Waking up in the coffin
- Dying while awake
- Dying while asleep
- Being watched, stared at, and judged all the time
- No one noticing that you died
- Burdening your family
- Being abandoned by your family
- Losing emotional control
- Not finishing everything that is important for you to do

If your person opens up to you and shares their fears, avoid the common habitual response of shallow reassurances and side stepping the conversation. These replies will only serve to keep fear hidden, allowing it to really take hold. The collusion of silence is common on the end-of-life journey, and it has devastating consequences. Most people know where they are and where they are headed. Often when they attempt to talk to others about their fears and hopes these much needed conversations are rebuffed by those around them who can't bear to come to terms with the reality of the situation. When there isn't an opportunity to share fears with another, the fears recirculate, causing distress. When we are unable to meet the dying in these important conversations, we abandon the very people we are hoping to support. As a companion to the dying, you can mitigate suffering through connection—by supporting fears through comforting conversations.

Death is often a vulnerable topic so it is natural to have some resistance and discomfort around talking about it. Of course you feel the urge to cheer your person up, or to turn away, but death is persistent—it quietly asks you to lean in a little bit when it feels hard. It nudges you to get curious about this natural part of life. Do your best to feel into your inner wisdom and let it guide you. Your true nature knows the way. We are all beginners—every death is unique. There are no experts here. No matter how often you see death you will not be immune to fear.

Let's take a closer look at the most common fears of the dying and explore some considerations for finding your way in these conversations. May these suggestions support you when exploring fears, all the while acknowledging that the most important thing is to simply offer your presence. Remember, listening to your person may not seem like enough, but opening your heart to their suffering changes things.

CAMPP: CONNECTION, AWARENESS, MEANING, PLEASURE, PRESENCE

Supporting fears through physical symptoms

If your person shares about their physical discomfort or dysregulation, you may ask, with respectful curiosity, about what they are feeling under those symptoms. You may find that the conversation shifts toward a parallel emotional experience. Your role as companion is not to keep the situation calm and grounded at all times—if it were, you would be unable to sustain the role for very long. The goal is to be fully present with everything that is arising, even discomfort and fear.

How do you begin these tender conversations? It may be supportive to start by softening a bit. It is not only safe to talk about this topic, bit it is also almost always a source of comfort and relief. Even if it feels awkward at first, expressing big emotions, being witnessed, and feeling understood by others increases connection, and connection always makes things better. If a conversation feels daunting, it is almost always an indication that it is an important one to have. Instead of bracing yourself for one big talk, it may be less overwhelming to think about approaching fears through a series of exchanges that progress a little at a time.

If your person initiates a conversation, the door is open for you to walk through. If you are sensing that your person would benefit from sharing their experience, honour self-determination. Begin by asking your person if they want to talk about how they are feeling. If you receive the blessing of consent, it will nourish the unfolding of your conversation, and once there is even a sliver of an opening for a big conversation, future discussions won't feel as insurmountable. Do your best to just be normal and support your person in the conversation in the same ways you always have. If your person begins to share their fears, your role is to do your best to settle in, soften your heart, and listen—truly listen with your heart sense, without allowing your head to get in the way. The guiding intention here is to communicate to your person that you see them and hear them so that they know they are not alone.

If you feel your own fear arising, just notice how it feels. Get to know your fear. This practice will support you to get closer to death as a companion, and to be more prepared in your own dying time. If the discomfort intensifies and you notice your body responding, do your best to stay with the conversation while supporting yourself.

Tending to your body—more specifically, your nervous system—is an effective way to stay present. You may want to try mindfully pressing the soles of your feet into the ground to allow the heightened energy to flow through you, taking an intentional breath to add a little pause, or letting go through a long exhale to support your vagus nerve. Simple practices like these may be all it takes for you to find equilibrium, allowing you to stay present with your person and their experience.

It can't be stressed enough that showing up in these conversations is not about fixing, solving, advising, minimizing, or any of the other entrenched responses that we revert to when flooded with discomfort. Companioning your person as they express their fears is about listening. When get out of our heads and connect with our hearts in order to listen deeply, we are able to understand what another is going through. This opens us up to connection, to feeling with another, which is the definition of compassion.

Among researchers, compassion is defined as the feeling that arises when confronted with another's suffering and then feeling motivated to relieve that suffering. In this dominant culture that values solving problems, staying comfortable, and doing as opposed to being, simply offering an ear for listening may not seem like enough but it is the medicine we are all seeking—*Am I being seen? Am I being heard?* If you can be there for your person, if you can keep breathing and hold space for the whole experience of dying, you will have done well.

After holding their fears through listening and feeling with your person, consider extending words of validation. "Of course," goes a long way. Of course your person is afraid. Of course. This territory is full of so many losses and so much mystery. Once you allow the fear to just be without trying to change anything, once you normalize their experience through validation, the fear will lift slightly. This may open up a space of silence—this is good and generous, and allows the fear to expand and find its full expression. These conversations are simply about coming alongside so that you can help your person carry these worries.

CAMPP: CONNECTION, AWARENESS, MEANING, PLEASURE, PRESENCE

Navigating fear with empathy: A guide to heartfelt conversations at end of life

- Meet the conversation heart first and listen—really listen.
- Acknowledge, validate, and normalize the fear.
- Hold space for the fear to be fully expressed—silence is a generous offering.
- Offer empathy—a simple phrase such as "You are holding a lot," or "I am here," a hand on the back, or shared silence will go a long way.
- Explore the fear—don't make assumptions, and ask open-ended questions rooted in respectful curiosity.
- Remember that things change constantly on the end-of-life journey so continue to check in.

You may not be able to control the situation, but you can control how you respond to it. You can offer your soft heart and your generous presence. You can choose to touch the conversation with love instead of with more fear. You can extend enough space for the whole experience to stretch out. You can offer your presence—a force more real than any words that you offer.

"Will there be pain? Will I suffer unbearably?"

Fear of pain is the most common worry on the end-of-life journey. The complexity of pain is reflected in the definition offered by British hospice pioneer Dame Cicely Saunders, who defined the concept of total pain as the suffering that encompasses all of a person's physical, psychological, social, spiritual, and practical struggles.

As companions to the dying, our approach to offer comfort must be rooted in this holistic understanding to be effective. Pain is a signal that something needs attention. It is always a personal experience that is influenced to varying degrees by many factors. Pain is a concept that is learned through one's life experiences. Your person's pain is whatever they say it is, but keep in mind verbal descriptions are only one of many ways to express pain.

The fear of pain and unbearable suffering at the end of life is profound, and addressing it with honesty, reassurance, and practical support can help ease distress. As a companion you can support your person by acknowledging and normalizing the fear. Feeling with your person and offering a simple statement such as, "I hear that you're afraid of being in pain, and that makes so much sense," will let them know they are not alone. Do what you can to create space for conversation that allows them to express specific concerns.

Differentiating between pain and suffering can offer guidance as to how to most appropriately support your person. Suffering is something that we can affect; it is the meaning or resistance attached to pain, and in this way the two concepts are connected but distinct experiences. Suffering is the emotional, mental, or spiritual distress that arises when there is struggle against pain or when one perceives it as unbearable. You can think of pain as an experience and suffering as a reaction. Both pain and suffering are personal, determined by one's personality and life experiences. Suffering can be increased by fear, attachment, or resistance to change. We will never completely understand how another suffers but we can approach distress heart first and companion others in their struggles.

Fear of pain at the end of life can itself be a source of pain. Eric J. Cassell, American physician, bioethicist, and author of *The Nature of Healing: The Modern Practice of Medicine* suggests that if a patient believes that more pain means their illness is getting worse—and that a worsening illness brings them closer to death—it's no surprise that their pain feels unmanageable. What the patient might not see without your guidance is that pain isn't about death; it is simply about pain—and pain at the end of life can be controlled. This distinction is important when supporting your person because while pain management is essential, helping your person find peace in their experience can reduce suffering.

Addressing pain on the end-of-life journey involves supporting emotional and spiritual pain. Sometimes, fear of suffering is more about emotional or spiritual distress than physical pain. As a companion you can ask, "Is there anything in your heart that feels heavy right now? Are there any unresolved worries or relationships you'd like to talk about?" Supporting your person in taking on unfinished business, finding meaning, or engaging in spiritual practices might just ease their suffering.

How can you hold space for pain and reduce suffering? How can you invite your person to soften around fear, accept what is, and find meaning—even in difficult moments?

Pain is a prevalent symptom on the end-of-life journey; however, in most cases dying is more comfortable than most people imagine it to be. The body knows how to die; it is a natural process. For those who experience pain, there are medical and non-medical ways to increase comfort. Hospice palliative care specializes in pain management, and it may take a bit of trial and error but it is estimated that for those who have access to quality care, most pain can be controlled. If your person shares a fear of pain with you, consider offering the compassionate listening support suggested above. It is important to validate the fear and give it space to stretch out. Perhaps your person will be guided to find a path forward to comfort.

Sometimes, fear of pain is a fear of losing control. As a companion you can empower your person by discussing their preferences and talking about what comfort looks like to them. Do they want to listen to music? Do they want to be touched or held? Let your person know that they are always in control and that they can speak up at any time if something doesn't feel right, so that you can make sure they are as comfortable as possible. If the fear of pain is rooted in a loss of control it may be supportive to start a care plan or review existing preferences together to ensure their personal wishes for pain management are honoured.

Reassure your person that they are in control of the care they receive. Perhaps you can invite them to explore pain management strategies that have worked for them in the past. You can let your person know that pain control will be an open conversation along the journey and choice will be offered. Empowerment around palliative pain management may include suggesting that your person has a conversation with their medical care team to discuss options. Do your best to start with normalizing and validating before exploring solutions. The goal is not to eradicate the fear of pain; rather, it is to offer support so that this worry is not overwhelming.

I WONDER . . .

Understanding pain: A journey through fear and acceptance

If your person is open, explore this fear. We relate to pain in different ways—annoyance, terror, silence. What does pain mean to your person? Consider asking questions about their personal relationship to pain such as:

- When have you experienced persistent pain before?
- What did you take away from the experience?
- What were things that helped ease your pain?
- Did anything make the experience more difficult for you?
- How important is pain management for you?
- Are you willing to be foggy-headed or sleeping most of the time if you are given strong pain meds?

You can reassure your person that pain can be managed. Palliative and hospice care have excellent tools for pain management. Offer gentle but truthful reassurance. You can let your person know that they will not be left to suffer. Let them know that there are medications and other ways to keep them comfortable. If they are hesitant about pain medication, you can encourage them to explore their concerns and discuss options that align with their values.

There are many options for treating pain, and with trial and error, most pain can be relieved. Unfortunately, treatments that alleviate pain can have unpleasant side effects such as nausea, fatigue, and constipation, so it is important to work with the medical care team to find the right medication and dose for your person. Keep in mind that even with perfect pain management, it is still not unusual to see suffering. You can continue to try to understand what your person is going through; even if the worry can't be solved your person will feel companioned in their experience.

Limiting attitudes toward medical treatments for pain can impact pain control. For example, people with concerns around addiction may fear that taking narcotics to manage pain will lead to an addiction. Addiction occurs when narcotics are abused by being taken in large doses in the absence of pain for the purpose of producing a high. At end of life, pain medication is increased when pain increases. It is important to remember that the right medication and dose should be determined by the person's response and comfort, not by the amount of medication. Addiction at end of life is not an issue, so the medication is taken at regular intervals to provide continuous relief from pain, in an amount sufficient to keep the pain under control.

You may come across barriers to effective pain management on your person's end-of-life journey. To start, not everyone has access to quality hospice palliative care or effective emotional support. Access may be restricted by language, geography, or cost. Culture can also impact our experience of pain. In some cultures, sharing pain is seen as a weakness so it is kept secret. In other cultures, the understanding of pain may be different. Personality also plays a role in pain. If your person has coped well with adversity in the past it is likely their resilient nature will equip them to meet pain with hope. However, if your person has had a different experience, if they are more fragile and feel that they have less control or that things usually don't go their way, it is likely that they will feel overwhelmed resulting in the felt experience of more pain.

As a companion you are perfectly positioned to offer non-medical therapies to reduce pain. There are so many ways to offer comfort beginning with a gentle physical presence. Perhaps your person would welcome touch—holding their hand or placing a hand on their shoulder. You can consider guiding them through slow breathing or relaxation techniques. Invitations for connection, awareness, meaning, pleasure, or presence (CAMPP), such as offering calming music, aromatherapy, or spending time outside to be held by the natural world can reduce pain. Leave it up to your person to decide what is most supportive to them.

Perhaps the assurance that they will not be alone in their pain will offer relief. Remind your person that they will not have to face this by themselves. A statement such as, "Pain can be managed, and suffering can be softened. You are surrounded by love," may provide relief.

CAMPP: CONNECTION, AWARENESS, MEANING, PLEASURE, PRESENCE

Comfort on the journey: Simple ways to alleviate pain and enhance connection

As a companion there is a lot you can do to support medical interventions to control pain and relieve symptoms. Your person's experience of pain will be amplified if they are anxious, tired, lonely, stressed, angry, sad, insecure, or bored. Consider how you can offer relief with simple comfort measures, looking to the senses as a place to start. Perhaps it feels right to lower the lights, offer light touch, or lead a guided meditation. These small gestures can have an enormous impact. You can also help your person feel understood, heal with humour, and make time for connecting conversation about passions.

CAMPP: CONNECTION, AWARENESS, MEANING, PLEASURE, PRESENCE

Navigating the journey: A guide for the detail oriented

Over the years I have supported many engineers on the end-of-life journey. I have noticed a shared relationship to control among them, and that this personality type appreciates clear guidance, direct language, and as many opportunities to choose from as possible.

I often share the map on page 127 with my engineer clients. It seems to offer clarity and options. I use the metaphor of travelling on a highway, reinforcing that they get to decide what exit they want to take and when.

"I'm afraid I will lose control over my body and my feelings."

Losing control over one's body and feelings is natural, and it happens to everyone living with a life-limiting illness as the body changes and eventually stops functioning. If your person expresses this fear, hold space for their worry and validate their experience. A simple statement such as, "You are right, we can't control everything," can offer relief. If it feels right, you can ask about what losing control means to them. You can be there to dance with their curiosity—perhaps in doing so your person will discover something.

Autonomy, one of the roots of practice for a companion, is even more important if this fear is being communicated. Offer choices to honour agency at every turn, even small choices such as what music your person wants to listen to, where they want to be touched (or not), or what to eat. Participating in these decisions can help your person feel a sense of control. If your person can't speak, consider offering yes/no questions or gestures to increase empowerment.

You can seek to learn more about your person's fear of losing control by asking an open-ended question about what it means to them. Maybe the fear originates from lack of information and not knowing what to expect. In this case, sharing simple information about the expected changes on the end-of-life journey may offer comfort and reassurance. Support and normalize the changes your person is experiencing with gentle guidance. Do you best to not to sound too clinical. Instead, you may offer simple reassurance such as, "Your body knows what to do," or "We will be right here to make sure you are as comfortable as possible." If they are seeking information, share common signposts on the end-of-life journey such as breathing changes, temperature shifts, or decreasing appetite to prevent your person from misinterpreting these as signs of distress.

Your person may be comforted by having a say in their future healthcare decision making. In this case, you may consider doing some level of advance care planning with the hopes of offering companionship and control. Consider what makes life worth living, identify their guiding values, and explore their wishes for future healthcare treatments. This information can be shared with your person's care team, friends, and family, offering a sense of control and the peace of mind that they have done what they can to ensure that their wishes will be upheld.

The fear of losing control could also originate from the experience of losing control as a side effect of medication, such as being sedated. In this case it may be supportive to find ways to bring your person back to their mind and body through meditation, or other mindfulness practices to help them orient to the present. Consider gentle touch (if welcomed), soft music, guided relaxation, or grounding exercises like placing a warm hand on their chest or belly to help ease the feeling of loss of control. Other somatic practices such as breath work—gentle breathing or sighing—can help relax the nervous system. It is important to get consent from your person before guiding them inward with these practices as not everyone finds comfort through these interventions.

Perhaps your person has always been someone who values control. The need for control can be a personality trait often resulting from one's upbringing, past experiences, and even situational factors. For some people, control may be an adaptive behaviour, developed as a response to growing up in environments where control was necessary for survival or stability. Others may feel a lack of control in certain areas of their lives, so they try to exert control over others to cope. Personality traits like perfectionism or anxiety also play a role and contribute to more controlling behaviours. Do your best to lead with your heart and offer empathy and understanding to your person to honour their own unique experiences and reasons for their way of being. Remember, in a crisis, personalities intensify. If your person valued control before their diagnosis, it is likely that this value will be even more important to them now.

Just a reminder, holding space for fears is about creating a tender space for expression. This will let your person know that whatever they are feeling is okay. Resist the urge to cheer your person up or minimize their experience. Instead, just be with them and whatever arises.

"I don't want to leave the people I love."

Looking at this statement on the page it's hard to even find the words to begin writing. The reality of this statement tears at the heart.

If your person expresses the fear of not wanting to leave the people they love, be sure to meet it with space, validation, and empathy. You can sit in loving presence with them—silence is so generous. If your person welcomes touch, perhaps offer your hand to hold. Once the fear has stretched all the way out, it may bring a little comfort to invite your person to connect with and express their love in a tangible way. This does not have to be complicated. Sharing words from the heart such as, "I love you," or "I'll always be with you in your heart," may support this fear a little. Writing letters from the heart, recording messages, or helping your person give small meaningful objects to the people they care about may bring a bit of comfort.

It may soothe your person to reframe "leaving" as "continuing love," by inviting them to consider that love doesn't end when the body stops functioning. Remind them that love is the one thing that continues on even after death.

You may be guided to create connection, awareness, meaning, pleasure, and presence by having a conversation about ways their loved ones can continue to feel connected. Perhaps it is through a song, a special place, or something that will help them feel close to them after they die. Your person might choose to leave behind a keepsake or create a supportive ritual such as lighting a candle for remembrance and connection on special days.

Offer reassurance through ongoing connection; instead of saying phrases such as, "You can go when you're ready," consider statements that affirm ongoing connection like, "We will miss you so much, and we will carry your love with us always," or "You have given us so much, and we will hold you in our hearts." This gives your person permission to release when they feel ready.

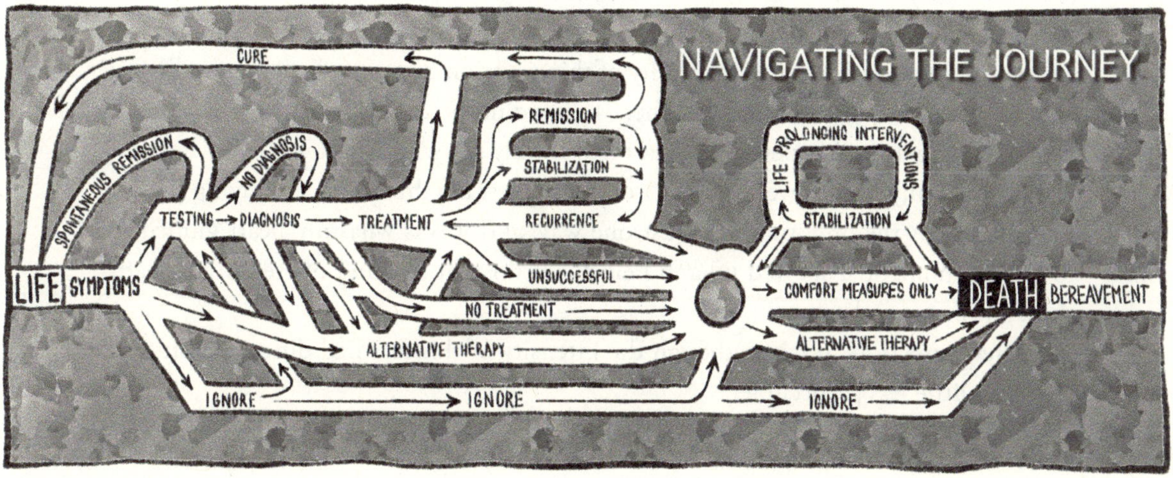

STORIES FROM THE TRAIL

The hardest thing

A doula client of mine uttered these words to me in a hospital room many years ago. She was a 55-year-old woman who was dying, and she just looked at me and said, "I don't want to die, I don't want to leave my partner." She started to sob. I couldn't find any words. I was flooded with the reality of this situation that we will all eventually face, and my eyes welled up. I cried with her. That would be the worst thing, I thought to myself. I sat there and I opened my heart and I really felt with her. It was overwhelming. I didn't have anything clever to offer. I didn't suggest anything. I'm not saying the way I showed up is the only way; it is just one way, and it was what my heart guided me to in that moment. I showed up and held space for that fear and offered my empathy through silence and tears.

After some time, it felt as though the intensity of this fear had diffused a bit—she seemed a little less preoccupied.

"I don't want to be a burden."

Being a burden is a prevalent fear for many people. The way we are cared for as we lose independence has changed a lot in the last hundred years. We live in a dominant culture that praises individualism and resilience. Being overly independent is not how humans are designed to function. We are communal creatures. We were brought into this world in the arms of others, and we can leave this world in the arms of others (if we choose). It was not that long ago we lived and died with the help of each other. People were supported in the home by friends and family members, communities, and congregations. The care was not always perfect, and pain was not always managed as well as it is today, but there was a natural and reciprocal cycle of care from birth to death. It was expected that people would care and be cared for—leaning out on each other was a necessity.

Caring for someone who is dying can be exhausting but when done with the support of those close to them, this natural cycle of birth, life, and death often also includes tender moments of connection, joy, laughter, and intimacy—moments of authentic caring, moments of love. Today, with families more dispersed than ever, care is often outsourced, and such tender moments are not always possible. In these places, despite the well-intentioned people that work there, policy, work overload, and potentially underlying beliefs of what is important, create a different flavour of caregiving. Also, with advancements in medicine, people are living with chronic illnesses for a long time, often resulting in extended periods of caregiving. It is common for people to feel like they are a burden. It is important to hold space for this fear, because the feeling of being a burden is often offered as a contributing factor for folks considering an assisted death.

It is not uncommon for people to equate their worth with what they do rather than who they are. It may be comforting to remind your person that their value and worth is not based on external factors such as their productivity. Just because they are unable to do the things in life that they used to do does not decrease their worth. Simply being a human being is worthy. Worth is not dependent on our bodies—on what they look like or what they are able to do. In fact, the wisdom gained from living with intention and purpose is exactly what this world is asking for in these times. For this reason, you may consider supporting your person's fear of being a burden by encouraging them to see their value beyond their abilities. You can gently remind them that it is their presence, their wisdom, and just being with them that you cherish. Reassure your person that they don't have to do anything to be valued or loved.

Having a conversation about the idea of care as an expression of love may also soothe the fear of being a burden. You can ask your person if they can recall a time when they offered care for someone, and whether they felt burdened by this role. Most often people see the opportunity to help another as a gift. Remind your person that caregiving is not just an obligation; it's an act of love. You can offer comforting statements such as, "Caring for you is a way we get to show our love," or "You have given so much in your life. Let us give back to you." If you are caring for a parent, they might appreciate hearing, "Just as you once cared for us, we now have the privilege of caring for you." We could all use more reminders that giving people the opportunity to help us is most often a gift. On a practical note, if your person is concerned about specific caregivers feeling overwhelmed you can have a conversation about how they can be supported in their role.

Another way to offset the sense of being a burden is by way of agency. You can offer your person small ways to maintain a sense of contribution. Ask for their advice, stories, or wisdom, and invite them to make decisions such a choosing music or deciding what to have for dinner. Through honouring their need for dignity and autonomy be sure to offer them choices in their care, no matter how small. This may look like asking them how they want to be supported rather than just assuming. Continue to acknowledge your person's feelings while also gently challenging any shame that arises around receiving help. Reassure your person that needing care does not make them a burden, it makes them human. This is a dance—the honouring of your person's felt experience should not be minimized as you do what you can to guide them to truth.

"Will I be forgotten?"

If your person voices this fear, begin by offering the generous gift of your compassionate presence. If and when it feels right, you may consider asking an open-ended question to gain a little more understanding of this concern. What does it mean to your person to be forgotten? By whom? Are they concerned they will be forgotten by friends, family, future generations, nobody, the planet? These questions will give your person the opportunity to explore their fear in more depth. The answers to these questions may lead you to support them in different ways.

You may consider asking if your person is interested in creating a legacy project. This may ease their fear of being forgotten, allowing them to leave a tangible mark. Legacy is personal and highly creative, and the possibilities are endless—writing letters, recording messages for loved ones, sharing stories that can be passed down, creating a memory book, making a musical playlist, or passing along a special keepsake. If your person has spiritual beliefs, explore what legacy means beyond the physical.

Continue to reassure your person that their essence, their wisdom, and their love will continue to live on. Remind them of how they have shaped the lives of those around them. Let them know that every story they have told and every kindness they have given will live on. If your person has children, grandchildren, or dear friends, affirm that parts of them continue on through these people.

As a companion you can honour your person's impact in the present moment by sharing specific ways your person has impacted you. Consider a phrase such as, "I will always remember how you [taught me, loved me, made me laugh, guided me]," or "Something of you will always be with me, in the way I [see the world, treat others, carry your wisdom]."

Your person may find comfort in knowing their loved ones will honour them in an ongoing way such as by lighting a candle on special days, continuing a tradition they cherished, or visiting a place that was meaningful to them. If it feels appropriate, you can directly ask your person how they would like to be remembered or if there is something special that you can do in their honour. Like all fears, this concern is normal and natural. If it feels right in your relationship, consider reorienting to love. Continue to remind your person that they are loved and will not be forgotten.

> *"Unable are the Loved to die, for Love is immortality."*
>
> *—Emily Dickinson*

I WONDER . . .

Embracing dignity in the face of change

What if we could meet ageing and illness without it affecting our dignity? Our sense of dignity comes from how we meet dying, which is very different from the need to control the experience. What if our true nature could find its voice? What if we invited our inner wisdom to be our guide? Would it be possible to experience the fear of being a burden without being lost to it? Could we come to accept a loss of control and continue to orient calmly toward our hearts, regardless of what happens in the body?

CAMPP: CONNECTION, AWARENESS, MEANING, PLEASURE, PRESENCE

Tender self-holding

You can offer this simple practice to your person to support their nervous system. Guide them to place one hand on their heart and one hand on their belly. Encourage them to breathe deeply to create a sense of comfort. This gentle gesture can be a powerful reminder that they are safe, supported, and not alone.

"I'm afraid of dying alone."

The fear of being alone can mean different things so understanding what it means to your person is important. Does it mean having someone physically present? Or feeling spiritually connected?

If your person is afraid of physically being alone, it may bring comfort to create a web of support around your person to ensure that they have lots of company. If this isn't possible you may reassure them by checking in at certain times and offering your companionship. Reassure your person that you will be there and be sure to do what you say you're going to do. Avoid overpromising. Let them know that they are not alone now, and you will do your best to be with them. If it is fitting for your relationship, you can express that they are deeply loved, and you will make sure they feel that love.

When others can't be present you can consider creative ways to support connection. Offering a special object to hold, such as a blanket, a letter, or a photo may help. Headphones on light volume can also soothe loneliness; your person can listen to music, recorded voice messages from their favourite people, a podcast, or a guided meditation. If people are planning on coming by, be sure to let your person know that others will be checking in regularly.

If your person's fear of dying alone is rooted in being emotionally alone, the ideas above will not bring comfort. Feeling emotionally alone could mean that even in a room full of people, your person doesn't feel understood. It could also reflect the fear that no one can go with them—that dying is a solitary act. For this fear all you can do is offer care through validation. Normalize and validate your person's fear, with a statement such as, "Of course you are scared. You are right; no one can go with you." There is a good chance that your person will feel a sense of relief from being understood.

If it is appropriate, you can invite connection beyond the physical. Perhaps reminding them that they are held by something greater will ease their fear. Even if your person is not overly spiritual, as a companion you can remind them that love doesn't leave, and even when you step out of the room, your heart will still be with them. Do what you can to let your person know that they are surrounded by the love of all who have known them. Remember that in the end, it is always about love.

Depending on where your person is on their health journey, joining a support group may be an effective way for them to feel less alone. It is likely that talking with others who are having a similar experience will be supportive.

Supporting your person with this fear asks you to honour the mystery. It is believed that people often choose when they die. Some people wait for friends and family to arrive, while others surrender when everyone has left the room. This, to me, is evidence of love. I imagine it is hard to let go when those who anchor us to this world are physically present. Death, even when people are alone, is not empty. Many hospice workers have observed that people who pass when no one is physically present often appear peaceful. In many cultures it is believed that ancestors and guides come just before death to accompany those from this world to the next. Trust that your person will let go in the way that is right for them. If you have stories of peaceful transitions, it may be comforting to share these with your person. People who die when no one else is in the room are not truly alone; they are held in love, in memory, and in the presence of all who have cared for them.

"What will happen after I die?"

We know what happens to the physical body after we die, but we don't have the same certainty about the non-physical parts of ourselves. For some, reflecting on this question can lead to profound spiritual peace and acceptance as folks come to terms with their understanding of life, death, and beyond. How one meets this fear is determined by their worldview—the lens through which they make meaning of life. We all have a unique lens that consists of the inseparable forces of culture, religion, spirituality, and personal experiences. Wrestling with fears, doubts, and existential questions is a natural stage of facing mortality. This spiritual struggle and deep questioning are often referred to as the Dark Night of the Soul. They form an intimately personal experience, and your role as a companion is simply to create the space for your person to reflect about the unknown.

Irrespective of worldview, most people believe that some part of us continues on after the physical body dies. This shared inner knowing varies from person to person. Some find it in religious or spiritual teachings, others find it in the phenomenal world such as nature, and some may feel it through a belief in the ongoing connection with self or others. Your person will find their own way. Trust that being there with them as they wonder about the unknown is supportive and makes their experience less hard.

It is common for those who have had someone close to them die feel a real and ongoing sense of connection. We don't often talk about these experiences for fear of being judged. Our dominant cultural narrative around death is missing guidance around what happens to the non-physical parts of ourselves. This enormous gap often leaves people searching for meaning, which causes more suffering than necessary. As humans, we are wired for connection and belonging. We need a story about our death that is generative, one that supports our need to belong and be held by others in life, including death.

If you are in the position of holding space for your person as they wonder about the afterlife, you can gently explore their beliefs of the afterlife. If they are unable to find a belief to hang onto reassure them that it's okay not to have answers and that the fear of the unknown is universal.

This wondering is simply part of the human experience. Again, trust in the power of being present with them in the mystery.

"Did my life have meaning?"

Again, begin with creating connection. Choose acknowledgment and validation over reassurance as a start. Allow the depth of their question have its full expression by letting your person know that it makes perfect sense to wonder about their life having meaning. Once you have honoured this fear by giving it plenty of space, the conversation can bloom from this fertile ground.

Perhaps it may feel right to ask your person to recall meaningful moments from their life. This prompt will invite your person into their own reflection and allow what is most potent to be revealed. If they begin to share stories from their life, know that this is good. Reflecting on life—the ups and the downs—is part of the dying role, and it supports people to die well.

Whether or not a person's life has meaning is not determined by what they did for work or how much wealth they acquired in their lifetime. Meaning comes from the connections that they made and the relationships that they tended. This is reflected by how they are valued in their dying time. If people are isolated and lonely, regardless of how productive they have been, they may feel that life has little meaning. If a person is loved and cared for by others who are there to listen to them, they can really come to understand that life is full of meaning determined by the lives that they've impacted.

To bolster your person's sense of meaning you can reflect their impact on others, or on a particular cause, back to them. You can gently remind them of the ways they have touched others, whether through kindness, love, guidance, sharing wisdom, presence, or perhaps other ways in which their life has made a difference, such as tending to the land or advocating for a cause. If you know them personally, you can let them know that you have seen the way that they have made a difference. You can reassure them that their love and life has mattered. Consider sharing any personal examples with your person, stories of how they have nourished you. Even if you have only known them for a brief amount of time, it is likely that you have been inspired by them in some way.

If appropriate, continue to invite them to recall moments of meaning. You can ask about who and what they have loved and what they meant to your person over their lifetime. You can ask them about a time when someone appreciated them, a time when they felt of value. If it feels right, you can consider reaching out to people they know and ask them to express the impact your person has had on their life.

If the suggestions above are falling flat, perhaps the fear behind this question comes from uncertainty about the definition of "meaning." You might ask your person what a meaningful life looks like to them. It may be supportive to ask them if there is something they are still longing to say or do that would bring them peace, allowing them the space to explore what might help them feel complete.

As you offer your person reassurance, try to avoid platitudes or dismissing their fear with shallow reassurances like, "Of course your life had meaning!" Instead, open your heart and offer something more personal, present, and true: "I don't have all the answers, but I do know that you have touched this world in ways that matter." Let them know that it is okay to wonder about this, and that they are deeply seen and valued in this moment.

In this way, through holding space for their question with gentleness, curiosity, and presence, you can guide them to their own sense of meaning, the most generous gift you can give.

For other common fears of the dying, please refer to the list on page 115.

CAMPP: CONNECTION, AWARENESS, MEANING, PLEASURE, PRESENCE

More than a memory: Relationships that continue

Perhaps you can wonder with your person as they consider how non-physical parts of us continue. Have either of you had the experience of maintaining a relationship with someone who has died? What does that relationship look like?

CAMPP: CONNECTION, AWARENESS, MEANING, PLEASURE, PRESENCE

Soothing with sound

You can invite your person to hum or sing; vibrations from the voice stimulate the vagus nerve which encourages relaxation as it calms the body. This stimulation can help regulate heart rate and breathing, and even improve blood flow. Humming is a simple and effective way to relax the body and mind.

Wayfinder

***noun* / *ˈwāˌfīndər*/**

A person who is curious about attuning to all of their senses—using their whole self to navigate life. They embrace bodyfulness through the light and easeful times and through the chaos and confusion of groundlessness and change. A wayfinder is one who chooses not to simply accept the status quo, deciding to tenderly return home to their body, with an openness that allows the heart to guide them moment to moment on a more intentional, harmonious, cooperative, creative, and pleasure-filled path.

GRIEF STORMS
BIRDSONG OF WHAT IS
LIGHTHOUSE OF PRESENCE
TRAIL
ENDS
HERE
SEA OF FEARS
BRIDGES OF COMMUNITY CARE
SHELTER OF OTHERS
WILDFLOWER MEADOW OF BEAUTY
BENCH OF STILLNESS
OCEAN OF POSSIBILITIES
RIVER OF LIFE

ASKING TO BE SAID
CLIFF EDGE OF ESTRANGEMENT
VIEWPOINT OF LIFE REVIEW
WARM BREEZE OF SELF COMPASSION
CAVES OF REGRET
LIGHTRAYS OF WONDER
CREVASSE OF DEMENTIA
LOSS LAKE
GO
SLOW
PATH OF WHAT'S EXPECTED
EMERGING LEAVES OF HOPE
DEAD WOOD OF WHAT NO LONGER MATTERS

Chapter 3

Grief Storms on the End-of-Life Journey

Grief is a small and unassuming word that defines an incredibly varied and wild experience. Trying to define grief is like trying to describe love. Neither concept is a feeling nor a certain pattern of feelings; rather, they are both more accurately an experience. Grief is the personal experience of meeting change.

Grief is most often associated with feeling sad after someone dies; however, a grief response can be evoked by non-death experiences of losing people, such as divorce or loss of a friendship. Grief also extends to the loss of significant concrete things like jobs and homes, and changes in abstract phenomena such as identity, future dreams, and states of being such as innocence or health. If you are human, you have experienced grief. Grief is guaranteed.

Grief is a response to change, and it begins when we are born—it is part of the human experience. Like death, we don't talk about it much, so we are not a very grief-literate bunch. When we are unaware of what grief is, what causes a grief response, how it affects us, and how to be well when we are grieving, we can easily feel confused and overwhelmed when it arises. Increasing our grief literacy and competency allows us to be more available for life. Grief deepens our ability to feel, increasing intimacy with ourselves, with others, and with all of life. Without engaging with loss, we risk limiting the depth of our experience, floating on the surface of life. It is only when we can truly feel our sadness for existence that we can truly feel our joy for the world.

How we meet grief is influenced by our individual experiences, circumstance, and culture. If you are supporting the bereaved, it is wise to take a humble approach by learning what you can about the significance of culture to your person, to ensure that you can show up and support them appropriately. Gender norms and social constructs also impact the experience of grief. The outward expression of emotions and how others are supported through loss are influenced by internalized cultural stereotypes. In Western cultures, men have been provided narratives about being strong and hiding vulnerability and emotion. This can prevent men from expressing their grief and accessing support. Dominant culture encourages women to be quiet and repress anger. It is so hopeful to see that our cultural understanding of gender and expectations around cultural norms is changing. Simply increasing awareness about these biases is protective.

I WONDER . . .

Finding your way through grief storms

Each of us has a personal "medicine cabinet" that we turn to when we feel uncomfortable, and grief can bring profound discomfort. These coping mechanisms are gathered over a lifetime, as we learn to care for ourselves during times of loss.

Do you go for a walk, take a bath, listen to music, call a friend, make some tea? Do you engage with self-compassion in self-care? Perhaps you attempt to soothe your discomfort, seeking things that distract you from your grief or numb the pain of loss. Do you go shopping, watch TV, or pour a glass of wine? What's in your medicine cabinet for grief? Reflect on the medicines you've used in the past and continue to rely on, as well as those you may want to explore in the future. If your go-to medicine isn't supporting your wellbeing, consider exploring new ways to care for your grieving self.

On the end-of-life journey, grief can weigh people down if it is not acknowledged, expressed, and shared with trusted others. The term originates from the Latin word "gravis," which means heavy or serious. Words such as grave, gravity, and gravitas also come from the same origin. For those living with a life-limiting illness, there are many non-death losses that can become heavy if the needs of grief are not satisfied.

In her book *Advice to Future Corpses (and Those Who Love Them)*, Sallie Tisdale, author and retired palliative care nurse, describes the nature of these losses:

> "Dying is a state of ongoing loss. Hair, teeth, erections. The ability to tie shoes or carry groceries. Breasts, vision. Attention span. The evening walk. Driving. The strength to climb stairs, to do the laundry and housework. Bladder control, a sense of smell, balance. Relationships disappear, plans are revoked, social roles are extinguished."

Each one of these losses evokes a grief response—it's no wonder that dying can be so overwhelming. So much is taken without permission and there is a mountain of loss to keep up with. With an understanding of grief and its needs, you can support your person. We all hold the medicine for grief—what a perfect design. Grief asks to be witnessed, and as a companion to the dying you can support your person by seeing, hearing, and feeling with them. You can offer comfort by letting your person know that their experience is normal and valid and that they are not alone.

The Longings of Grief

Grief has two basic needs. Thie first is that it longs for the bereaved to acknowledge the loss on a personal level and be with the feelings that arise. Permission to feel one's feelings is a radical act in a culture obsessed with the high notes. Folks are often reluctant to lean into their experience of loss as there is a commonly held fear that people might drown in sorrow if they open the floodgates, but it is when people stay with their grief that it changes and becomes lighter.

Sadness is often the expected response to loss, but when it comes to grief, there is no normal. Emotions may come and go, arise in waves, stand alone, or show up in a pack. The answer to relieving the discomfort of loss is in the discomfort. By allowing the uneasiness to exist, it changes somehow. Grief asks the bereaved to stay present when emotions intensify. This is not an easy ask. Grief asks for truthfulness about the intensity of pain. Grief asks for spaciousness, enough for all the emotions that arise in response to loss to stretch out and take up all the room they need. For this reason, many people find comfort in the natural world in times of grief, being guided to the ocean, the prairies, the mountains, the sky. These natural landscapes provide vast and wild spaces for grief to stretch out and when grief is given enough room to spread a sense of relief usually follows. The bereaved is the expert in their grief experience. Grief asks for a slower pace to tune in to the natural wisdom that we all hold. At times grief may ask for distraction, and it is okay to take a break from the experience of loss if the feelings become too intense.

The second longing of grief is to be seen and heard. When it is witnessed, it allows others to get a sense of what is being experienced. Feeling with another is the definition of empathy. This is why we are guided to express our grief, regret, or sorrow, yet this can become complicated in a culture that doesn't advocate mourning. Grief is what one thinks and feels on the inside and mourning is the experience of loss expressed externally. Mourning is something we do; it is how we show our grief. Mourning moves grief from the inside to the outside, preferably not just once, but over and over as needed. Mourning is not always intentional and in keeping with its feral nature, grief may express itself in unpredictable ways. Mourning is facilitated by vulnerability, trust, and connection and when practiced it reinforces these qualities as well.

Grief is communal—we need each other in times of loss. We are not designed to carry the weight of our losses alone and yet we may need frequent reminders of this fact. Humans have always been interdependent. As community members, we are designed to support others and lean on others as needed. Expressing grief, or mourning, is required for witnessing, and witnessing is the medicine for grief.

As a companion to the dying, you are perfectly positioned to support your person with the losses experienced on the end-of-life journey. With less to carry there is greater capacity to be more present to the experience of being alive. We are being called to recover the right to ask for help and enlist others when we begin to struggle. To do so, we can offer a shoulder for support and an ear for listening. It is essential to remember that when we let others help, it is a gift.

> "What if joy is not only entangled with pain, or suffering, or sorrow, but is also what emerges from how we care for each other through those things?"
>
> —Ross Gay

CAMPP: CONNECTION, AWARENESS, MEANING, PLEASURE, PRESENCE

Weathering the grief storm: Gently opening the conversation

As your person journeys, identify their losses. These may be social roles, abilities, or activities. If there is an opportunity for you to gently engage in a conversation about these losses, take a temperature read. Consider asking permission with a phrase such as, "Do you want to talk about how you're feeling?" rather than directly asking, "How are you feeling?" This approach is gentle and less intrusive. It also gives the person the choice of how to respond.

If you person choses to share, simply offer the medicine of witnessing. The goal is to listen well so that you see, hear, and feel with your person. This will communicate to your person that their grief matters and that they are not alone.

If your person chooses not to talk about their experience of loss, it's okay. Remember to take their lead and do your best to not take this personally. Grief can be a private matter, and if your person doesn't want to talk about it now, that doesn't mean that they won't want to talk in the future. In time, when it feels appropriate, you can gently check in again. Root your intention in care and compassion—in time, this may create an opening for grief to be shared, or not, and that's okay.

GROUNDING PRACTICES

Mourning the unseen: Tenderly tending to grief

Grief may be a private experience, but mourning is not. When you cry, you are mourning. When you talk to someone else about your experience of loss, you are mourning. When you write in a journal, or listen to a song that evokes tears, you are mourning. Take a moment to consider how you are honouring the non-death losses that you are experiencing. If you are not mourning, how can you externalize your internal experience of grief in a way that feels right to you?

GROUNDING PRACTICES

Honouring your grief: The uncharted path to wellbeing

In these times, we are being called to reimagine new ways of responding to life's challenges because the consequences of avoiding grief are far reaching. Grief will fester if not tended to, resulting in depression, dullness, despair, overwhelm, and anxiety. To be well, we are asked to slow down and tune in to our needs during times of loss.

Contrary to popular belief, there is no map—no predictable stages of grief. The way forward is best determined by attuning to your emotions as they arise and trusting that your feelings will guide you to what and who you need. Slow down, establish direction, and listen inward using your heart as a compass. Allowing your grief to have its feelings can be intense, so remember it is okay and even adaptive to take a break.

It takes a lot of energy to resist all the distractions constantly at our fingertips that help us self-soothe and keep up from feeling. It takes consistent awareness to be resourced. This is so challenging in this time, with so many shiny things vying for our attention.

We can numb out in so many ways, through alcohol, drugs, sex, cell phones, video games, shopping, or work—things to keep our busy minds spinning. We live so fast that it has become counterculture to feel our feelings and tune into our hearts.

Many distractions are welcome. Enjoyment can be found in movies, podcasts, and video calls with friends; however, when you are feeling raw and overwhelmed, often the most direct route back is the one that reconnects you to the natural world. This route will point you back to yourself and your natural wisdom. Spend time in nature, move your body, sit in silence, or spend time with people who see you, and enjoy activities that feel congruent with what is most important to you.

GROUNDING PRACTICES

Nurturing your body through grief: Embracing rest, nature, and connection

How can you care for your body? More sleep? Nourishing food? Gentle movement? How can you reconnect to the natural world? Can you get out into nature? Spend time in the company of animals? Breathe the fresh air? Spend time in the garden? Gaze at the stars? Swim in the ocean?

If we can be with our grief, this presence opens the way to change. In times of loss, it can also be supportive to balance out grief with gratitude. Praise increases our appreciation of life and serves as a ballast to our grieving hearts, tenderly guiding us to acceptance. Praise is not something we use to distract ourselves from loss or minimize the experience of grief, as it cannot be faked. It is an authentic way of seeing the world and being in the world that springs from our own inner wisdom. Gratitude is an action and when we take action, we feel less debilitated. There is always something to be grateful for—a sunset, health, good memories, friends, trees, or a kind smile.

Praise opens us to all of life, the pain of loss alongside all of the blessings. It expands our view so that we don't overlook goodness in the face of suffering. When struggling, we often ruminate on what is wrong, but gratitude dampens this negativity bias, allowing our hearts to rest. Gratitude invites us to notice that the good in the world is just as true.

Holding the opposing forces of grief and gratitude at the same time creates enough space for all of our feelings. This keeps the heart tender and soft, allowing us to respond wisely in this complex world. Gratitude centres us on the opportunity of simply being alive and not wanting, which ultimately inspires generosity because the more aware we are of what we have, the more we want to give. In this way, gratitude aligns us with our true nature.

> *"Gratitude takes us from abstract belief to living compassion in the world. Gratitude is strongest, clearest, most robust, and radical when things are really hard. Really hard. All-is-lost hard."*
>
> *—Diana Butler Bass*

GROUNDING PRACTICES

In this moment: A simple practice of gratitude

Think of three things you are grateful for, in this moment. They don't have to be big or extraordinary—sometimes it's just a warm up of tea, the sound of a bird outside, or noticing the steady rhythm of your breath. Gratitude does not erase worry, but it can soften its edges and remind us that even in difficult times, life offers moments of beauty, comfort, and connection. When we pause to notice what is good, even when its hard, we can invite a little more lightness into our day.

GROUNDING PRACTICES

The shape of grief: Tuning into your body's wisdom

Grief lives in the body. Notice where you are holding grief. What size is it? What shape is it? Does it have a colour? A certain texture?

Tune in to your natural wisdom. Feel into your heart. Your heart is the compass that will guide you in how to tend to your grief. Your heart will show you your way during times of loss.

For most people experiencing grief, having a companionate listener is the most healing remedy. When grief becomes complicated and people experience aftershocks of loss that contribute to long lasting, intense feelings, the support of mental health professionals may be helpful. With complicated grief people often feel a persistent sense of disbelief, or a strong longing for what was, and these feelings may not diminish over time. For those living with complicated grief, finding meaning in life may feel like a daunting challenge.

How to Grieve

At the beginning, lean into any little thing that brings you comfort, or rest. Initially, grief can be an isolating and private experience. Do your best to stay with your feelings as they arise. Notice how they come and go. When it feels right, share your grief with a trusted other. This will allow the medicine of witnessing to be offered. If you are met with empathy, let that balm sink in. If you are met with someone trying to fix, advise, one up, or discount your situation, you will likely feel unsupported. It is not always easy to find people who are grief aware.

Grief is personal and it impacts people in many ways. Grief is often considered an emotional experience, but it is so much more than that. Grief affects people affectively, cognitively, behaviourally, and in physiological and somatic ways. Grief impacts the mind, often impairing focus, memory, and concentration. Denial, lowered self-esteem, helplessness, and hopelessness are also common cognitive impacts of loss. Grief also lives in the body. The physical responses to loss can vary from changes in appetite to inflammation, sleep disturbances, exhaustion, susceptibility to illness, and a multitude of somatic changes. Understanding the physical manifestation of grief also opens up the potential for people to look to movement-based rituals to express grief. Expressing grief can reach far beyond traditional talk therapy. Grief can find expression with breath, dance, art yoga, writing, martial arts, etc.

Supporting your person's experience of grief on the end-of-life journey

As a companion on the end-of-life journey you can help immensely by validating and normalizing grief, and serving as a witness so that your person can keep up with the many losses as they roll in. Many changes leading up to the moment of death—things taken without permission—are often unwitnessed which can be a lot to carry. These non-death losses are layered on top of a lifetime of losses.

To help your person to travel light you can also hold space for past losses that never received the attention they needed. We all carry a lifetime of grief, and this weight becomes more apparent on the end-of-life journey. One powerful way to facilitate this spiritual work is through a life review. Reflecting on significant people and experiences fosters connection and meaning while also evoking grief. Change and loss are part of life, and we all carry unacknowledged grief. By asking about the past, you may invite your person to share these losses. As a companion, your role is to listen, helping to lighten the load. It is healing to release what's been carried too long and your support can make the journey feel less exhausting.

Your experience of grief as a companion on the end-of-life journey

The way you handle your grief is uniquely yours. When you share your experience of loss, don't be surprised if others attempt to contain or "fix" your grief. Expressing grief often makes people uncomfortable and they may say and do that unintentionally to reduce their own discomfort. It is hard for those around you to see you in pain, and this deep care can sometimes make it difficult for them to truly show up and support you. Though it may require emotional labour on your part, it can be helpful to guide others on how they can best support you—whether that's simply listening, holding a hand, or offering a hug.

Getting the support you need during grief can lessen suffering. Pain is a natural and unavoidable response to loss, but suffering arises when you feel dismissed or unsupported in your pain. When this happens confusion, frustration, isolation, and self-doubt can emerge. Suffering comes when you are told not to feel what you are feeling. Ironically, the people who care most about you—your friends and family—may unknowingly contribute to this suffering due to their discomfort with your pain. Recognizing this is the first step to finding more supportive and understanding ways to show up for each other.

As a companion, you may find it a significant responsibility that can impact your relationship with your person. You might grieve the life you had before caregiving, the changes in their health, or the anticipated death. It's natural to feel the weight of these losses—consider leaning out on others for support. There is opportunity in grief—vulnerability and listening connect people. This is a beautiful design! When the inside experience of grief is shared with others, it can be heart-expanding and community-making.

STORIES FROM THE TRAIL

A ritual of presence: What my friend Kelley taught me about sitting shiva

It was such a gift to hear my friend Kelley share her experience of sitting shiva after her father died, and something in her words stayed with me. She described it as a profoundly supportive and grounding ritual—not just for her, but also for her family and community. "Jews do death really well," she said. There's a pathway, a structure that carries you—a velvet-lined conveyor belt, she called it—that moves mourners gently through the first days of grief with care and clarity.

Kelley's family chose to sit shiva for three nights, gathering with loved ones in the synagogue and then transitioning to her parents' home to share stories, food, and silence. She was deeply touched by how many people came; so many friends and acquaintances stopped by, and no one needed an invitation. "You just show up," she said. "Your presence is the gift." There's no need to know what to say. All are welcome. You come, you sit, you listen, and that is enough.

Traditionally, the mirrors in the home are covered, mourners sit on low stools, and meals are simple—often including symbolic foods like eggs to represent life and renewal. Clothing is sometimes torn or marked to outwardly show the inner reality: things are not normal. You are not expected to tend to your appearance. You are expected to tend to your grief.

What really stayed with me was how Kelley felt so supported by the framework of shiva—it gave her something steady to be supported by in those early days of grief. She didn't need to make decisions or manage anything—she could just *be*. She remembered sitting with her family just after her father died, telling stories with the rabbi present, her father's body still in the room, and feeling something close to peace. "We're going to be okay," she recalled thinking at the time. "We lost our patriarch, but we're together."

Kelley also spoke of the evolution of this practice—how some shiva gatherings moved to video calls during Covid, and how younger generations are adapting traditions to fit their lives. But the heart of the ritual remains: showing up, witnessing, feeding one another, and offering presence without pressure.

In a world where we often don't know what to say, how to offer support, or where to place our grief, Kelley's story reminded me how essential ritual and community are—not to fix our pain, but to hold it. Shiva, like many end-of-life rituals, makes space for mourning in a way that's embodied, communal, and deeply human. It's a much-needed pause—time to sit still, remember, and allow others carry you part of the way.

GROUNDING PRACTICES

The support surrounding you: What holds you when grieving?

What holds you when grieving? Perhaps it's a trusted friend or family member that comes to mind. Maybe it is an element of the natural world such as a forest or the ocean. Do you feel supported by a favourite activity, such as writing, running, or listening to music?

Write your name in the center of a blank piece of paper and acknowledge the people, places, and practices that bring comfort to you when you are grieving. Take some time to reflect on what holds you and express gratitude for the people, places, or things that you lean out on.

Are you seeking more support? Consider how you can bolster your web of support. Acknowledge and explore what arises as you do this activity.

Young People and Grief

Children experience grief differently than adults. When describing grief, literature has often used water metaphors. For adults, grief is often compared to a river with headwaters, rapids, and in time, rejoining the sea. The metaphor of an ocean works best to describe waves of grief that ebb and flow. With young people, the experience of grief often resembles puddles. Grief is an experience that kids step into and out of repeatedly. Children can be sad one moment and giggling the next. Young people are also very physical in response to loss, exhibiting behaviour such as play, tantrums, anxiety, and hyperactivity.

Do your best to stick to your family routines. More change will likely add more stress. The consistency of a routine will help young people feel safe.

When kids jump in a grief puddle it is best practice to be there for them and just let them experience their feelings. When they are ready, empower them to get out of the puddle on their own. Children might retreat and want to be alone with their emotions. As difficult as this may be, know that this is okay, and a healthy response to loss. When the child is ready to connect again you can ask them questions and hold space for their experience.

CAMPP: CONNECTION, AWARENESS, MEANING, PLEASURE, PRESENCE

Opening the door to conversation: Supporting young people in grief

If a young person finds it hard to talk about their feelings, create space for conversation with a gentle approach.

You might say something like, "I know some things are really hard to talk about, but talking can help. I am here if you ever want to share what's going on."

Often we try to protect young people from big emotions, thinking it's for their own good. While this may be well-intentioned, it is not always what is best for them. When a child receives upsetting news, they often run off and play. It is tempting to believe that they are okay; however, play is simply a language. When it comes to grief, it is important to consider how resilient children really are. Can they make it through loss on their own and be okay? Or are they just invisible in their grief? Often adults hope for the best and are simply unaware that young people grieve differently.

For adults to support children in grief, a narrative can be helpful. It is a good idea to check in with the child first and assess their understanding. If the child asks questions, answer honestly—it's okay not to have all the answers. If their understanding is different from reality, then guide them to the truth. For example, if a child looks at Grandpa, who has just died, and says, "Grandpa looks asleep," use plain language to explain that Grandpa is not asleep, he has died. Let the child know that his body simply stopped working. Make sure the child understands what dying means. The concept of death will vary depending on the developmental stage. Do your best to use simple and accurate language and avoid euphemisms, like "passed away," "is in a better place," or "is at rest." As you communicate with children, don't try to hold back your emotions. It is healthy to share your feelings as they are a natural response to loss. This is an opportunity for you to model healthy reactions to grieving.

When providing children with a story, make sure you offer a beginning, a middle, and an end. Be sure that the story you tell is an accurate, age-appropriate account of what has happened. As previously mentioned, if children don't have a story, they will use their brilliant imaginations to create one and what they imagine is often more upsetting than the actual situation. When children aren't presented with a story based on truth from adults, trust can erode.

As children get older, they progress through different developmental stages and each stage provides them with a different lens through which to see death and grief. As children mature, they will continuously revisit the loss and new understandings will evolve. Keep asking the young griever what they loved most about the person or thing that was lost, and you will likely hear a story from their heart; if you ask what they miss the most, chances are their feelings will be revealed. Be there to hold space for them as they share their stories.

EXPECTED CHANGES ON THE JOURNEY

Grief through growing hearts and minds: How children's understanding of loss evolves

Children experience grief in unique ways that are often influenced by their developmental stage, which can shape how they understand and process loss.

Children under two are likely to sense stress in the house even though they don't understand the cause. Take the time to comfort and give them extra attention if the heaviness of grief is in the house.

Children between two and five usually believe they are invincible. At this stage, they typically believe that death is reversible. Although they may not understand the concept of death, it is best practice to explain death concretely so that it will help them understand the concept as they gain new understandings about death as they mature.

Around eight years of age, young people usually understand that death is irreversible. At this developmental stage they are the centre of the universe so it is common for children at this stage to think that somehow, they may have caused the illness or death.

Children will respond differently to grief than adults. They may draw pictures of the person dying, bury dolls, or ask direct questions about what is happening to your person's body. Know that these responses are normal and healthy.

CAMPP: CONNECTION, AWARENESS, MEANING, PLEASURE, PRESENCE

Showing our tears: Teaching children that all emotions are safe

Showing your own grief in front of children can be healthy. When you hide your emotions, it might lead them to wonder why you aren't sad which can cause confusion about whether they should be sad. By grieving openly you show them that it is safe and healthy to express all emotions, not just the ones that feel good.

CAMPP: CONNECTION, AWARENESS, MEANING, PLEASURE, PRESENCE

Kids are ritual beings: Consider inviting kids to express their grief creatively

Plant a tree, paint a rock with an image or word that brings the person to mind, or encourage young people to write a letter, or draw pictures, or light a candle of remembrance together. The important thing is giving permission for each person to honour their grief in a way that feels personal and meaningful to them.

Reactions to Bereavement

Reactions to bereavement can vary widely, and while the following chart offers insight into common responses, it's important to remember that every experience of loss is unique. This study looks at grief through a Western academic lens, but there are many ways to understand the experience of loss. Interestingly, Margaret Stroebe, the lead researcher of this study, went on to do a meta-analysis on poetry titled *The Poetry of Grief: Beyond Scientific Portrayal.* After years of research, she felt as though the theories fell short. Western science is, after all, primarily concerned with prediction. Grief is never predictable. Stroebe turned her sights to the poets, acknowledging that their words greatly add to our understanding of grief by exploring the relational side of grief and through bringing associated feelings to life.

Reactions to Bereavement (Adapted from Stroebe et al., 2007)

Affective:

- Depression, despair, dejection, distress
- Anxiety, fears, dreads
- Guilt, self-blame, self-accusation
- Anger, hostility, irritability
- Anhedonia—loss of pleasure
- Loneliness
- Yearning, longing, pining
- Shock, numbness, denial, and avoidance

Behavioral:

- Agitation, tenseness, restlessness
- Fatigue
- Overactivity
- Searching
- Weeping, sobbing, crying
- Social withdrawal

Cognitive:

- Preoccupation with thoughts of the deceased, intrusive confrontations
- Rumination
- Sense of presence of deceased
- Suppression, denial
- Lowered self-esteem
- Self-reproach
- Helplessness, hopelessness
- Suicidal ideation
- Sense of unreality
- Memory, concentration difficulties

Physiological–somatic:

- Loss of appetite
- Sleep disturbances
- Energy loss, exhaustion
- Somatic complaints
- Physical complaints similar to deceased
- Immunological and endocrine changes
- Susceptibility to illness, disease
- Mortality

GROUNDING PRACTICES

Being present: The power of witnessing grief

When you are witnessing your person express emotions about loss, grounding yourself can be helpful. Keep your feet flat on the floor and focus on your breath to stay present. Notice any tension or discomfort in your body and gently invite relaxation and breath to those areas. Simply notice what is coming up for you.

It may be helpful to remind yourself that this experience is not happening directly to you—it is happening to your person. There is a difference. You might become evoked because you have had a similar experience or you are holding grief that hasn't been tended to, so simply notice what is arising. You can explore those emotions in a journal, or with a friend or therapist when the time is right.

These golden moments to witness grief are precious. Culturally, we are conditioned to help sad or grieving people by cheering them up; however, when this dismisses what is alive in them, it simply minimizes their experience. These habitual responses do not honour grief; rather, they silence it for the sake of the comfort of others.

Despite any discomfort, continue to breathe and stay focused on grief support, on seeing, hearing, and feeling with your person. Share words that let your person know that they are not alone, such as, "I am here." Just be normal and use language that is comfortable for you.

You may not know what to say and saying just that can go a long way.

Do what you can to find the depth of love to acknowledge your person's pain without rushing in to clean it up.

Trust that simply being there to witness, validate, and normalize the grief experience is the medicine. Feeling with your person in a non-judgmental way and listening deeply is the goal.

Encourage your person to teach you about their grief experience. Listening is how we can truly show up and offer appropriate support. We can't possibly know what is best for someone on their grief journey, but we can be there and do our best to understand and walk alongside.

GROUNDING PRACTICES

Grief rituals for release

Grief rituals can be deeply supportive. Rituals are actions with intention that make the invisible experience of grief visible. Consider a regular grief practice to help to lighten the heaviness of grief. You can consider journaling, walking in nature, or creating art. These actions with intention can invite a gentle release. You may feel called to make an offering—you can express your grief on a piece of paper, or infuse your grief into a stone. You can release your ritual item back to the earth; bury it, drop it water, or let it go it into the air with a song.

GROUNDING PRACTICES

Honouring your grief: Finding ground in vulnerability and emotion

As a companion to the dying, it is normal to feel powerless and fragile after a diagnosis. The best way to find your ground is simply to be with what is arising by acknowledging your emotions and giving them space to stretch out.

We often associate grief with the feeling of being sad, but grief has many faces. Some of the other responses to anticipatory grief are a desire to talk, fear, loneliness, rehearsal of the death, irritability, anger, guilt, and resentment. Welcome all that arises in you. The experience of loss can be private and vulnerable but if you listen to your needs as they arise, your heart can serve as a compass to guide you to the most supportive next step. Your feelings may nudge you to cry, call a friend, go to the ocean, or even take a break from the intensity of heartache and avoid the feelings altogether for a while. There can be grace in taking a break from your grief.

Common Grief Experiences on the End-of-Life Journey

Anticipatory grief

Anticipatory grief is an experience of loss that occurs before a significant event. Anticipatory grief happens after a life-limiting diagnosis. It affects your person as well as you and everyone else connected to your person. Anticipatory grief is the response to a cascade of losses that occur when death is expected. These losses may include the loss of an imagined future, changing roles in the family, financial changes, the loss of security, and the foreseeable death of your person.

Like all types of grief, anticipatory grief evokes an unpredictable range of responses. Often the grief felt before a death can feel more intense and stressful than the grief that comes after. Anticipatory grief may include any of the affective, behavioral, cognitive, and somatic reactions to loss mentioned above. This grief experience often includes anger and a general loss of emotional control, which adds heightened anxiety to the mix. Anticipatory grief can be complicated, confusing, and exhausting. It extends the period of mourning, and it is layered on top of the exhaustion that often comes with failing health or providing care. Unfortunately, you can't get a head start on grief—the experience of loss before a death doesn't reduce the amount of grief experienced after a death.

Like other forms of grief, simply acknowledging, naming, and normalizing anticipatory grief can offer protection. Take time to slow down and allow your feelings to surface, letting them guide you in caring for yourself. Consider the people and things that offer support and rest.

Anticipatory grief can have an adaptive function by helping you prepare for what is ahead, motivating you to address unresolved issues, and encouraging you to make the most of the time that's remaining. Anticipatory grief can help you and your person find meaning on the end-of-life journey—dying can be an extraordinary time that encourages people to soften their hearts and offer forgiveness to relationships that have been challenged or estranged.

CAMPP: CONNECTION, AWARENESS, MEANING, PLEASURE, PRESENCE

How to begin: Use prompts to open up meaningful conversations

Your person will benefit from companionship. Picking up the phone and calling, popping by for a tea, or offering to go for a walk are ways in which you can intentionally show up and create a container to hold whatever emotions your person shares, allowing you to offer witnessing.

Here are some conversation prompts that may help to open up the space for conversation—don't forget to use language that is natural for you and just be normal! (These prompts are from American physician Atul Gawande, who challenges the current medical system. They're found in his fabulous book *Being Mortal: Medicine and What Matters in the End.*)

- What is your understanding of where you are and of your illness?
- What are your fears or worries for the future?
- What are your goals and priorities?
- What outcomes are acceptable to you?
- What are you willing to sacrifice and not?
- And later, what would a good day look like?

Gawande writes about the dying role—how it is common for people to share memories, make peace with powers greater than themselves, pass on wisdoms and keepsakes, consider their legacies, complete relationships, and do what they can to make sure that those who are left behind will be okay. This role is essential to dying—not just for your person, but for you as well.

Cumulative or compounded grief

When a person experiences multiple losses at once, or in relatively short succession, they are more likely to struggle to cope with each loss because of the compounding effect. This can happen on the end-of-life journey if folks are unable to connect with, express, and be witnessed in the various non-death losses leading up to death.

Disenfranchised grief

Disenfranchised grief results when grief is not acknowledged on either a personal or societal level or both. This includes the experience of being rushed through grief. When grief becomes disenfranchised, it can complicate the experience of loss.

A loss that is seen as too small or a relationship that is seen as too distant to justify grieving by others often causes grief to become disenfranchised. So many of us are lacking support systems, rituals, traditions, and institutions that honour grief appropriately. Know that if you recognize disenfranchised grief in your past, it is never too late to connect with your emotions and share them with trusted others to be witnessed.

Grief can become disenfranchised if those closest to you—well intentioned friends and family—find it too hard to hold space for your grief, or if their discomfort causes them to urge you to hurry up and get over your grief. Below are some examples of disenfranchised grief:

- Relationships that society doesn't recognize enough, such as pregnancy loss, the death of an ex-spouse, death of a pet, or the breakup of a secret relationship
- Non-death losses that are not recognized enough, such as loss of a job, a house, a sense of independence, a sense of identity, or loss of levels of cognitive function leading to dementia
- Grievers who are not recognized, such as young people, the elderly, those living with developmental disabilities, or the LGBTQ+ community
- Circumstances that are stigmatized, such as death from toxic drug poisoning, suicide, addiction, murder, estranged relationships, divorce, or infertility.

This lack of social recognition deepens the sense isolation inherent in grief. Without validation, the bereaved feel unseen and unheard, making it difficult to process the loss and move forward.

Ambiguous loss

Ambiguous loss refers to grieving someone who is still alive but absent, either physically or emotionally. This type of loss is complicated because it leaves grief unresolved, making it challenging to move forward. Some common causes of ambiguous loss in which a person is alive yet psychologically absent are addiction, traumatic brain injuries, dementia, and mental illness.

When a person is psychologically absent but physically present, they show up very differently in the relationship. They may be unrecognizable, or they may look the same, but regardless of their appearance, they are psychologically gone. They do and say things that are out of character, and the relationship changes; they treat you differently than in the past, and they are unable to be there for you in the ways that they were before the change.

Ambiguous loss can also result when someone is physically absent but psychologically present. Examples of this are adoption, a missing person, or incarceration. In both types of ambiguous loss, the love continues but grief arises for the person who is gone. The felt sense of this loss can manifest in many ways, but the emotions commonly associated with ambiguous loss are sadness, anger, guilt, and yearning.

CAMPP: CONNECTION, AWARENESS, MEANING, PLEASURE, PRESENCE

Bridging the crevasse: Companioning your person with dementia

An increasing number of people are living with dementia, primarily since to ageing is the biggest risk factor. As dementia progresses it may be challenging to offer emotional or spiritual comfort to your person and yet this support significantly enhances wellbeing. The sensory based invitations in this guide are well suited to people living with dementia. Activities such as listening to music, holding hands, massage, or watching birds may create connection, awareness, meaning, pleasure, and presence. Simply being there with your person can increase comfort.

Avoid asking direct questions

Asking direct questions requires a search for information that your person living with dementia may no longer be able to access. Such questioning may bring awareness of the disability to the surface which may cause unnecessary distress.

Listen to your person and take their lead

Listen to the questions your person is asking and take time to consider the most fitting answer from their perspective as opposed to yours. Keep in mind that your person's feelings are more important than facts. As a companion, it is helpful to focus on creating positive feelings, and sometimes this may include supporting information that is not correct. Consider using information and language that is most comforting to your person and encourage everyone who is in contact with your person to do the same.

Connect and don't correct

Meet your person where they are and take their lead so that you support the sense they are making of their world. Consider using the same language that they are using—this will guide you to take their lead.

Companioning your person with dementia can be overwhelming. Depression and fatigue are common experiences for caregivers. To be well, it is important to lean out on others for help, seek respite for caregiving so you can have a break, and engage in activities that bring you joy comfort, and a chance to reset.

It is not unusual for companions of people with advanced dementia to feel a sense of relief when death occurs. If you experience this feeling after your person's death, know that this is completely normal.

Estrangement Grief

Estrangement grief a type of ambiguous loss. It is the emotional response to a significant relationship becoming strained or severed. There are many causes for estrangement ranging from emotional, physical, or sexual abuse; to substance abuse, divorce, or disagreements around lifestyle or values. Grief that arises is the result of a relationship lost, or of a relationship one wished one had but never did. Estrangement grief often creates confusion, leaving people feeling as though they have lost something but not being sure of what exactly they have lost.

Estrangement is a healthy choice for those who have experienced abuse that has created a lack of physical or psychological safety in a relationship. In this case, stepping away from the person can result in a sense of freedom and relief. This isn't always easy, as there is a common expectation that biological connections to family members are guaranteed and necessary. In these relationships, there is a lot of pressure to forgive and heal. There is a commonly held idea that somehow you have to figure out a way to love every family member. That expectation is not realistic.

Often the experience of loss begins long before the ties to the other person are cut. Grief can begin decades before the relationship ends and continue to surface throughout the relationship. This prolonged grieving is often invisible, because the losses experienced aren't always noticeable, even to the bereaved.

Some people in estranged relationships may experience the common symptoms of grief; however, because estrangement grief is a type of ambiguous loss, some may experience very little grief or be unable to acknowledge their grief. This can create confusion, a sense of not being sure how to feel. Rejection and lack of closure due to unresolved conflicts can cause estrangement grief to become even more complicated. Further to the confusion, estrangement grief is often disenfranchised, or unacknowledged by the griever or others around them, which can lead to compounded grief.

Honouring the feelings that arise from estrangement grief can be tricky because this type of loss is often stigmatized. It can be uncomfortable to talk about complicated relationships so it may be easier to avoid the conversations altogether. Blame, judgment, guilt, and shame—either arising in the bereaved or others—are often in question. This discomfort can create grief secrets which can cause people to get stuck because they are reluctant to share their experience with others. This may increase feelings of frustration and fuel anger toward others who were oblivious to the need for support because they were unaware that there was a loss.

When someone a person is estranged from dies, their unlikeable traits can linger. The finality of death brings the realization that the relationship will never be what was hoped for, and this may cause yet another loss.

Like all experiences of loss, it is supportive to acknowledge the feelings that arise and share grief with trusted others who can hold space for it. Boundaries are important here; honouring what is okay and what is not, is a form of protection. To prevent further suffering, it's helpful to be mindful about how we speak about family with others avoiding assumptions shaped by cultural or personal expectations.

> "If you think you are enlightened, go spend a week with your family."
>
> – Ram Dass

STORIES FROM THE TRAIL

A fitting goodbye

Jean's quality of life had been deteriorating for years. Now in her eighties she had lost the ability to drive, and she relied on a walker to get around her apartment. She lived in an assisted living facility and even getting downstairs for mealtime was challenging. She spent most of her days in the quiet company of her beloved cat, Riley, moving through her routines with increasing physical discomfort. Her medications were gradually increased, leaving her drowsy and disoriented. She often slept through the day and awoke at odd hours, groggy and confused. The medication also made her unstable, and after a few falls, it became clear she needed more care. The prospect of moving from the home she'd known for eight years was overwhelming, and Jean refused. It seemed her body protested too—her symptoms worsened, and eventually it was decided that a stay at the local hospice was the best course, even if just temporarily, to manage her pain and reassess her needs. She accepted a bed. The care was wonderful, she was kept clean, she was offered kindness and regular meals, and her pain medication was adjusted as needed so she was comfortable, albeit sleepy.

It soon it became clear that she was nearing the end and she chose to access a medical assistance in dying (MAID) provision.

Jean had been adventurous, accomplished, and fiercely independent. Educated and successful, she married after university and had three children. I met her later in life, so I didn't know the full history, but it was clear her relationships with her adult children were strained. Jean was edgy, direct, and unfiltered. She didn't soften herself to please others—she was unapologetically herself.

She decided abruptly one day that it was time. She called the MAID team and scheduled her provision to take place at the hospice the following week. She was terrified. Her medication was increased in the days leading up to the provision to help quell her growing anxiety and dread. The day of the provision her adult children arrived to offer support. Her eyes were closed most of the visit—her son offered to play some music and that seemed to ease the atmosphere slightly. Understandably, emotions were amplified. Once a date is on the calendar things change. It is such a strange thing to schedule a death, to have it on the calendar, to wake up and go about the morning routine anticipating the enormity of what was about to happen. The fragility of life held up with such clarity.

With Mozart faintly playing in the background, and awkward glances darting around the small room as she lay resting, the MAID team arrived. The nurse prepared for the provision and the doctor explained the procedure to the family and asked if anyone had any questions. The kids shook their heads. Jean cracked her eyes open and addressed the two women who stood at the foot of her bed.

In true Jean fashion, she launched into a critique of the MAID process—how confusing it had been to navigate, the inefficiencies in communication, her suggestions for improvement. She went on at length, undeterred. Her kids sat quietly, visibly uncomfortable, but this was Jean: opinionated, exacting, unyielding.

When she finished, the doctor gently let them know there was no rush—they had all the time they needed. Her children were invited to say what was asking to be said, and when the time felt right, the doctor would administer the medication.

"I'm ready," Jean said without hesitation.

"Okay," the doctor replied, reaching into a case on the bedside table.

Her children gathered around her. Jean squeezed her eyes shut. "See ya, Mom," one said softly. The others sat quietly, tears slipping down their faces.

Everyone in the room was silent, looking at Jean, so close to the great mystery. Jean took her last breath less than five minutes later. That was that. "Did we do it right?" one of her sons asked. "What that a normal goodbye?"

"You did it right" I reassured. "You were there for her right up until her last breath."

There was no expression of forgiveness or love—but it was a fitting death. Jean died as she lived: fiercely independent, unapologetically herself. The nurse let the family know that they could take all the time they needed to be with their mom. Her children glanced at each other and in agreement decided to leave. This experience was a potent reminder that people often die the way they lived, that personalities often intensify in a crisis, and that with the possibility of resolution gone, grief can be complicated.

GROUNDING PRACTICES

The letter unsent: The grief of what might have been

Writing a letter to someone you are estranged from can be a powerful ritual, even if you never send it. Whether you burn it, hide it away, or simply leave it unsent, the act of putting your emotions on paper helps release stuck energy and express what's alive within you. This practice offers a chance to shift the dynamic energetically, allowing you to free yourself from the hold of unspoken words and unresolved feelings.

EXPECTED CHANGES ON THE JOURNEY

A family's walk with grief: The long goodbye

In many parts of the world, the way people die, and how they grieve, has changed significantly in recent years. Advancements in modern medicine have led to longer dying processes, which have resulted in prolonged grieving. This new grief differs from traditional grief in significant ways. One key difference is that it includes the person with the life-limiting illness. Additionaly, this extended care period can provide families with an opportunity to address unresolved issues that may have lingered for years.

On the end-of-life journey families often find it helpful to plan together and say goodbye, though each experience is unique. This may involve talking with the dying about mortality and other issues that do not arise when death happens unexpectedly. It requires family and friends to make space for extended grief in the busyness of our modern lives, including taking time off from professional careers or acting as an appointed family member for planning or logistics purposes. The way a family responds to this crisis not only depends on the family dance, but also on the resiliency of the family before the crisis. Death can create opportunities for healing and for longstanding resentments to be resolved, bringing people closer; however, the stress of a family member dying can also fracture families if they are less resilient.

In the book *Saying Goodbye: A Guide to Coping with a Loved One's Terminal Illness*, Barbara Okun and Joseph Nowinski offer an exploration of how families as a constellation navigate a crisis.

When a person receives a life-limiting diagnosis, the whole family (without qualifiers) is impacted and drawn into what often turns out to be a prolonged crisis. This process alters lifestyles and forces families to acknowledge issues that, in the past, were dealt with only after the death. Family grief often involves dealing with lingering issues from the past that were never fully resolved. Okun and Nowinski seek to offer hope and healing for those who may be "living with death" for an extended period.

This interrogation of grief includes the stages of crisis, unity, upheaval, resolution, and renewal. If family members feel confused and unsupported in these stages and have trouble coping with prolonged grief, they are vulnerable to experience depression, guilt, and anxiety, which can in turn lead to physical illness. While virtually every family will experience each stage, it is important to understand that the stages do not clearly end as another begins. It is likely folks will find themselves dealing with issues associated with more than one stage at any given time. The stages also vary in length and intensity, depending, on the length of the illness and whether there are any significant periods of remission. This new grief can be overwhelming, simply seeking guidance about what to expect, ways to feel supported, and how to show up for your person can make all the difference.

Crisis

Crisis is the first stage, and it begins with a life-limiting diagnosis. Families are thrown into a new reality, and often those affected feel like they are in a dream-like state. Anxiety is the most common response at this stage and the family's equilibrium is disrupted. How a family reacts at this stage is determined by the history of the relationships with other family members and the status of the relationship with the dying, such as the relationships to the person, as well as what the person's past and current roles are in the family.

If the relationship with the terminal family member has been challenging or estranged, the heaviness of guilt, resentment, or anger may arise. If the person with the life-limiting illness is a child or young adult, anger is a common response because of the seeming injustice of a life cut short.

Unity

Unity, the second stage, is characterized by coming together. The reality of the impending death often motivates folks to put even longstanding annoyances or grudges on hold as they come together to move into this second stage of grieving. This phase will be easier for family members who don't have complicated feelings or unresolved issues with the dying. However, if individuals feel less appreciated than others, it is normal to experience complex emotions.

During the unity phase family members tend to work together to decide how they want this new reality to play out. This unity phase is typically a busy time, with lots of decisions to be made such as establishing a medical team to work with, navigating access to social services, and practical planning. How the family organizes to get these tasks done can deeply impact the emotions of family members. This is the time when everyone involved attempts find their roles in relation to one another and to the dying. Without awareness, it is common to regress into roles played years earlier as children and adolescents, roles that individuals would not consciously choose now. During this phase, resentments, rivalries, and jealousies are often temporarily paused. It is a time to make a lot of decisions to support the dying person, who is typically in good shape and not feeling too debilitated. Clearly, the level of unity depends on the communication in the family and the previous roles, rules, relationships, and responsibilities of each person, but people are usually cooperative at this stage even though it is still a crisis.

Upheaval

If the process of dying goes on for an extended time the friends and family will eventually enter the third stage of grieving: upheaval. At this time, the unity that characterizes the second stage begins to fade as the lifestyles of family and friends shift with significant changes. This occurs due to prolonged grief causing people to begin to feel a little frayed at the edges. Old resentments may return and the likelihood of burnout increases. This is a complicated time. People often feel guilty because they feel ambivalent, wondering how long the situation will last. Anger and resentment are common at this stage. It is supportive to connect with and express emotions to increase understanding and to communicate honestly. Suppressing thoughts and feelings can lead to strained relationships and eventually can cause the entire family to fracture. Even though this time of upheaval can be discouraging, there are also opportunities to make changes in long-standing family dynamics by addressing important issues so that the family is effective in planning for what lies ahead.

Resolution

Resolution, the fourth stage, is characterized by a gradual deterioration in health for the dying, with possible periods of stabilization. At this time there is an opportunity to resolve conflict that has built up over time as well as heal and redefine roles within the family. People may either feel inspired at this stage or else overcome with anxiety, which may lead to avoidance.

Recalling memories from the past by way of a life review is a common practice for the dying and their people. This life review may reveal unresolved issues. Depending on the narratives, memories may evoke feelings such as joy, anger, jealousy, pride, shame, and embarrassment.

All families have long-standing issues that build up over time. In this resolution stage these issues can be brought out of the shadows and addressed. Rivalries, jealousies, and resentments may be resolved. Due to past coping strategies, some family members may react to this opportunity with anxiety instead of with enthusiasm and may avoid facing these issues; however, acknowledging long-standing patterns offers an opportunity for the family to grow closer and be healthier. This prolonged grief within the family offers an opportunity for growth and renewal.

Renewal

The fifth and last stage of the family grief model is renewal. This stage begins with the funeral and allows for mixed emotions such as sadness and relief. It can be a time of creativity and planning as the family decides how to commemorate their person who has died. If the family has navigated the other four stages well, this stage offers yet another opportunity for collective and personal renewal. As with any crisis, the family unit may either weaken and fracture or become even closer. This stage is a time for remembrances and looking to the future, perhaps with more intimacy, and to new family traditions.

STORIES FROM THE TRAIL

Creating a care journal: A story of family connection at the end of life

Creating a care journal for your person is one way to support connection by enhancing communication between family and friends. A care journal can be used in a hospice or hospital setting, or if your person is dying at home. You can invite anyone who is offering care to contribute—ideally with the blessing and permission of your person.

You can be intentional with the purpose of this journal. In addition to documenting health updates, it can serve as a running dialogue about each visit. It allows companions to share care, advocate for your person, and express hopes or concerns. You might encourage family and friends to journal about their experiences—sharing moments of connection, awareness, meaning, pleasure, and presence. They can also record stories about your person, adding richness to the journal.

A care journal can often bridge gaps between differing points of view—offering a place to express what may not be easily said face-to-face. Here's a story of how I've used this supportive tool with a past client:

I was hired by the son of a dying woman to provide respite from the demands of caregiving. He asked me to visit his mom daily. He lived near the hospice that his mom was at but he was having a difficult time juggling a demanding career and family life. The responsibility of caregiving landed on his shoulders as his sister lived out of town and their younger brother who also lived nearby was considered unreliable due to addiction challenges. I was honoured to be companioning their mother for the final month of her life.

The family dynamics were complex. Trust had eroded, and the relationships were fraught with anger and long-held wounds. The older siblings were estranged from their younger brother.

A care journal felt like a meaningful mode of communication for this disconnected family. I first gained permission from the woman to place a journal at her bedside. We spoke about her hopes and fears, and when I asked about her wishes, she had only one:

she wanted her family to stay connected after she died. She worried deeply that they would drift further apart.

Near the beginning of the journal, I clearly recorded her wish: "Your mom's number one hope is that the three of you stay connected after her death."

As we spent time together, I documented the comfort measures I offered—modeling care in hopes that others might do the same. I wrote about how she enjoyed leg and arm massages, how we listened to her favourite songs, and how she lit up when we told stories from her childhood. I captured those stories in the journal for her family to read—gifts of memory and meaning.

I also used the journal to advocate for her needs. Her well-meaning youngest son often tried to feed her, even though her body was no longer asking for food. This forced eating caused her discomfort and bloating. I gently used a page in the journal to explain that at this stage of life, it's normal to stop eating—the body no longer requires energy in the same way as before. I shared how listening to the body can bring more comfort than force feeding.

This journal was also a tool to foster communication among her children. I encouraged everyone to jot down a few notes after their visits—how their mom was doing, what brought her comfort, and any stories or observations they wanted to share.

I still remember the first entry from the younger son. On a blank page, he scrawled a single word: "Mom."

And then… nothing.

But over time, he began to write more. His voice slowly emerged, tender and uncertain at first, then stronger. His entries began to weave between those of his siblings, like threads finding each other. His sister began writing with more gentleness. The older brother's tone softened too. It was deeply moving to witness this gradual change—a family slowly learning from each other, offering comfort strategies and updates, their voices beginning to come together in a shared purpose.

The journal offered space for expressions that might never have emerged in conversation. It held feelings, ideas, memories—written safely and without interruption.

One day, the significance of this little book became crystal clear. I had accidentally slipped it into my bag and brought it home. An hour later, I received a text from the son.

"Where is the care journal? I just got here and it's nowhere to be found!"

In that moment, I realized how central the journal had become. It was anchoring this family—giving them a place to gather around their mother's bedside, even when they weren't there at the same time.

Her daughter later told me that her own daughters had decided not to visit. It was too painful to see their dear grandmother so close to death. She planned to share the journal with them when the time felt right, so they could know this chapter of their grandmother's life, even if they hadn't witnessed it directly.

This simple care journal profoundly supported this family as they navigated the end-of-life journey. It gave them a way to process the enormous experience, to witness one another, and to hold space for grief, healing, and love.

I WONDER . . .

How we cope again and again

Reflect on how your family and friends have responded to past crises. Recognizing their patterns can help you understand how they are reacting now and allow you to anticipate how they might respond as the situation intensifies.

STORIES FROM THE TRAIL

With less to carry, she went on her way

Travelling light is key on the end-of-life journey, and unresolved grief is heavy. While revisiting loss and regret may seem abstract, the impact of being witnessed by an empathic listener is profound. When we lean out on others there is less to carry alone. Connecting with our losses and expressing them in the company of others can lighten our grief, and that is exactly why Kimberly reached out to me.

During our first call, Kimberly shared that she was scheduled to have a medical assistance in dying (MAID) provision the next month. Her primary goal for support was to have her lifetime of grief and gratitude witnessed before she died.

We had four conversations over the phone before I met her in person on the day of her death. On our first call Kimberly expressed that she was lonely. She expressed a desire for connection, and she wanted to talk about her life and her approaching death. She began by expressing regret over a lack of community to help her with this need.

I took her lead as she shared a lifetime of change and loss. She shared about her many health challenges, both physical and mental, and she expressed grief about losing a child, being estranged from her father, and the tragic and sudden deaths of her mother and sister.

She also shared happy memories from her childhood, lighting up as she recalled vacations at the lake, and the intense sweetness of the small, wild strawberries she would pick and eat on the spot in the summertime.

She shared the plans for her upcoming MAID provision. She wanted to wear an oversized men's t-shirt and soft sweatpants. She planned to have her favourite pictures surround her bed. She wanted grace, which according to her was the scent of lavender, a candle burning, the sound of the nature channel playing in the background. She also hoped for dignity, and she asked me to write down specific mantras that she wanted spoken out loud to her in her last moments.

She talked about the practical details of her upcoming death, how she did not want to be cremated—to her, the idea of fire reducing her body to ashes was distressing. She shared about her past relationships, careers, and the different cities she had lived in.

She revealed the ways in which she cared for herself through the years, the healing that came from holistic therapies and expression through art.

Gratitude, the other side of grief, was sprinkled like confetti throughout our conversations. She shamelessly boasted that she had beautiful skin, and she shared with the excitement of a child when she started gushing about her love of Dolly Parton.

When I asked her about what made life worth living, she responded that the song "What a Wonderful World" said it all. She went on and on about her love of horses. Her grief morphed into anger at times. She spoke of the injustice that she experienced, and that she witnessed her sister's experience. She held anger for the systems and people who didn't offer her the support she needed.

She spoke about her love of art, naming her favourite pieces from Klimt and Monet. For Kimberly, there was a felt sense that her ancestors were present, and this gave her great comfort. She referred to our phone calls as "show and tell" and as she spoke, I sat, legs crossed, with my sketch pad on my lap, doodling pictures, capturing phrases, words, and names. She talked about her fears—of losing control, of abandonment, of increasingly painful physical symptoms. She shared about her love of painting and how time would disappear when she wrote poetry. She talked a lot about taking one day at a time and her belief in reincarnation, her view of her death as a new beginning.

I ended each session with a poem, a goodbye ritual for safe keeping. She would often reflect on the poetry and respond later in the day with a poem of her own. At the end of our four telephone sessions, I snapped photos of the pages and pages of sketches and notes I had taken over the hours we spent together. I emailed the pictures to her, and she was delighted. She said that she felt so seen and heard. For the first time ever, she felt complete, and that she was enough just as she was. Kimberly reached her goal. She had been witnessed, and with less to carry, she went on her way.

Anger as a messenger: What grief might be saying

Anger often stems from the fear of losing what we care about, making it a common response to loss. In Western culture, anger is often viewed as "bad"—linked to violence or dismissed as an inappropriate emotion for women to express openly. These narratives silence the griever, and that silence feeds anger, allowing it to grow unchecked.

However, there are alternative stories about anger—that it can guide us, that it can be expressed in healthy ways, that it is not inherently bad, and that there is no "right" or "wrong" time for it to emerge.

Embracing grief means welcoming all the feelings and sensations that come with loss. Each experience of grief is unique, but if we slow down and listen to our whole selves, our natural wisdom will guide us forward. We can approach these cues with curiosity when we understand that feelings aren't inherently good or bad; they are signals meant to capture our attention and lead us toward what we need.

By allowing ourselves to fully experience even the uncomfortable emotions, we also make space to embrace the more pleasurable ones. We cannot choose which emotions we experience. Grief invites us to explore new depths of awareness. This expanded capacity for feeling connects us to the most profound parts of ourselves and to the experience of being truly alive. Ironically, in a culture fixated on happiness, the path to greater joy often begins with embracing sadness.

Practicing radical self-compassion means listening to ourselves with less judgment and tending to our emotions with care. By acknowledging the messiness of being human, we honour ourselves. If we can hold the tension between sorrow, joy, grief, anger, and gratitude, we can expand and grow.

Deep feeling requires vulnerability, a tender space where both love and fear coexist. How we navigate this space is shaped by self-compassion. When we are gentle with our grieving hearts, caring for ourselves with the same kindness we would offer a dear friend, we create conditions for healing.

How can you express your ever-changing responses to loss? Do you have an outlet for anger? This can look like giving yourself permission to punch or scream into a pillow. When my kids experienced anger when they were young, I would give them a few eggs, send them out into the yard and give them permission the throw them at the trees. This physical release of energy, along with acknowledging their valid emotions, provided immediate and supported and relief.

What if we began to see grief not as something to avoid or fix, but as a lifelong companion, rooted in love, that has the power to soften and expand our hearts? Grief could become a path that deepens our connection to ourselves, others, all beings, and the planet. There's wisdom within the heart, waiting to guide us if we slow down, listen, and open ourselves to it.

We need each other in the process of grief. When we share our grief—whether through conversations, ritual, writing, silence, or simply being present with one another—we build community. In these moments we remind ourselves that none of us are alone. It is through honouring grief that we nurture our wellbeing. Integrating our losses helps create fertile ground in which we can plant seeds of love, hope, and meaning—not only for ourselves, but also for each other, and for all of life.

> "Anger is the deepest form of compassion, for another, for the world, for the self, for a life, for the body, for a family and for all our ideals, all vulnerable and all, possibly about to be hurt. Stripped of physical imprisonment and violent reaction, anger is the purest form of care, the internal living flame of anger always illuminates what we belong to, what we wish to protect and what we are willing to hazard ourselves for. What we usually call anger is only what is left of its essence when we are overwhelmed by its accompanying vulnerability, when it reaches the lost surface of our mind or our body's incapacity to hold it, or when it touches the limits of our understanding. What we name as anger is actually only the incoherent physical incapacity to sustain this deep form of care in our outer daily life; the unwillingness to be large enough and generous enough to hold what we love helplessly in our bodies or our mind with the clarity and breadth of our whole being."
>
> —David Whyte, from Anger

Part Two: The Physical Landscape

In his inspiring TED Talk, "What Matters Most at End of Life," palliative physician, speaker, and author Dr. B. J. Miller addresses this idea of accessing life through the senses. Dr. Miller suggests that we, as people companioning those living with a terminal illness, can not only set our sights on wellbeing, but we can also consider enriching the lives of the dying in their final weeks and days. In the talk, he implores us to remember to attune to our senses:

> "I am asking that we make space—physical, psychic room—to allow life to play itself all the way out so that rather than just getting out of the way, aging and dying can become a process of crescendo through to the end. We can't solve for death, [but] we can design towards it. Parts of me died early on and that's something we can all say one way or another... It has been a liberation to realize you can always find a shock of beauty or meaning in what life you have left."
>
> —Dr. B. J. Miller

For Miller, it is all about the level of authenticity that makes these sensory connections meaningful. With this approach of appreciating life through the senses, he concludes with a call to action: "Maybe we can learn to live well not in spite of death, but because of it. Let death be what takes us, not lack of imagination."

Given the mysterious nature of dying, and the emotional weight of navigating the many changes that come with a life-limiting illness, it's understandable that people often feel lost. During this time we can offer comfort by inviting them to focus on the body—our sense of wellbeing is deeply rooted in relationships, and these connections are built through sensory experiences. These living exchanges allow us to commune with one another. No matter where someone is on their end-of-life journey, there is always an opportunity to invite them to engage directly with the world around them, to connect through their senses, and experience the present moment fully.

Let's now explore how you can approach companioning through sensory-based invitations. Our bodies are the gateway through which we engage with life itself. Our senses connect us to our surroundings, ourselves, and each other. It is through our bodies that we come to know and be known, that we are reminded of our aliveness, and that we realize that we are not alone. As relational beings, being present in our bodies allows us to experience life in a direct and intimate way. It is our bodies that live and it is our bodies that die.

Consider the sensory memories you hold of someone that you deeply care about. It is their smell, the sound of their laugh, the feeling of their touch, and looking into their eyes that really allow you to feel connected to that person and to life. Without direct sensory experiences, we are merely in relationship with abstract ideas. It is through our bodies that we experience the wonder of living. Sensory emotional connections that arise in the body have the ability to directly inform and enhance relationships.

We seem to like to separate the senses; however, they inform each other. The five senses of sight, hearing, touch, taste, and smell may appear to operate autonomously, but in reality they work together to enable us to understand our surroundings. This is how we truly listen—not just with our ears, but with all of our senses. We feel things, and experience life by using multiple senses, taking in information through energy entering our brain and spinal cord. This information is integrated to give us an experience. If a person is differently abled, often our bodies will accommodate by enhancing the other senses, proving that our senses work together to assist and reinforce one another.

We are the creators of our memories and thoughts, and our senses help us to continually construct our reality. Imagine the possibilities of designing rich sensory experiences for the dying—moments that foster connection, awareness, meaning, pleasure, and presence. As a companion, you can draw inspiration from the senses, seeking opportunities to enhance your person's wellbeing.

Chapter 4

The Gateway of Sight

Imagine yourself standing in the middle of a forest. With your eyes closed, tilt your head back and envision what you see. Perhaps you are surrounded by a grove of enormous trees with branches reaching high above. Take a moment to relax and fully immerse yourself in this image. What are you noticing?

Now picture yourself standing in the middle of a bustling city. Look up at the skyline, perhaps surrounded by a wall of concrete skyscrapers. Hold that image for a moment. What do you notice now?

For many of us, spending time in nature or even just imagining natural images can boost our wellbeing. It offers mental, emotional, and physical benefits. People often report feeling calmer, more grounded, and nurtured. Even when imagined, nature brings a feeling of peace, allowing us to not only feel better but to think better as well. Nature calls us home, inviting us to settle into ourselves.

What we see or even what we imagine seeing can shift how we feel. As a companion to the dying, you can look to the sense of sight to increase comfort. Perhaps your person enjoys looking at old photos, recalling people and past experiences. As a companion you can look to the sense of sight to inspire invitations for connection, awareness, meaning, pleasure, and presence.

Sight is considered our strongest sense. Humans tend to rely more on sight than hearing or smell to understand our surroundings. It is estimated that roughly 80 percent of our sense of reality comes through our vision. Given its power, it's worth considering how we can intentionally use this powerful sense.

The sense of sight is truly amazing. Our eyes take in information about the world around us and convert it into images. Miraculously, the eyes translate stimulus in a way that is consistent with the interpretation of how others take in the world. This allows us to feel connected to others by knowing that we're seeing the same trees, sunsets, and stars as those around us.

The process of decoding light into sight is complicated and involves many steps and delicate parts that work in unison. Incredibly, this all happens in the blink of an eye!

Where Can You Find the Gateway of Sight?

Once you have settled in and attuned to your person's needs, consider how to use the sense of sight to offer comfort. You might dust off a home video, frame a favourite poem and place by the bed, or enlarge a photo from a family vacation and hang it on the wall. You could position their chair or bed so they can look out the window. Begin by identifying the qualities you hope to offer your person—be it a sense of calm or joy—and then get creative.

Simply looking at nature makes us feel good. Gazing out a window or taking a short walk can invite in the sense of sight in partnership with the natural world. Simply adding a houseplant to the room can bring comfort through sight.

The familiar faces of friends and family are often a source of reassurance. There are many ways to facilitate connection with others. Face to face visits, audiovisual contact through technology, watching old family movies, or flipping through the pages of a family photo album are just some of the ways we can facilitate connection.

Don't hesitate to share visual images from the past, and don't worry about upsetting your person by reminding them of a healthier, happier time—your person is already sad about what has been lost. Instead, remember that sharing photos helps create connection and meaning. Consider selecting photos to put in a special album, perhaps even writing captions for each photo. Younger family members may appreciate revisiting memories and learning about their family's history.

You can also look to the gateway of sight as inspiration to create a supportive space for your person. A setting that is organized and intentional can promote a sense of security; this is supportive for folks who are living with great uncertainty. Consider how you can increase comfort for your person by placing meaningful objects within view. These items may symbolize positive people, places, and experiences in life. Imagine everything from colourful throws, to plants, music, stones or shells—anything that holds special meaning. Consider the lighting; a room lit by soft, subdued sunlight or candles can provide a sense of serenity. If an uplifting energy is desired, consider wearing bright colours to boost your person's mood; see how vibrancy can affect those around you. Mindfully considering the physical spaces that people spend time in is one way we can look to the gateway of sight to increase wellbeing.

Some hospices are now using the technology of 3D headsets to offer residents experiences from the comfort of their beds. Sensory guided trips back to a family home, a summer cottage, or a dream vacation destination are frequently requested excursions. There are a multitude of creative ways we can use the sense of sight with intention and compassion.

When There Are Gaps in the Gateway of Sight

People who cannot see or have limited visual abilities can still be comforted by the sense of sight. In fact, people living with visual impairment are often gifted with enhanced hearing, taste, touch, and smell, and even improved memory and language skills.

In her essay "The Power of Touch," Helen Keller, American author, disability rights advocate, political activist, and lecturer writes:

> "It is not for me to say whether we see best with the hand or the eye. I only know that the world I see with my fingers is alive, ruddy, and satisfying. Touch brings the blind many sweet certainties which our more fortunate fellows miss, because their sense of touch is uncultivated. When they look at things, they put their hands in their pockets. No doubt that is one reason why their knowledge is often so vague, inaccurate, and useless...There is nothing, however, misty or uncertain about what we can touch. Through the sense of touch I know the faces of friends, the illimitable variety of straight and curved lines, all surfaces, the exuberance of the soil, the delicate shapes of flowers, the noble forms of trees, and the range of mighty winds. Besides objects, surfaces and atmospherical changes, I perceive countless vibrations. I derive much knowledge of everyday matter from the jars and jolts which are to be felt everywhere in the house."

Keller's description of how she uses her sense of touch to see reveals how sight and vision are different entities. Sight is a sensory experience in which light reflects off shapes and objects to pass into the eyes and create signals that are sent to the brain to be converted into images. Vision, however, is a metaphysical concept; it is how the mind interprets these images. Sight may allow a person to witness an event, but it is vision that helps the person understand the significance of that event and draw interpretations. Folks like Keller, who are unable to take in visual stimulus, are able to draw on multiple enhanced senses to visualize images that are as real as—perhaps even more complex than—those who rely on their sense of sight for understanding.

Guided meditation is another way to engage vision without relying on sight to offer comfort. By providing a vivid description of a favourite place, you can help your person see. Talking through the sights, sounds, smells, tastes, and textures of that place can transport them there, creating a sensory experience that brings peace and connection.

The Gifts of the Gateway

The gifts of the gateway of sight can vary from the calming, supportive effects of nature, to the sense of control gained by creating a peaceful, organized space. They also include the meaning-making that comes from a life review inspired by meaningful objects and photos. These simple sensory-based practices offer a connection to what is most meaningful, and this connection always brings comfort and clarity.

Look out the window, take a walk, go for a drive, or simply close your eyes and use your imaginal sense to see—notice how your sense of sight can bring you joy.

To support you in your role as companion, consider an invitation for comfort through the gateway of sight. What could be supportive for you at this time as you do your best to companion your person on their end-of-life journey?

STORIES FROM THE TRAIL

A landscape for letting go

I once companioned a frail woman propped up by a pile of pillows. She was quietly resting in her bed, gazing softly yet focused on the wall on the other side of the room. She was somewhere else, completely unaware that I had entered the room. The television that hung on that wall was turned off. I wondered what was capturing her attention.

The sense of peace and calm in the room was palpable. I stood there for a moment, in silence, and then gently greeted her. "My name is Tracy, I am a volunteer." She slowly turned her head toward me, our eyes met, and then she turned back toward the wall across from her bed. I followed her gaze to discover an enormous photo. It was a stunning picture of a lush forest canopy crowned by a pink and golden sunset.

"Wow," I remarked as we both took in the photo in silence. After a few moments she spoke: "The day after I came here my daughter went to my home and took this photo from my deck—my favourite place." She shared how much she loved the view from her chair under a grove of trees, spending time relaxing and watching the glorious sunsets. Knowing that this view soothed her mother, the daughter thoughtfully had the photo enlarged and hung it on the wall directly across from her hospice bed. This simple, beautiful image transported this woman from her dying bed to her sacred deck, evoking the comfort and peace of home through the powerful the gateway of sight.

STORIES FROM THE TRAIL

The forest in a box

Dr. Nadia Chaudhri is deeply inspiring. In a social media post, she shared how a box filled with pieces of the natural world brought her comfort after her life-limiting ovarian cancer diagnosis. A friend had brought the thoughtful gift to her while she was in the hospital—tokens from the natural world, a place where Chaudhri, like many, found peace.

Inspired by Chaudhri's story, I created a little forest box for a woman I was serving in my role as an end-of-life doula. Knowing how much peace nature brough Chaudhri, I wanted to offer something similar—something tangible that could help this woman reconnect with the calming, grounding energy of the natural world. She was confined to her apartment in the city and her chronic pain had become unbearable. She made the challenging decision to choose the legal end-of-life option of MAID.

Over the course of a month we had many conversations to prepare her for what lay ahead. We brainstormed about how the day of her death could play out in a way that was okay with her. She embraced this planning with remarkable courage, ultimately deciding that she wanted to be in the forest at the time of her death. We began to imagine this day, discussing different options, but as the date drew closer, her energy waned, and her desire for warmth led her to change her mind, opting to have the procedure at home instead. She was disappointed but accepted that this was the right decision. The day before her event, Chaudhri's post came to mind, and an idea sparked—why not bring the forest to her?

My youngest son painted a little wooden box a beautiful sky blue and glued a stone on top to serve as a handle. My middle son and I hiked up into our wild backyard and went treasure hunting. We filled the small box with moss, lichen, a mushroom, a blackberry flower, maple leaf buds, a heart shaped stone, and an evergreen sprig. As we foraged for treasures my son and I talked about who the box was for and the meaning behind the gift. My intention was to spark compassion and direct his awareness to the natural cycle of birth, life, death, and rebirth. I hoped he could find beauty and connection in the face of death and consider how to offer comfort to others.

Her MAID provision was the following day. With the treasure box in hand, I knocked on the door of her little apartment. As the door opened, I was surprised to see her standing there, like any other day. She seemed excited and grateful that her wish to die on her own terms was being realized.

She walked into her tiny bedroom and settled into the hospital bed that faced the window, framing a big maple tree and allowing natural light to filter in. I noticed the care that she had taken to surround herself with her favourite things: candles, photos, and flowers. A sacred space.

I passed her the little painted box. She pinched the stone and slowly lifted the wooden lid. She peeked inside and her face lit up with wonder. She carefully held each item, noticing how each piece of nature looked and felt. When she was done, she lifted the box up to her nose and inhaled deeply, closing her eyes and letting out a sigh of pleasure. At the end of life, it is often the simplest gestures that bring the deepest comfort and meaning.

STORIES FROM THE TRAIL

Spring through the lens: Bringing the outside inside

Patrick's work life came to a halt during that first Covid springtime. As with so many of us, this forced him to slow down and settle into a few months at home. As a professional cameraman, Patrick traveled the world, taking it all in through his camera lens. Patrick's mother, a resident in a long-term care facility, was also confined to her space. Not only were the residents unable to leave, but visitors were not permitted to enter, either. Feeling an overwhelming sense of helplessness, Patrick decided to use his camera to bring the wonder of the rebirth of spring to his mom and her fellow residents.

Patrick spent days roaming the city with his camera in hand. He captured the beauty of spring, filming streets dusted in powder-pink cherry blossom petals, ducks paddling in the ocean, and birds in flight. He recorded all the natural wonders he noticed as the world began to come to life. Patrick edited the footage to almost an hour of stunning video and set it to a gorgeous piece of classical music that enhanced a sense of wellbeing, providing connection, awareness, meaning, pleasure, and presence.

In an email, Patrick shared: "The residents were isolated, and I thought something as beautiful as the outdoors, as well as the music composed and used throughout the world specifically for calming and healing, may help. It was greatly received by the recreational leader in the home and there were many reports of agitated residents calming down when watching and listening."

Through his lens, Patrick not only brought a sense of peace and presence to those who needed it most, but also showed how even in the hardest of times, small acts of kindness can ripple through and make a meaningful impact.

GROUNDING PRACTICES

The feel of that place

Take a moment to bring up the image of a sacred place in nature that you have visited, a place where you felt a deep sense of peace and connection.

Close your eyes and vividly imagine this place, letting the sights, sounds, and even smells of the environment come alive in your mind. Cultivate the feelings this sacred place evokes—perhaps a sense of calm, awe, or tranquility. What is it about this place that makes it sacred to you?

What are the qualities that stand out? Its vastness? Its stillness? The way the light plays across the landscape?

Reflect on any memories and emotions tied to this place and allow yourself to fully experience those feelings.

Sit with the gratitude and pleasure you associate with this special place. Remember that landscapes have the power to embrace and soothe us. This sacred place is always available to you—you can return to it in your mind whenever you need a moment of connection, solace, or renewal.

Chapter 5

The Gateway of Hearing

> *"We hear in equal measure to what we listen with. When we listen with our mind, we understand more of life. When we listen with our heart, we feel more of life. When we listen with our entire being and spirit, we are transformed and joined with life itself."*
>
> —Mark Nepo, Seven Thousand Ways to Listen

What is the Gateway of Hearing?

Consider a favourite song. Imagine the melody, perhaps even sing the lyrics, or else put it on and listen closely to it. What happens to your body? Where does your mind go? What are you noticing?

Through music, we can shift our mood in an instant. Music can serve as a portal to connection, awareness, meaning, pleasure, and presence (there we have it—CAMPP again!). Brain scans taken as people listen to music illustrate how complex and powerful hearing perception can be. We are often deeply affected by music as melody, harmony, and rhythm activate widespread areas of the brain involved in movement, attention, emotion, memory, and language. The effect of music on the brain has been harnessed therapeutically for rehabilitation after stroke, brain injury, and for those with brain disorders ranging from autism to Alzheimer's disease.

The perception of hearing goes far beyond just music. It allows us to absorb a variety of experiences—words of affection, a playful joke, the soothing sound of waves, the wind rustling through trees, laughter, conversations, and even the songs of birds. We can be provoked negatively through our sense of hearing too; imagine an extended honk in traffic, or the clamour of noise pounding from a busy construction site. You may even feel these imagined sounds impacting your mind and body. Sounds can agitate or calm us on the spot.

Sound artist Yoko Sen has dedicated her life to considering the effect of sound on the dying experience. She acknowledges that in institutions where most people die, it is the beep of machines that is often the last tone that the dying hear. Inspired to create change, Sen encourages people to imagine how different the experience of dying would be if people could hear gentle sounds, such as ocean waves, lullabies, or other familiar reverberations that evoke comfort. Her hope is for future hospital soundscapes that are not only safe and functional, but gentle and supportive for this vulnerable time. Sen is working toward transforming the way we die in institutions using the gateway of hearing.

Hearing is a mechanical sense that connects us to the world and to others. Through the auditory system, sound vibrations travel into our bodies, allowing us to experience the world not just as individuals, but as part of an interconnected whole. Our auditory system allows us to connect and communicate intellectually, emotionally, and spiritually with each other. Sounds are processed in the brain. Hearing involves sensing, moving, feeling, and thinking. Hearing is perceiving sound, whereas listening is making sense of sound and the whole brain is involved in that process. We do this by synthesizing visual signals, words, emotions, the cadence of speech, our understanding of the person speaking, and the language spoken. By integrating all these signals, we can form a meaningful and accurate interpretation of the sounds we hear. From the gentle rustling of leaves to the comforting words of a loved one, sound invites us into a deeper relationship with our surroundings, with others, and with the essence of being alive.

It's not surprising that nature sounds are a common source of comfort. Sound researcher Joshua Smyth at Pennsylvania State University has found that when people listen to songbirds, the tension in their nervous systems decreases. Smyth measured by heart rate variability, noting that the same marker rises with the rumble of cars and roar of airplanes. Being aware of how sound influences a person's comfort at the end of life is an important aspect of compassionate care.

Laughter can be a source of comfort that can be offered to the dying through the sense of hearing. They say "laughter is the best medicine" for a good reason. Humour can help maintain lightheartedness and foster connection, even during difficult times. In the past, when care was provided by families and communities, it wasn't always perfect, but it was infused with moments of connection and humour. These moments are less common in the clinical care settings where most people spend their final days today. Laughter is so good for us, and it has been shown to have many physical benefits, many of which can be measured, such as reducing tension, increasing feel-good chemicals, boosting the immune system, reducing stress, improving mood, stimulating creativity, and increasing resilience. Consider sharing stories that remind your person of laughter and joy, bringing up fond memories of those precious moments.

Where Can You Find the Gateway of Hearing?

In her guide "The Listening Path: The Creative Art of Attention," Julia Cameron encourages readers to deepen their awareness of their daily soundtrack and make changes where possible. When we notice the harsh tone of an annoying alarm clock, we can consider replacing it with a gentler sounding alarm. Cameron believes that these small changes can impact our lives in a big way. The first step is to listen to what we may normally tune out by simply asking ourselves if the sound is pleasant as we move through our days. Cameron suggests attending to any irritating noises, so that we can turn our attention to what sounds support us throughout the day. Why not support your wellbeing and play your favourite album when you get home?

> *"Gentle sounds make for gentle lives. As our kindly sounds soothe our psyches, we become more kindly, our mind loses its jagged edge."*
>
> *— Julia Cameron, The Listening Path*

When you understand that sound can impact wellbeing, you can look to the gateway of hearing as a tool to bring comfort to your person. Actions such as closing a door to a busy hallway, playing favourite music, or reading aloud, can change the environment. It's important to consider your person's personal preferences; check in with their needs and offer choices whenever possible to support their sense of autonomy. The gateway of hearing can either distract from the intensity of the present moment or guide a person into the peace of the present moment, creating connection, awareness, meaning, pleasure, and presence.

During this time of great change, both you and your person probably have a lot to express, making the gateway of hearing so important. Your person may feel the need to express hopes, fears, and wishes, calling for you to listen and hold space for what is arising. Seeing and hearing your person as they navigate the end-of-life journey is deeply healing. When you soften to the present moment and truly feel what your person is expressing you offer them companionship, ensuring they don't have to face this journey alone. Remember, this isn't an easy role—the end-of-life journey can be challenging, but it becomes a little more bearable when you lean on others for support.

People often feel a sense of release or completion when they express forgiveness, gratitude, and love. These conversations are not always easy to instigate, but tending to relationships in this way can allow you and your person to say what needs to be said, making it a little easier to let go when the time comes. There is, however, no obligation to engage in these conversations if your person isn't receptive or if this type of communication feels awkward in the context of your relationship. Instead, you can consider writing your person a letter. There is no need to give the letter to your person; the act of simply expressing yourself and letting it go will set you free.

Years ago, I spotted a thoughtful handwritten sign taped to the door of a hospice room. I was so touched by the tenderness of the words and the care with which it was written. In beautifully formed letters the sign read, "Thank you for coming to visit. Please have a quick (5–10 minute) visit and let him know how much you love him." Almost always, there are two questions that the dying are left with: "Was I loved enough?" and "Did I love enough?" At the end of life, it almost always comes down to love. Do what you can to soften your heart and consider communicating love as often as possible.

Technology can allow the gateway of hearing to bring comfort to your person even across distances, allowing people to connect instantly through a phone, tablet, or computer. It can help create meaning and connection, whether by looking back over a lifetime of memories or sharing favourite stories. You might feel called to read from a newspaper, poetry, or sacred texts—reminiscing about the past or discovering meaning in the present moment can offer comfort and connection.

The gateway of hearing can support healing. When sound travels in waves through the body, it has a measurable effect. All matter is energy vibrating at different rates, so sound has the potential to shift the vibration of the body. Emotions are linked to vibrations which means we can use sound to intentionally evoke specific feelings. Music therapy is based on this understanding. Music therapists are valued members of the palliative care team. One of the most effective interventions I observe at hospices is watching the music therapist, guitar on lap, sing at the bedside—a gentle voice and soft focus on each note connects everyone in the room. The feeling of comfort and peace that comes from intentional music resonates deep in the bones. As humans, our psychological response to music is hardwired. We have long used song to express ourselves; in fact, music is the only sensory experience that activates all areas of the brain simultaneously, affecting us emotionally, cognitively, and physically. There are two types of music therapy offered by therapists, active and receptive. Active, or expressive, music therapy engages people in creating music by writing songs, playing an instrument, or singing. Receptive music therapy involves listening to music, either recorded or live, where everyone is connected by the same note, intentionally offered for comfort, yet each person internalizes the experience in their own unique way, allowing space for them to just be in that moment. Music can be incredibly generous in this way, offering a shared experience that still respects individual expression.

The Threshold Choir is an amazing organization that brings songs of comfort to those at the end of life. With over 200 choirs around the world, volunteers learn songs to sing at the bedside. This organization believes that a calm and focused presence at the bedside, with gentle voices, simple songs, and sincere kindness, can soothe and reassure the dying and their people. The Threshold Choir invites those close to the dying to join in song or simply listen. Songs are chosen to respond to the person's musical taste, spiritual direction, and receptivity in the moment. Many of the songs offered are composed by Threshold Choir members specifically to communicate ease, comfort, and presence. The songs are not religiously oriented, so the singing is appropriate for those who are deeply spiritual, regardless of religious affiliation. A session typically lasts about 20 minutes, using soft voices blended in harmony. The Threshold Choir offers singing as gentle blessings, not as entertainment, and members consider it an honour when the person being serenaded falls asleep. Most of the songs are very short, and the repetition is conducive to rest and comfort.

Akin to music therapy, sound baths—bathing in sound waves that are produced by a wide range of ambient sounds such as drums, chimes and gongs—are being incorporated into a growing number of hospitals' alternative healing options. Sound baths can also offer deep healing and leave patients feeling relaxed and focused.

The examples above show how sound can deliver us into the present moment or bring back a treasured memory, but we can also turn to the gateway of hearing to offer a distraction from the reality of dying. Often in hospitals and hospices, I observe sound being used as a way for the dying to disengage from their surroundings. At times, there is grace in escaping reality, allowing people to take in only as much as they can handle. It enables those facing this profound transition the space to take control and step back from constantly confronting what lies ahead. Tuning out is a helpful coping mechanism at times. It is common to walk into the room of a dying person to find televisions blaring with soap operas, daytime talk shows, or the news. People are either awake, dozing, or sleeping soundly—often resting with mouths wide open, seemingly oblivious to the noise. Wanting to create a calmer atmosphere I often offer to turn it off, only to be instructed by the resident not to touch the remote!

Now consider the absence of sound. Silence becomes a portal into the present moment, creating space to fully acknowledge what is being experienced. When it is quiet, space is created, and emotions can surface. Silence allows for communication beyond the limits of words. Generous and spacious, silence can allow us to sit with what is. Slowing down and self-witnessing can support people to keep up with the many changes on the end-of-life journey and create space for acceptance.

The gateway of hearing has so much to offer, from music and nature sounds to the muffled conversation floating in from another room. When I imagine my last days, I think of the sounds I want to hear—birds chirping, life going on outside my window, and expressions of forgiveness, gratitude, and love from my people. I imagine that I would feel comforted by the sound of my closest people chatting and sharing stories. I believe it would be reassuring to eavesdrop on a conversation between friends and family—lively and hushed at the same time. I hope for the natural honouring of sadness, joy, heaviness, and lightness weaving together, knowing that my people are close by, caring for each other while they companion me. I dream about dozing off in my tired body, without having to participate in the chatter—a glimpse into what it will be like when I am no longer here, imparting in me a knowing that life will carry on and everyone will be okay.

When looking to the gateway of hearing to comfort your person, consider asking about their preferences. Perhaps they have a favourite podcast. Maybe they are soothed by the sound of waves crashing onto the shore or calmed by the sound of a breeze through the trees. Sounds can inform, enrich, and comfort and yet without awareness, what we hear can cause agitation. The gateway of hearing connects us to life happening now and you can consider yourself a conductor, intentionally directing sounds.

Keep in mind that when people who die slowly are in their last few days, music and other sounds can be overwhelming. At this stage the dying are unable to communicate verbally. As a companion, take the time to listen deeply, attuning yourself to their needs and trusting your intuition to offer the right support. The senses heighten as the body changes, so it is important to be mindful of sound levels. This goes for conversations, music, etc. Consider playing music in intermittently and adjust speakers away from the head of the bed. Allowing for silence is usually supportive as the dying retreat inward. If you are grounded and listen with all of your senses, you will be guided by your intuition to what is most appropriate. Trust this knowing.

When There Are Gaps in the Gateway of Hearing

"You miss a lot without having your hearing aid in." I was on a breathtakingly beautiful ferry trip up the Inside Passage of British Columbia, and the couple beside me were taking in the unobstructed sights in the front row seats when the wife said this to her husband. The ten or so other passengers sat in silence witnessing the holy landscape. I smiled to myself. *Hmm, but was he?* The silence we were all enjoying offered a spaciousness to absorb the magnitude of the beauty.

Mark Nepo wrote *Seven Thousand Ways to Listen* as a personal search to discover how to keep listening as the author himself was losing his sense of hearing. Nepo writes of hearing with body and mind—he believes that it is here that we find the ability to taste life directly; it is here that we find the capacity for wisdom. He invites us to listen to silence, to work on being in a deeper relationship to life.

> "What we call listening is an innate process that integrates an array of sensations we encounter through different ways of knowing (sight, smell, touch, taste, and sound). What we hear is the sum of life's vibrations, which constantly arrive like waves that soak into a perpetual shore that the oldest traditions call the mind-heart."
>
> —Mark Nepo

It is remarkable to consider that even as hearing fades, we can guide people to remember or imagine sounds they can no longer hear. Our incredible imaginations allow us to reconnect with past experiences.

Even when your person appears unresponsive, remember that they can still hear. Hearing is the last sense to leave and there is clinical evidence that confirms that those in the last days of life can still hear and are aware of what is happening around them. In a groundbreaking study published in *Scientific Reports* in June 2020, neuroscientists provided the first evidence that some people can still hear while in an unresponsive state hours before dying. Neuroscientists at the University of British Columbia measured the electrical activity in the brain from patients at St. John's Hospice when they were conscious and again when they became unresponsive. Data from a control group of young, healthy participants was also collected. The researchers monitored brain responses to tones and found that the auditory systems of the dying patients just hours from death responded similarly to the young, healthy control groups. They concluded that even in an unconscious state, the dying brain responds to sound tones, reinforcing that hearing is the last sense to fade in the dying process.

With that in mind, continue to speak kindly and softly, even if your person is unresponsive. Communicate as you normally would, greet your person upon arrival, offer reassurance, and explain what you're doing while you're there. Say goodbye when you leave, and let your person know who will be coming next. When guiding others on how to show up, encourage them to speak from the heart, and from a place of compassion or forgiveness. It is okay to be honest in a gentle and loving way. You can reassure your person that they are loved and that it's okay to go. The sense of hearing is a gateway to connection, awareness, meaning, pleasure, and presence right up until the very last moment.

STORIES FROM THE TRAIL

The soundtrack of a life

My friend Alison, a skilled music therapist, has a remarkable ability to foster connection, awareness, meaning, pleasure, and presence through the sense of hearing. She invites people to create a meaningful legacy project by curating a musical playlist that captures a lifetime of memories. Alison prompts people on the end-of-life journey to select one or two songs from each decade of their life—a musical life review. She then guides individuals to reflect on the emotions and experiences each song evokes, how they interpret the lyrics, and why each song was meaningful at the time. At the end of the project, the person has reviewed their life, finding meaning in the good times and the challenging times too. After the person has died, the personal legacy playlist is often shared at the memorial ceremony, and it can serve as a source of comfort and connection to friends and family moving forward.

STORIES FROM THE TRAIL

Words that set us free

Expressing forgiveness, gratitude, and love is like a magic bullet for completing relationships. I share this guidance with almost everyone I support because of the deep healing I have witnessed from these prompts. I often offer gentle direction on how to engage in the courageous exchanges that can give those at end of life the peace to let go, and safeguard those who are left behind from regret caused by not saying what needed to be said in the time that is left. Completing relationships and expressing love is the centre of it all.

I was invited to support a family who was navigating a life-limiting diagnosis. The husband and father was living with glioblastoma, a terminal brain tumour, and he was slowly retreating from his young family as the disease progressed. In a conversation with his wife one day, I suggested the idea of expressing forgiveness, gratitude, and love—a simple framework for a big conversation that serves as a starting place to share what really matters. She listened intently and felt that the prompts would be helpful for her two young boys to express themselves to their dad in his final days. She encouraged her boys to express four things in writing: *Please forgive me for…*, *I forgive you for…*, *I am grateful for…*, and *I love you.*

With their heart-soaked papers in hand, the boys headed to hospice one winter evening to read the letters to their dad. Their mother called me, in need of reassurance after she ushered her young boys into their dying father's room with the intention of expressing their deepest emotions. I held space for her fear and shared that in the end, it is what is left unsaid that is cause for concern. She agreed, knowing on an intuitive level that speaking from the heart was the most healing way forward. Later that night she called me again, and I could hear a sense of lightness and relief in her voice. Both boys had time with their dad, and both had been courageous enough to read their letters. Although their dad lay resting with his eyes closed, he was able to acknowledge what had been shared and reflect love back.

He died the following morning. While his death came as a shock to everyone, the gateway of hearing gave the boys the chance to express everything that needed to be said. Words from the heart were offered up, and in that moment, they were all set free.

STORIES FROM THE TRAIL

A laugh to hold on to

Years ago, I supported a woman who found comfort in sound. She had a recording of her daughter's laugh on her phone, and whenever she felt down, overwhelmed, or simply needed a lift, she would play it. This simple act brought her pure joy. It's that simple.

The Gifts of the Gateway

Hearing is one of our most important senses, serving as a gateway that connects us to the world around us in essential and vital ways. Hearing connects us to people, allowing us to communicate in a way that none of our other senses can achieve. Knowing that the gateway of sound is a culmination of all of the senses, and that it is the last sense to fade, provides a portal for love right up until the last breath and beyond.

> *"Music is the literature of the heart; it commences where speech ends."*
>
> *—Alphonse de Lamartine*

GROUNDING PRACTICES

A soundtrack of support

Consider creating your own playlist that brings you joy and touches your heart. Listen while you drive or move to the music in your living room.

GROUNDING PRACTICES

Tending to the soundscape of your life

Keep a log of the soundtrack of your life, taking note of the sounds around you and your reactions to them. Review the list and consider any changes that you could make that would make your world more gentle. Why not treat your ears lovingly?

Chapter 6

The Gateway of Smell

Just the other day a friend asked me to hold her garage door open while she went in to find a box. Standing in the doorway, I inhaled a familiar but complex scent. I noticed top notes of old metal tools, oil-soaked concrete, and time, all steeped in a cool, enclosed space. In an instant, I was transported back to my grandpa's garage, a place I hadn't visited in decades. This smell unlocked vivid memories of my grandpa and I was reminded of being a little girl full of wonder, standing next to him and watching with curiosity as he tinkered away at his workbench. I was overwhelmed by the immediate flood of warm and fuzzy feelings that washed over me.

The gateway of smell may not immediately seem like the most enthralling sense, but it is quite unique. Unlike sight, hearing, touch, and taste, the sense of smell is directly linked to memory and emotion.

> "Smell is a potent wizard that transports you across thousands of miles and all the years you have lived." —Helen Keller

I wonder if you can recall a time when a scent caused an old memory to surface and you were flooded by the accompanying emotions? Perhaps a moment from your childhood arises with the smell of fresh cut grass, wax crayons, or a certain perfume or cologne. Scents can evoke intense emotional responses due to the way they are processed in our brains.

Smell is the most mysterious of the five senses, and it can be a potent emotional trigger. Scents can instantly transport us back to wherever we first experienced a specific smell. This is because smell and emotion are stored as one memory. It is during childhood that we create the distinction between smells that we like and dislike for the rest of our lives.

Whether pleasant or unpleasant, a scent may correlate directly with our past experiences and awaken memories. Immediately, this impulse creates feelings on a subconscious level, allowing us to access what is buried deep in the unconscious mind. This happens because the olfactory bulb connects directly to the brain in two places that are strongly linked to emotion and memory. The sense of smell is the only one of the senses that travels through these regions. This is why odors and fragrances can evoke emotions and memories that the other senses can't.

People may have surprisingly strong aversions to seemingly benign scents. Anne-Marie Keppel, an end-of-life doula and author, illustrates the importance of asking about preferences and permission in her hilarious cautionary tale, a short skit titled "Get the Psychopomp." Keppel shares the unsuccessful attempts of a newly trained and overly eager end-of-life doula who consistently acts without warrant. In an attempt to provide comfort to a dying woman, the keen doula applies lavender oil to the inside of the dying woman's nostrils—she does this even after the woman's attentive granddaughter shares that her grandmother hates lavender. This intervention, although initiated with good intentions, turns out to be deeply upsetting to the dying woman, causing her to silently exclaim, "I'm not sure I have enough strength to take a swing at her the next time she comes at me with the damned lavender oil but I'm going to try."

In the skit, the woman about to die was unconscious and unable to verbally communicate her likes and dislikes directly to the doula. The lavender incident could have been avoided if the doula had taken the time to learn about the woman's preferences by listening to her family and reading through her detailed end-of-life planning documents, both of which clearly communicate the woman's dislike of lavender oil. When it comes to following a harm reduction approach without clear guidance, it is best practice to do nothing. Making assumptions may cause distress, even with respect to something as seemingly innocent as lavender oil.

EXPECTED CHANGES

In the air around us

Changes in the body at the end of life can cause a variety of odors. Unpleasant smells can affect your person's sense of dignity as well as your ability to be at ease and present. When the body begins to shut down, changes in metabolism can cause different smells to be released from the breath, skin, and bodily fluids. Often a distinctive acetone scent is produced, a smell similar to the scent of nail polish remover. Certain diseases can cause pungent and unpleasant odors as well.

If unpleasant smells become a problem, consider opening a window. If this is not an option, you can use a fan to circulate air and refresh the room. If unpleasant smells persist, slip a small bowl of coffee beans, activated charcoal, or kitty litter under the bed to absorb unwanted odors.

GROUNDING PRACTICES

Scented supports

Over the years I have picked up some tips from experienced hospice nurses, care aides, and palliative care physicians on how to manage pungent smells. Peppermint, eucalyptus, or clove essential oils can be applied to a scarf, inside a mask, or to the upper lip if strong odors are an issue. Menthol-based ointments can also be applied to the inside of the nostrils. Some folks manage strong odors by sucking on a menthol-based lozenge to override the unpleasant smell.

Where Can You Find the Gateway of Smell?

You use the sense of smell to foster connection, awareness, meaning, pleasure, and presence by evoking memories of favourite places or people, or simply encourage feelings of ease and calm. Smell-triggered memories are often more emotional than those recalled through sight or hearing, with scents having the power to transport people back to the original event.

If you are looking to the gateway of smell for inspiration to bring comfort to your person, start by asking about your person's unique preferences. This fosters a sense of agency, allowing your person to act independently and make their own free choices. Scent preferences are deeply personal and what brings comfort to you may not have the same effect on your person. It is important to take the time to ask about likes and dislikes and listen before turning on the diffuser.

If your person is agitated, certain scents may evoke a sense of tranquility and peace. A room can be scented in many ways, such as diffusing or spritzing essential oils, lighting scented candles, burning incense, or adding fresh flowers to a vase. Remember, the senses of those nearing the end of life are often heightened. Be sure to ask your person if they are comfortable with the intensity of the scent and adjust accordingly.

CAMPP: CONNECTION, AWARENESS, MEANING, PLEASURE, PRESENCE

The scent of comfort

Scents hold the power to enhance wellbeing, making the sense of smell a powerful tool for offering comfort to your person. Has your person ever mentioned a memory or emotional experience tied to a particular scent? If so, how can you use this smell with intention to increase comfort?

At the end of life, aromatic oils can be used to alleviate various symptoms such as anxiety, nausea, fatigue, shortness of breath, pain, coughing, restlessness, and improving wellbeing in general. Aromatherapy works through the sense of smell and through skin absorption. Examples of aromatherapy products are aromatic spritzers, diffusers, bath salts, body oils, creams, or lotions for massage or topical application, as well as with hot and cold compresses.

If you are considering aromatherapy for your person, check with the medical care team before using essential oils. In some cases, breathing in the tiny particles released by the diffuser may trigger airway inflammation and asthma symptoms. Also, it may be best to stay away from eucalyptus and lavender if your person has respiratory issues as these oils may cause difficulty breathing. Essential oils are also contraindicated with certain medications.

Using scents doesn't have to be expensive or complicated. Simply exploring your home can offer inspiration. Once you understand your person's preferences you can create a list of comforting, and possibly even uplifting, scents. Consider a jar of cinnamon to evoke holiday memories or freshly cut flowers from the garden. Even the scent of a familiar detergent or household cleaner can be soothing. Perhaps your person appreciates the smell of banana bread baking or a roast cooking in the oven. These smells will most likely evoke emotion, memory, and nostalgia. Scents are powerful because they have the ability to guide us home.

The emotional state of your person can be shifted in an instant through the sense of smell. The enlivening effect of peppermint can be refreshing, as it opens up the sinuses. Citrus is also an uplifting scent, easing stress and depression. Scents like lemon, orange, and grapefruit are known to reduce anxiety and fatigue, and increase wellbeing.

GROUNDING PRACTICES

A boost of citrus

Caregiving can be exhausting. For a quick pick-me-up, rub a few drops of sweet orange oil between your palms. Raise your hands to your face, cup your nose, and enjoy a deep inhale. The scent of this citrus fruit can boost your mood and energize you in an instant.

You can use the sense of smell to guide your person to places that have special meaning—a seaside cabin perhaps, or a favourite forest hike. It is common for people to be transported to memories of carefree beach holidays by smelling sunscreen. Consider how you can invite your person to time travel.

Smell can also create comforting feelings of connection to important people. Several studies have suggested that the act of smelling clothes once worn by an absent loved one is comforting and potentially soothes loneliness.

The same can be said for the scent of foods that are associated with specific relationships. Perhaps your mom's lasagna elicits a sense of social and emotional connectedness, or the feeling that your mom is right there with you. Occasionally, my youngest son wears his late grandpa's cologne. When I catch a whiff of that scent lingering in the hallway, it feels like a visit from my dad, and I welcome the memories that follow.

The opportunities to call forward meaningful memories and induce emotions through the gateway of smell are endless, from scented candles and essential oils to a sniff of a child's hair or a dab of pine sap. Diffusers, cleaning agents, and personal care products can all be used with intention. The sense of smell is extraordinary for its ability to subconsciously evoke feelings of nostalgia and deep emotion, often bringing memories of comfort and connection.

When There Are Gaps in the Gateway of Smell

If the ability to smell is impaired, it is still possible to tap into this remarkable sense. Our vivid imaginations can be used to evoke the memory of certain scents for the sake of summoning positive experiences. You can invite your person to imagine a favourite scent. Since scents are registered through neural signals and linked to memories and emotions, simply imagining a specific scent can evoke experience for your person, along with all the associated feelings.

Guided meditations are an effective way to revisit special memories or desired emotional states, and incorporating an imagined sense of smell has been proven to enhance this experience. There are numerous notable sources for guided meditations available these days, many of which are free.

Studies have shown that the pathways of neural processing are the same when someone is visualizing a place as they are when one is experiencing the actual image. You may choose to create a personalized guided meditation to distract your person from physical, emotional, or spiritual distress, and to find comfort and connection. A meditation about a favourite place can be used to create a sense of calm or even excitement by recalling an adventure. Whatever the desired state, a personalized guided meditation can be a comforting intervention.

If your person is interested in co-creating a personalized guided meditation, be it to the family cabin or recalling the thrill of a white-water rafting trip, start by inviting your person to settle in and soften their gaze or close their eyes. Prompt your person to describe the place or experience in as much detail as possible. It is helpful to be slow and deeply descriptive. Ask about specific smells associated with the memory as well as sights, sounds, tastes, and textures while you record the details. You can then read the meditation back and allow for any refinements. Once you have a script, you or someone else can recite the meditation at any time. This personalized guided meditation can be read out loud to your person or it can be recorded onto a smart phone so that it can be played whenever connection, awareness, meaning, pleasure, or presence is desired.

STORIES FROM THE TRAIL

The comfort of something cooking

I have spent time in a hospice where the kitchen is a few steps from the main doors. As visitors and residents enter the building, they are often met by the aroma of simmering soups or roasted chicken. These comforting scents drift down the main hallway and into the patient rooms, with many folks often commenting on the soothing smells wafting from the kitchen.

The chef approaches his work with reverence, listening carefully to individual food preferences, firsthand or from attentive families and friends. Often, the lovingly prepared trays return to the kitchen untouched. As already discussed, near the end, people have little need for energy by way of calories, but this does not affect the chef's motivation. He is aware of the impact of the comforting smells that come from food being prepared. The smells that rise from the kitchen nourish the patients and their friends and families in other ways.

One day, in a conversation with the chef I shared that I was inspired by palliative care Physician B. J. Miller's TED Talk in which he mentions "the little things not being so little." Dr. Miller goes on to describe the "sensuous aesthetic gratification, where in a moment, in an instant, we are rewarded for just being." He shares his experience at Zen Hospice, an organization in San Francisco that he co-founded and served at for many years. He reveals that "with all the heavy-duty stuff happening under our roof, one of the most tried and true interventions we know of is to bake cookies."

About an hour later, my nose detected a heavenly scent. I inhaled deeply and recognized the smell filling the main hall—the aroma of freshly baked chocolate chip cookies. I peeked into the kitchen to find the chef, beaming, with four baking sheets of steaming cookies on the counter—a powerful testament to the companion of smell

STORIES FROM THE TRAIL

The fragrance of connection

Lisa, an end-of-life doula, incorporates her training in aromatherapy to support her clients. This holistic approach, using natural plant extracts, has been a valuable support in serving many of them.

Lisa was once approached by a woman seeking doula services. The woman was looking for support with accompanying her brother on his end-of-life journey. The situation was complicated due to estrangement, her brother lived across the country, and he did not want any contact from his sister.

Initially, Lisa was stumped by how to provide comfort and connection to this woman but after sitting with this predicament and tuning into her creativity, she came up with an idea for her client to find meaning and connection despite these obstacles.

Lisa began by offering education and support through face-to-face meetings, texts, and emails. She invited the woman to create a dedicated place in her home where she could go to connect with her brother—a small altar to honour him. She suggested starting with the five senses.

An altar is simply a place devoted to a being or thing. Altars are often found at shrines, temples, churches, and other places of worship, but they can be personalized and made in a home or a garden by using meaningful items. Altars have been used by various religions around the world, with many historical faiths also incorporating them in their practices.

Lisa encouraged her client to spend time at the altar whenever she felt drawn to be close to him. She invited her client to spend time recalling memories and stories, encouraging her to connect with her heart and intentionally send him love and connection to support him in his final days.

Drawing on her aromatherapy training, Lisa leveraged the memory-inducing gateway of smell to create connection. She created three essential oil blends and asked her client to pick her favourite scent. She gave the woman a little bottle that held the chosen oils and advised her client to apply the oil when she was at the altar connecting with her brother. She guided her to be with feelings of love and connection as she inhaled the oils. She also suggested that the woman carry this pocket-sized vial with her so that she could invoke connection whenever her brother came to mind. This little vial held so much more than oil; it contained immediate access to love for her brother, an experience she could tap into whenever she sought closeness.

GROUNDING PRACTICES

A corner of intention

You can create an altar in your home to help you regularly connect to what matters most to you. An altar can be created on a small table, a shelf, or a mantle, and a simple scarf can be used to designate this special spot. Dedicate this place to its purpose and keep it clear of clutter. Altars often include items that have personal significance—objects that evoke feelings of love or inspiration—such as photos and trinkets imbued with meaning. Consider placing sacred texts or a journal on your altar. Chimes or an instrument can be included to honour the gateway of hearing. For the sense of taste, a bowl of sweets or some fruit can be added. You may want to place a comfortable cushion to sit on or a blanket for spending time at the altar as a way to appeal to the sense of touch. Consider fresh flowers or scented candles to include the sense of smell. Having an altar in your home can evoke feelings of connection and meaning simply by walking past. Over time, just being near the altar can influence your energy and mood. Creativity is key, so if you design an altar, open up, be flexible and curious, and have fun.

GROUNDING PRACTICES

Sustaining rituals of scent

How can you use the gateway of smell to support you in your role of companioning your person? Consider creating rituals using scents that support you to invite in what you are seeking. Do you crave more joy, rest, connection, or peace in your daily life? You can intentionally light a scented candle after dinner, diffuse some essential oils, or cut some flowers or herbs from the garden to support you on your caregiving journey. I regularly use oil of rose before I meet with clients as this soft floral scent increases my heart awareness, reminding me that companioning those on the end-of-life journey is heart work.

STORIES FROM THE TRAIL

Scents as solace

A while back, fellow doula Angela and I were contacted by a woman seeking doula support. She was desperate for help as she was suffering greatly due to uncontrolled pain. Medications and interventions that had previously brought relief were no longer effective and she was now confined to bed and becoming weaker by the day. Her quality of life was unbearably low. This woman felt as though she had exhausted the pain control options that she was comfortable with that were offered by the medical team and she was desperate for comfort.

During an intake meeting, Angela asked the woman what brought her joy. With her face twisted with pain and her body tense, the woman shared that she enjoyed the smell of oranges. Angela left the room and went into the kitchen. She found an orange and peeled the fruit. Holding a piece of the orange peel up to her nose, Angela gently squeezed it to release a gentle mist of energizing orange oil. In an instant, her face relaxed and her posture eased.

Sensory interventions need not be complicated. Simple, everyday things can bring great comfort.

The Gifts of the Gateway

The gateway of smell can be a powerful support to your person on the end-of-life journey. This effective memory inducer can, in an instant, create a flood of vivid feelings and allow your person to reminisce about memories and create meaning. The sense of smell can evoke moments connected to positive emotions, changing or enhancing moods that invite security, joyfulness, tranquility, and connection. The remarkable effect of the sense of smell lies in its ability to create connection to the people, places, and moments in life that matter most.

Chapter 7

The Gateway of Taste

The sense of taste, like the other senses we have explored so far, can spark memories from times gone by and offer opportunities to experience what it means to be alive, to be human, and to engage with the world. Taste can serve as a gateway to connection, awareness, meaning, pleasure, and presence.

In the first moments of life, an infant is put on its mother's breast to nurse. This association of food and drink with qualities beyond nutritional sustenance continues throughout our lives. Whether we are aware of it or not, food is often associated with care, tenderness, and love.

We know that connection increases wellbeing and food is an effective connector. Food can help us to relate to each other, to our ancestors, and to our lands of origin. Legacy from the previous generations is often carried on by way of favourite recipes. Perhaps you can think of a traditional dish passed down from your grandparents to your parents, a recipe that you continue to make and perhaps have passed on to someone younger. Food is present at almost every social event. When we share a meal with intention, we have the opportunity to tap into a source of deep connection.

For many, food is a love language. Thoughtfully prepared and intentionally served, it often symbolizes love—an offering that speaks volumes without the need for words. Preparing, gathering, and sharing favourite meals with others offers a meaningful way to communicate care. For those who express love through food, the ritual of washing, peeling, and chopping ingredients—like making a pot of soup for a loved one feeling unwell—becomes an act of deep caregiving.

I often see family and friends come through the front doors of hospices carrying special treats for the residents. There is often a communal fridge in the family kitchen full of containers that hold a range of food from lovingly prepared meals to fast-food hamburgers. I recall a time when a visitor arrived at the door of a local hospice cradling two pounds of mashed potatoes in his arms, eager to fulfill the wish of a resident. An incredibly diverse range of home-cooked dishes are thoughtfully prepared and delivered in labeled containers, each an expression of hope and love.

If your person's appetite is waning, and their food preferences are changing due to changes in the body, you can continue to invite comfort through the gateway of taste. Simply reminiscing about meaningful foods can be a source of connection and comfort. Research indicates that it is supportive to harness the restorative power of nostalgia as a form of therapy and this applies to those living with a terminal illness and the bereaved.

Nostalgia not only links people to their past, but it also helps fuel connection to community and encourages the building of new social experiences. Nostalgia leads to pleasure, such as sharing a favourite food or drink that is linked to a meaningful moment. This experience can connect people back to themselves and may facilitate an increased connection moving forward. It has been noted that wellbeing increases when people who were feeling down spend time reminiscing about joyful, memorable times, such as special occasions like weddings, birthdays, and gatherings with family and friends.

Nostalgia has a positive impact on people suffering from dementia and grief. Experts are now looking at a form of nostalgia therapy that can be developed, which might train people to recall special memories in moments they are feeling down or struggling with loss.

The sense of taste changes over time. Usually beginning around age 50, people naturally begin to lose taste buds. At the end of life, other factors can exacerbate the loss of taste. Certain medications or treatments, including chemotherapy, can change the taste of food. Mouth dryness and vitamin deficiency can also affect taste. Flavours that were once enjoyed may become unappealing. At the end of life, people crave specific foods, usually simple flavours and textures as the senses become heightened.

Considering how symbolic food is of life and love, it is understandable that it can be distressing when people experience loss of appetite and the accompanying weight loss which is common at the end of life. With everything going on, often the dietary changes resulting from the loss of taste and a decreased need for calories, remain among the most upsetting for family and friends. It is common for people to feel as though they are somehow failing as caregivers if their person is not eating but this is not the case. A diminishing appetite and weight loss are normal signs of dying. Loss of appetite is expected as the body begins to change.

EXPECTED CHANGES ON THE JOURNEY

Appetite decreases on the end-of-life journey

There will likely come a time when your person will have very little or no intake of food or fluid. This happens when sustenance by way of food is no longer required by the body. It is normal to habitually, and perhaps desperately, try to offer your person anything and everything to stimulate their appetite. Your person may just nod to suggestions that dedicated family and friends insist on making, taking just one bite, only to reject the rest, all the hope-infused preparation dismissed. This can be devastating for family or friends, and it can also cause your person to feel guilty for letting everyone down. What was once a shared pleasure can now be incredibly anxiety provoking.

It is important to not pressure your person to eat or drink. Doing so will likely only cause distress and discomfort such as bloating, nausea, or vomiting. If your person chooses not to eat, supporting this decision is the most compassionate action.

The same goes for fluids. Follow your person's lead—their body knows exactly what it needs. Introducing fluids when your person isn't thirsty, either orally or by way of intravenous hydration, is ineffective and often causes respiratory distress. At this stage you can consider offering small chips of ice or frozen juice chips. Dehydration actually initiates mechanisms in the body that help the body prepare for death and a more easeful transition. At the end of life, it is not uncommon for people to go two to three weeks without eating anything. The kindest thing you can do is to follow the lead of your person and let them choose if and when to eat or drink.

Where Can You Find the Gateway of Taste?

You can check in with your person to inquire about cravings. Consider offering meaningful or traditional food that is associated with relatives, home, and celebration; foods that inspire a nostalgic connection. Maybe it's a favourite birthday cake that evokes memories of past celebrations, or perhaps a food specific to your person's culture offering a sense of belonging with each mouthful. A cup of warm milk before bedtime may be a simple way to symbolize comfort and rest.

When There Are Gaps in the Gateway of Taste

The sense of taste varies for each individual and usually remains intact until the end-of-life. As disease progresses, it is normal for people to stop eating. The sense of taste can be supported in other ways. Consider offering your person a favourite hard candy or a soft oral sponge soaked in something they like. Be sure to check with the care team about safety if you are unsure about offering certain foods or drinks.

If your person is no longer eating, simply reminiscing about food they love can provide connection. I recall accompanying a woman who had spent her life preparing traditional Ukrainian food for her family. It was clear that for her, food was a love language. As her disease progressed, she began to eat less and less, her body simply did not need the energy. Eventually she stopped eating altogether; however, talking about food still nourished her spirit. She loved sharing, in great detail, her secrets to making the perfect pierogies and her coveted borscht recipe. Just discussing food evoked the love and connection these special dishes represented for her.

STORIES FROM THE TRAIL

Tasting the memories

I remember meeting a man who came to visit someone I was companioning on the end-of-life journey. He arrived at the front door carrying a big bag. He had a sparkle in his eye. I couldn't help myself; curiosity was overflowing and I just had to ask what was inside. He excitedly opened the bag and pulled out a large wooden cutting board, some lemons, a bottle of soy sauce, a knife, some small dishes, chopsticks, a hearty side of tuna, and a ruby red side of salmon.

He shared that he had a seaside cabin up north where he had caught both the tuna and the salmon himself. He pulled his phone from his pocket and showed me a photo of his friend, now nearing the end of her life, standing in front of his rustic log cabin. She had visited last year, and he had taken her out in his boat where she had loved every moment of the ocean-fishing that day. He was there to offer her salmon and tuna sashimi, but in reality, he was offering so much more. He was there to serve up memories and reminisce about their trip together a few summers ago.

STORIES FROM THE TRAIL

Food, love, and letting go

A doula colleague once shared the story of a dying woman whom she was supporting. The woman was terrified of dying, fearing that her husband would not eat after she was gone. They had been married for over 60 years, and throughout that time, it had been her role to cook for the family. As a result, her husband had never learned to cook—he couldn't even boil an egg. The wise doula recognized the depth of her worries and gently addressed her concern. She worked with the woman to ease her fear by carefully writing out cooking methods, assisting her to record his favourite recipes, and printing off takeout menus from some local restaurants. Knowing that her husband would be fed after she was gone gave her peace of mind and allowed her to surrender a little more.

STORIES FROM THE TRAIL

Tea ritual touchpoint

A woman reached out to me, feeling overwhelmed by the swift changes in her life after her husband's diagnosis with a life-limiting illness. The disease and her anxiety were both progressing quickly. As an oncology nurse, she was aware of her husband's prognosis, and she was aware that the journey ahead was going to be unpredictable and challenging.

The couple had a comforting nightly ritual. Each evening, they would sit outside on their covered deck with a peekaboo view of the ocean and share a pot of their favourite tea. Sipping the tea together, they looked out over the bay, watching boats come and go. This nightly tea ceremony gave them the chance to slow down, process the wave of changes flooding in, and simply enjoy the moment together. This little ritual became a much needed daily touchpoint that provided stability in the midst of change.

As the disease progressed, her husband was eventually transferred to hospice, where the nightly tea ritual continued. With all the uncertainty and unfamiliarity that this couple was living with, this simple act provided much needed consistency offering pause and connection.

GROUNDING PRACTICES

Feel good foods

There are certain taste experiences that are heightened and somehow make us feel so good, like that cold mouthful of ice cream on a warm day, or that first sip of coffee in the morning. Embracing small pleasures can nurture our wellbeing, bringing solace and renewal to body and spirit.

Can you think of a specific food that will offer you comfort or nourishment? Why not give yourself a pleasurable experience through food? Perhaps you feel called to make yourself a delicious meal, share a treat like warm cookies out of an oven, savour a hot cup of tea with a friend, or snuggle in on the couch with a bowl of popcorn? How can you look to the sense of taste to support you?

CAMPP: CONNECTION, AWARENESS, MEANING, PLEASURE, PRESENCE

The comfort of a familiar taste

Consider offering your person an invitation for comfort through the sense of taste. Can you think of foods that might help them reconnect with the simple pleasure of taste during this challenging time?

Chapter 8

The Gateway of Touch

Sometimes, words don't feel like the right response to witnessing discomfort. At times language proves to be too finite to describe and discuss the infinite. When you listen to your emotional body, know that simple presence is sometimes more powerful and true than words. Often silence, sighing, a held gaze, or touch are more effective ways of communicating that you are there for your person. These quiet examples of compassionate action may not seem like enough for us modern-day humans who are so busy doing, but trust me, they are. Your grounded presence and witnessing changes everything. Showing up this way allows us to come alongside each other and raise up our hands to help carry the weight of navigating a life-limiting illness. Humans are simply not designed to carry it all alone.

What is the Gateway of Touch?

Images of hands resting in hands are commonly associated with caregiving. A wrap-around hug, or a hand on a shoulder are also gestures that come to mind when we think of showing up for others. Although we frequently use our sense of touch, it is somehow not as compelling as our other senses, and it is often the most overlooked. It is strange how when we recall a memory, we tend to remember what we saw, what we heard, and what we smelled, but rarely do we remember what we touched. Touch is essential to help us navigate the world, and for many it is an effective way to create connection, awareness, meaning, pleasure, and presence at end of life, a time when comfort and contact are welcomed more than ever.

From the delicate petals of a flower to the rough texture of a tree trunk or the cool touch of a breeze, countless physical sensations come through the gateway of touch, helping us make sense of the world. We can feel tactual vibrations without touching the skin. Waves such as pain, heat, and cold penetrate the body by way of the skin, nerves, and bones. Sounds also travel in waves, creating noticeable vibrations in our bodies that help us know our surroundings.

Physical pain and frailty at the end of life may be concerning, leading you to believe that your person may be too fragile to touch. However,there are many gentle ways to access the gateway of touch. In this chapter we will explore the power of touch and offer suggestions as to how this mysterious sense can be used at the end of life to enhance wellbeing.

How Can You Access the Gateway of Touch?

Touch is the most primitive of all the senses. It is the first sense to develop, present from just eight weeks of gestation. It is universal, and science confirms that we can all benefit from touch. Studies have shown that touch is critical for children's growth, development, and health, as well as for adults' physical and mental wellbeing. Touch fulfills one of our most basic human needs—the need to connect with others. When we are hungry, we crave food, when we are tired, we crave sleep, and when we are lonely, we crave touch.

There is a lot we don't understand about touch. Although typically neuroscientists haven't studied how touch affects the brain nearly as much as the other senses, this is changing, and touch is beginning to get the attention it deserves. The COVID-19 pandemic tragically highlighted the importance of this underrated sense. During the pandemic, human touch was the first thing to be taken from us and some people were forced to live for an extended period of time without physical human contact. Touching was one of the first things we were cautioned against, even before social distancing. Masks and stay-at-home orders became the new normal. For many, touch became a source of stress and a negotiation of personal boundaries. Years after the start of this global crisis, we are still rethinking how to safely interact with each other. People are offering elbow bumps, fist pumps, or respectful bows over the traditional handshake. The pandemic has brought to our attention that the absence of touch can give way to touch deprivation, which can lead to health issues such as anxiety and depression.

Researchers have been drawn to the power of touch, leveraging the opportunity of the pandemic to learn more about what happens to humans when deprived of this direct way of knowing and experiencing the world. For the dying and their companions, touch provides many benefits. Practices such as massage and healing touch are used by care teams to offer comfort to those in need. Some of the benefits of gentle touch include reducing stress, protection against future stress, improved mood and self-esteem, strengthened interpersonal bonds, improved cognitive function, vagal nerve stimulation resulting in a calming of the cardiovascular system, and enhanced immune system function. These effects are mediated by hormonal changes that include a lowering of the stress hormone cortisol and the release of the oxytocin, also known as the love hormone.

Touch is a powerful form of communication, and it is more nuanced and sophisticated than speech and gesture. Touch relaxes people and it can communicate to folks that they are being seen and heard, which creates connection, empathy, and enhances trust. No words needed. Compassion can be communicated in an instant with a gesture as simple as a brief touch to the forearm. The gateway of touch can directly express presence, deep care, and love when delivered with intention.

The English language supports this evidence about the importance of touch. When we haven't connected with someone for a while, we do not say that we are "out of sight," but rather, we are "out of touch." We express the need to reach out and make contact. These words reinforce the truth that human touch, like food and sleep, is a visceral need for most.

Alarmingly but not surprisingly in our technology-obsessed culture, people have considered using robotic human or animal substitutes for human touch in caregiving settings. Over the last few years, I have seen on more than one occasion, stand-in robotic plush cats and dogs used to offer comfort in institutional care settings. These strangely realistic replicas appear to breathe and at times purr or let out a bark. In a recent study it was discovered that for touch to have a physiological benefit, the person receiving touch must believe that the thing or creature is alive and able to respond to their needs.

Dr. Tiffany Field, the director of the Touch Research Institute at the University of Miami, has noticed that those living in the West who are influenced by dominant culture are dangerously touch-deprived. Dr. Field has a Ph.D. in developmental psychology, and she is a leading authority on touch. She reports recent research results on the value of touch therapies, such as massage therapy, for a variety of conditions and emphasizes that there is a great opportunity to increase well-being through touch.

Dr. Field describes touch treatment as simply "moving the skin," and there are many ways to do this, such as scalp massages or by simply using a weighted blanket. Her research and increasing awareness of the importance of touch is focused on changing medical practice and encouraging touch therapy in hospital settings. Field's research has revealed that touching patients with Alzheimer's and engaging them to touch has been proven to reduce symptoms. She has also discovered that when medical doctors make eye contact with patients with a complex disease, and simply offer a supportive pat on the back, survival rates increase. As already mentioned, these findings must be considered within the context of personal and cultural considerations.

As we age, there is a noticeable decrease in the amount of physical and emotional contact we receive. Touch is the most important nonverbal behavior in the nursing profession when treating older patients. As it turns out, for the elderly, tactile hunger is more intense than ever, and it is often the only sensuous experience that remains. As companions to the elderly and people who are dying, we can leverage the power of touch to offer connection, awareness, meaning, pleasure, and presence.

It's important to note, however, that touch is not comforting for everyone. During a palliative massage training offered at the local hospice, I learned this firsthand. As a volunteer, I accepted the opportunity to be trained in Gentle Touch; a technique involving light stroking of the arms, legs, and head that can offer comfort to the dying. This type of massage is well suited to those at end of life because it is designed for people who are sensitive and confined to wheelchairs or beds. Ironically, the woman who facilitated the course was completely averse to being touched. She would wince and squirm as she explained the various massage techniques, her face and shoulders scrunching up as she watched us practice on one another. She owned her experience and made light of her reactions, but it was glaringly clear that not everyone is comforted by human touch.

For some, touch can be distressing. This may be a result of past physical trauma, or the reasons may be misunderstood. It is essential to ask for permission to touch and be aware of personal preferences. If your person is unable to communicate with words, pay attention to body language and non-verbal cues for guidance. As a companion, the last thing you want to do is cause harm to your person that you hope to comfort. When I consider offering touch to the dying, the image of the massage training facilitator comes to mind. It reminds me to check in, listen in, and take the lead of those I am serving.

Before You Touch

As already noted, it is important to be grounded and authentic when companioning the dying. Consider exploring your relationship to touch and discover what is comfortable for you. After you have noticed your comfort level, listen to your person. You can sit with them and tap into your intuition by paying attention with all your senses—listen to your person with your whole being.

As with any intervention, it is best practice to be mindful of cultural considerations before offering touch. Certain cultures are more comfortable with touch than others.

CAMPP: CONNECTION, AWARENESS, MEANING, PLEASURE, PRESENCE

Open to touch

If touch seems appropriate, you may wonder how to touch your person. Where do you touch them? When do you touch? How long do you touch for?

1. Tune in before touching and get explicit consent where possible, otherwise use your intuition.
2. Wash your hands with soap and water. Warm your hands.
3. Before touching, sit quietly next to your person. In your mind, set your intention and take some breaths to connect to your heart. An example of an intention is, "May my touch bring peace and comfort."
4. Let the person know which areas you are thinking about touching them and ask if it is okay. You may simply cup their hands, feet, or head in your hands, or gently rest your hand on their arm, leg, shoulder, or even abdomen. If it is appropriate to your relationship and feels guided, you may offer to lie next to them in their bed.
5. If they can communicate verbally, ask them to let you know if anything is uncomfortable or if they want you to stop.
6. Keep your intention and connection to your breath in your awareness while you touch your person.
7. Depending on how fragile or close to death the person is, keep touch sessions on the shorter side (up to 15 minutes). Tune in to yourself regarding when to stop, or ask the person.

Being intentional really makes a difference. When you are feeling with your heart, your touch will likely communicate love and care. Remember, it doesn't have to be complicated. Holding a hand or simply helping with personal care by offering to wash your person's face, arms, legs, or apply moisturizer, can lead to connection, awareness, meaning, pleasure, and presence. Take your time and move slowly. Tell your person what you are going to do next and keep listening with all your senses for both verbal and nonverbal cues.

When Your Person Is Not Comforted by Human Touch

If receiving touch is not welcomed or not possible, that's okay; there are endless other ways you can offer comfort and connection through the gateway of touch. Self-soothing touch-based practices and pet therapy are two examples that we will take a closer look at in the following pages.

For many, stroking or snuggling a beloved pet is deeply soothing. Touching a pet can be immediately comforting and can deliver the same dose of pain relieving, stress reducing, calming endorphins as human touch. Touch and connection often happen effortlessly between people and animals.

Animal therapy is becoming more common in facilities as the benefits of touch are realized. Furry friends such as dogs, cats, guinea pigs, and even horses are being seen more frequently in care homes, hospitals, and hospices. Animals provide comfort and pleasure for people living with health challenges. These benefits extend to the companions as well. Those who sit in on animal visits also tend to feel a sense of comfort. Pet visits are often heartwarming and leave companions feeling less tired and anxious and more hopeful.

Another alternative to human touch is to invite your person to participate in activities that make them the giver (instead of the receiver) of touch. Stroking the leaves of a houseplant or working on art projects with soft clay or other textured materials can bring a calm and supportive experience of touch. Sound vibrations from an instrument are also an effective mode of touch, especially if your person is able to rest a hand on the instrument to experience felt sensations.

Whether your person is open to receiving your touch or prefers to explore the sense through other means, there are many ways to access the gateway of touch. The following stories offer some real-life examples illustrating the power of touch.

STORIES FROM THE TRAIL

The touching comfort of teddy bears

Teddy bears, usually the old and tattered variety, often make an appearance on beds at end of life. Lovingly tucked in under the covers or propped up at the foot of the bed, these fuzzy companions offer comfort. I always ask about these silent bedmates and there is usually a story. I remember one woman's connection to a brown tattered stuffed bear, a gift that she had given her daughter decades ago. Her daughter now lived out of town and could not be there with her mom in her last days. She had brought the teddy bear to her mom the last time she visited, and this bear had not left the bed since. It was tucked in beside her at all times. The woman would gently swirl her fingers over the bear's tattered fur, often with her eyes closed. It was clear that through the sense of touch, this bear offered comfort and connection to something so much greater.

STORIES FROM THE TRAIL

Touching memories of the sea

Sheryl, an end-of-life doula, is an expert at encouraging her clients to explore what brings them joy, and she uses their responses to inform her practice. Connecting people with what makes life worth living is a creative endeavor and looking to the senses for opportunities is a good place to start.

Sheryl was serving a woman who loved beaches. She often reminisced about her favourite vacation spot, Long Beach, B.C. This enormous, wild swath of Vancouver Island's west coast was a place her client enjoyed visiting. It was a place she wished she could visit again, but due to her progressing illness, she was unable to travel. When Sheryl heard that I was heading to the area for a vacation her creativity was sparked. Her client couldn't go to Long Beach again, but Sheryl decided that she could bring Long

Beach to her client. She asked me to collect some sand and perhaps a shell or trinket from the beach and I happily accepted the mission.

I arrived at the beach early one summer morning and filled a little glass jar with sand. I walked the beach with a deepened sense of gratitude for simply being able to be there. I spotted a perfectly intact sand dollar and placed it gently in the jar. When I arrived home, I gave the jar to Sheryl, who passed it on to her client. She reported back that her client was deeply moved by the gift of the beach and the memories they evoked. She shared that her client held the sand and let it run through her fingers, lost in thought. She gently stroked the gritty surface of the sand dollar as she shared more stories about the lazy days that she had spent on Long Beach, treasures revealed to her through the companion of touch.

STORIES FROM THE TRAIL

Animals as soft and warm companions

Relationships are complicated and love can look like many things. I once sat vigil for a woman in a local care home. It was a simple room, with two Christmas cards stuck on the wall next to a cat calendar. It was the month of May—a litter of black and white puppies and 31 empty squares.

Around the room were faded photos of her and her beloved dog, taped to walls haphazardly, a gorgeous, droopy eyed black lab. A stuffed rendition of the dog from the photos sat watch in the corner. A sketch of the dog hung above her bed, while a framed photo of her fur baby sat framed on the bedside table.

She lay like a bird, skin stretched over bone, eyes fixed and cloudy, her breath stopping and starting.

"She's estranged from her children," said the nurse who led me to the room of this woman who I was meeting for the first time. "They know, but..."

The door to the busy hallway was left open. The voices coming from the nursing station across the hall sliced through the spa music coming from her TV. The talk was all about Mother's Day: "Happy Mother's Day!" "Did you go to the luncheon? Did you get a glass of champagne?"

Hearing is the last sense to go. As I sat there doing what I could to create a space for her gentle dying, these Mother's Day wishes felt like daggers.

To make it worse, a cheery and very well-meaning employee entered the room, holding two stems of bright pink carnations. She crouched down close to her cheek and exclaimed "Happy Mother's Day" in her face. "I brought you some flowers! Happy Mother's Day!" She placed the flowers on her chest.

Concerned, I sat there waiting for guidance… and then the medicine was delivered. A small woman with big blue eyes peered into the room. "Hi," she said quietly as she stepped in, and a gorgeous black lab followed behind. This was the friend who had cared for the dog over the last few years. Even though she was in a state of consciousness that prevented her from communicating verbally, it was clear that she was aware of the dog's presence. We coaxed the dog onto the bed and found the woman's hand under the covers. We unfurled her fingers and placed a treat in her palm. The dog licked her hand and tucked in against her frail body. This tender moment was such a balm.

GROUNDING PRACTICES

Tender touch

As a companion, consider how touch may be supportive for you as you care for your person. Perhaps holding hands with a loved one while out on a walk? Or lovingly stroking a pet? Take some time to contemplate how the gateway of touch can brighten your days at this challenging time.

The Gifts of the Gateway

Touch is a direct and powerful way to bring comfort to your person. The joy we feel with positive experiences of touch are some of the simplest yet most meaningful pleasures of life. Whether you offer a big hug, wrap your person in a soft blanket, offer a foot massage, or hand over a warm cup of tea, touch can bring a sense of peace and calm.

> One Way She's Shaped Me
> *For Kayleen Asbo by Rosemerry Wathola Trommer*
>
> With hands that have played Bach
> on the finest pianos in Europe,
> hands that have written poems
> and love letters and treatises on art,
> with precious, skilled, talented hands
> she lifted my foot to her lap
> and smoothed oil into the cold, rough skin,
> kneading and pressing deep circles
> into my arches, squeezing my toes
> (once deemed by a boyfriend
> "the ugliest toes I've ever seen").
> And she made me feel beautiful.
> I remember how all of me softened,
> even those voices that sometimes rage,
> you're not good enough.
> How could those voices stand a chance
> against such a gift of touch?
> Her hands said, you are not alone.
> Her hands said, you belong.
> Her hands said, you are treasure to me.
> And the day was grey;
> her hands were strong.
> I was less woman, more clay.
> With hands that coax music
> from sorrow and fear,
> she made me into song.

Chapter 9

The Gateway of Wonder

> *"Cultivate humility and equanimity. Humility in the face of mystery helps us with the frustration we often feel when we think we are supposed to know it all and be in control of it all, when really we're not. We are merely instruments for a process to go on. You are only one part of the whole unfolding."*
>
> *—Ram Dass*

> "In the beginner's mind the possibilities endless, and in the expert's mind, they're few."
>
> —Shunryu Suzuki, Zen Mind, Beginner's Mind

According to the Merriam-Webster dictionary, wonder is defined as "rapt attention or astonishment at something awesomely mysterious or new to one's experience, or a feeling of doubt or uncertainty." It is when we open up and embrace what we don't know, we are often lead to feel wonder and a sense of awe. In this way, wondering begets wonder.

When we accept that we live in a state of not knowing, we make room for curiosity and deeper engagement with the world to emerge. That kind of engagement, that open, wondering attention and curiosity is intimate and very, very alive. This is true in the process of creating music, art, and literature—it also applies to the role of companioning the dying. It is about being able to sit in the unknown, and somehow finding a way to rest there, to become even slightly more at ease in that tender, uncertain place.

This place of not knowing can feel deeply uncomfortable.

There is a natural a tension between wanting to know and being in the unknown. We have explored maps that can support as we find our way as companions on the end-of-life journey. There are predictable signposts, landmarks, waypoints, and stages that can guide and reassure as we travel. There is also so much we don't know—an ocean of possibilities. It can be supportive to gently practice staying in that space—the generative, sometimes uneasy stretch between clarity and uncertainty—until something begins to take shape, until knowing begins to arrive on its own.

GROUNDING PRACTICES

A sip of space: A one-breath ritual for presence

This is a simple and accessible ritual to return to calm whenever you feel contracted, overwhelmed, or untethered. You can take a sip of space and ventilate the situation with one breath. This will create a little more room around whatever is happening and deliver you to the present by returning you to your body. Begin by taking a slow, intentional inhale. As you breathe in, imagine yourself separating from the moment you are experiencing and come into your body. Pause. As you exhale, intentionally return to the space you are in with your breath. Even one breath can help you settle, expand your perspective, and navigate what is unfolding with steadiness. When we allow for more internal spaciousness, we're better able to meet change with presence.

There is a phrase from Zen Buddhism that you might find helpful during this practice: "Not knowing is most intimate." It's when we don't know something, and when we can sit in that state of not knowing, that we find a kind of an intimacy with the world around us.

What is the Gateway of Wonder?

Death is wild with mystery. Yes, there is fear—the fear of the unknown—and grief for what has already been taken, and for what is still to be lost. But there is also so much more. There is also the opportunity for joy, beauty, laughter, connection, healing, meaning-making, and love. So much love. Death, in its own way, can bring generous and unexpected gifts. When we show up with humility, presence, and open hearts, the end-of-life journey has the potential to reveal some of the most precious insight into what it means to truly live.

In an attempt to track down a cigarette for a dying man, I found myself in a conversation with a staff member at a local hospice. She is Indigenous, a member of the xwməθkwəy̓əm (Musqueam) Nation, a Coast Salish nation from the west coast of Canada.

"He's asking for a cigarette?" she asked.

"Yes," I replied. "Do you have one?"

"Oh no, he doesn't really want a cigarette, he doesn't smoke. He used to smoke, he smoked with my ancestors decades ago, but he hasn't had a cigarette for years. They are just here visiting him so he thinks he should be smoking. They are here to bring him home," she offered with certainty.

The Coast Salish believe that deceased ancestors come to guide the dying home and they continue to visit this world after death. Offerings in the way of favourite foods, drinks, and lit tobacco are often left on doorsteps as gifts for ancestors and other visiting spirits.

The woman at hospice that day recognized, through her cultural lens, that we were in the presence of wonder. Thanks to her insight we were able to create connection with the dying man's request instead of presenting him with a cigarette. She entered the room, sat down by the bed, and listened as the man told her about who was visiting and why. She listened and smiled. "You're in good company," she said, offering connection and comfort.

This story not only speaks to the importance of diversity in the workplace, but also to the value of the companion of wonder at the end of life. In this chapter, wonder is defined as the influence of cultural, spiritual, and personal beliefs, or the worldview through which one attempts to understand and make meaning of life, including death. To honour wonder, we must come to the great mystery with an openness to the idea that there are forces larger than us at play. We know so much about dying—with physical, emotional, and spiritual landmarks mapped out at the end of life—yet there is still so much we don't know.

Throughout this journey, we have explored the five senses, but there are many more ways we perceive the world than we often recognize. Intuition, the ability to perceive with our whole being, helps us to navigate the unknown and find our way through darkness. Culture, spirituality, and personal beliefs shape the unique lens through which we make meaning of life's mysteries. To embrace this, we are asked to let go—to release our struggle against uncertainty—and reconnect with the natural flexibility of our being.

Wrestling with doubt and uncertainty is part of the human experience. Most of us are not comfortable with ambiguity—it can make us restless, even anxious. In this culture we are desparate to be certain—to know, predict, and control. As a response we create sides to alleviate the tension of the unknown. We don't have many opportunities to simply be with the not knowing in our polarized world. What if we opened instead to wonder? What if we allowed ourselves to rest in the mystery? To dwell in the questions rather than rush to anwers? So much of life is shaped by what we cannot predict and yet we spend so much of it trying to avoid that very truth.

What Would We Be Gifted if We Could Open to Wonder?

Dying well requires ambivalence. It asks us to let go of the rational, over-intellectualized way of being that restricts our perception. Take emotions, for example, which can change in a heartbeat and often coexist with opposing feelings. If we accept this ambiguity, we can foster humility in life and wonder at the mystery of it all. Questioning our certainty about what is true can be threatening. On the end-of-life journey, seeking answers and meaning is relentless. Dying is a mystery that can't be known with medical technology, planning, or strategies for how to approach death; it is known by feeling the way through the darkness. Death invites us to stay present as it unfolds.

This deep questioning is a natural part of the dying process, often called "the dark night of the soul." The end of life can be a challenging time when deeply held beliefs are tested as one faces the great unknown with no place to hide. The dark night of the soul calls for individuals to sit with uncomfortable emotions such as loneliness and anxiety. To navigate this stage with grace, we are asked to lean into the mystery. When one can do this, when one can move to acceptance around what is arising, courage is often revealed in the groundlessness and fear subsides. For those with loosely held faith or even no belief in an afterlife, it is not unusual to find clarity at this stage. After this deep questioning many find meaning in the experience of life itself. Wondering and questioning can lead the dying to a dissolution of the ego which may deliver them to a place where they stop struggling and discover a new way of being.

Embracing the mystery of dying can be a profound challenge for many. If your person embraces unpredictability and enjoys uncovering new aspects of themselves and the world, they may navigate the wilderness of dying with more ease. However, if they prefer predictability, this journey may prove more challenging. Dying can often resist carefully laid plans, but that doesn't mean we have no control; there are still choices to be made. While the process of dying cannot be controlled, how we choose to meet it is within our power. It is through this choice that death can be transformed.

In his book *Die Wise: A Manifesto for Sanity and Soul,* grief-literacy advocate Stephen Jenkinson suggests a different perspective on death, one that goes beyond being in charge and invites us to live with death in mind, befriending it as we approach the end of life:

> "Dying asks of you, the willingness to learn endings. I do not mean domesticate. I mean befriend. When I say *befriend death* what I mean is, our obligation is to know death well, to be useful when it comes, to craft a language wherein your dying can recognize itself and is not groping for some kind of foothold."

We must approach the experience with respectful curiosity, asking ourselves what death has to teach us.

The goal of this chapter is to acknowledge that there is another dimension beyond the senses that greatly impacts the end-of-life experience. My hope is to ask a few guiding questions that will help you consider how to support your person as they face the unknown, and to inspire you to identify opportunities for them to find moments of connection, awareness, meaning, pleasure, and presence.

A Culture of Perspective

Culture is conceptual. It is made up of shared beliefs, behaviours, philosophies, ideas, and practices. Our experience of life and death is determined by culture. We do not willingly or intentionally choose our associations and fears; rather, most of them have been inherited. Some of the fears of the dying are personally constructed, but most are communal realities that are culturally driven.

Here in the West, there is an increase in culturally diverse people, making this a place of varied beliefs, customs, and traditions that influence behaviour. Culture affects what we believe, the clothes we wear, the foods we eat, and how we choose to spend our time. In *Deeply into the Bone: Re-Inventing the Rites of Passage*, Ronald Grimes, author and Director of Ritual Studies International and Professor Emeritus of Religion and Culture at Wilfrid Laurier University, considers how culture influences the way we die. Grimes names common practices that are shaped by culture, all of which come into play on the end-of-life journey. The practices listed include anticipating death, observing taboos, mourning, protecting survivors, announcing a death, comforting, showing gratitude, ensuing succession, dramatizing death's finality, reconstructing social order after death, denying death's finality, embracing death's finality, and commemorating. Culture plays a significant role in how death is embraced and supported, yet it can be challenging for people from diverse cultural backgrounds to have their cultural preferences honoured while navigating the end-of-life journey within the current healthcare system.

> *"If we do not birth and die ritually, we will do so technologically, inscribing technocratic values in our very bones. It matters greatly not only that we birth and die, but HOW we birth and die."*
>
> —Ronald L. Grimes, Deeply into the Bone: Re-Inventing Rites of Passage

One of the complexities at the end of life is navigating the differing cultural perspectives on the value of family versus the individual. Many cultures place a higher value on the family as a unit, which contrasts with the individual-focused approach of our dominant culture. In cultures where family is prioritized, it is often preferred that information about the dying person's prognosis be shared with the family as a whole. When making treatment decisions, it is the family unit that determines what is best. Through the current cultural lens, this may seem like an infringement of autonomy; however, when considering the relevant cultural beliefs, it can actually be the most supportive action, as it honours the wishes and values of the dying individual, thereby supporting their agency.

Culture can also determine how and to what extent one wants to be informed about the prognosis of an illness. In some cultures, hope is paramount, with more assigned value than facts about medical outcomes. In this case, supporting informed decision-making by sharing the anticipated outcome of interventions—a practice highly regarded in Western medicine—may not be the best approach. Instead it is more important to focus on fostering hope and preserving the belief that the dying person will be okay. In such cultures, hope is seen as the most important determinant of wellbeing. Family and friends often feel compelled to protect the dying from the harsh reality of a prognosis, believing it safeguards hope. When the dying person takes charge of their healthcare decisions, it is important to see this as an exercise in autonomy. In this context, withholding information is not an infringement on the ethical responsibilities of the healthcare team.

Many cultures have beautifully supportive practices that guide what to do next for people who are dying and grieving. Death ceremonies and traditions worldwide often share a common focus—community. These rituals are not only comforting, but also help us regain a sense of control in the wild experiences of death and grief. For many, they provide a way to make meaning of the experience of death.

Most non-Western cultures maintain death ceremonies and grief rituals that honour death as a natural part of life and allow space for long-term grieving. What a startling difference to our dominant, death-phobic culture that rarely takes notice of aging, decline, death, and loss. Many of the systems in place today, including the healthcare system, were created in the context of this death-phobic culture. This explains why healthcare primarily seeks to treat, fight, and extend life at all costs. The big question is, how then, do we die well in a world where we are often sold the idea that death is the ultimate failure?

The bright and exuberant Caitlin Doughty, an American mortician, author, blogger, and YouTube personality, has travelled around the world in search of answers to this question. Doughty explores how culture impacts the way people engage with death. Fuelled by her fascination with contemporary Western culture's pervasive fear of dying, Doughty set out to discover how we can meet death differently. In her guide *From Here to Eternity: Travelling the World to Find the Good Death*, Doughty shares stories of her travels around the world, and how different cultural narratives impact the end-of-life journey. She writes about numerous compelling and meaning-infused death and grief rituals that are almost entirely unknown in North America.

Doughty believes that modern day humans can benefit from looking into the stories of our past to become aware of more supportive ways to view death. She encourages readers to explore the arts, literature, archeology, and film to inspire a more nuanced and intentional understanding of how to do death better. The stories she speaks of are much less fear-laden narratives than those common in dominant culture. Such stories are often filled with awe at the miracle of the entire human experience—of birth, life, and death. Doughty hopes that reframing death will bring a greater sense of peace at final stages of life. She also believes this shift in perspective can help address some of the big questions that arise on the end-of-life journey, offering insight into how the deaths and losses we experience fit into the greater threads of the universe.

Becoming aware of how culture shapes our views on death can help us recognize the limiting beliefs and stories we've inherited. This awareness gives us the opportunity to choose how we engage with death. If we have the motivation and the capacity, we can intentionally embrace more supportive stories—ones that honour death as a natural part of life. We can adopt narratives that encourage acceptance of dying as part of the human experience and perhaps invite us to approach or even embrace death.

Spirituality

> *"Spirituality is the tuning of the inner person with the great mysteries and secrets that are around us."*
>
> *—U Thant*

Another source of wonder is spirituality. Spirituality can take many forms, whether it is through the belief in a goddess or god, nature, a universal oneness, love, or any idea that resonates personally. It is an enormous concept, encompassing an inner knowing that offers comfort and guidance. Spiritual practices can be as simple as bringing an open awareness to ordinary acts such as breathing or walking, revealing the presence of greater forces that influence how we live and how we die.

The concepts of religion and spirituality are often blurred, but they are, in fact, quite different. Religion typically refers to a specific set of organized beliefs and practices that are usually shared by a community or group of people, whereas spirituality is more of an individual practice that creates an internal sense of peace and meaning. Everyone has a spiritual life to some extent, which means everyone has a spiritual death to some extent too.

Religion is often defined by the external aspects of a belief system, such as church, prayers, traditions, rites, and rituals. It consists of an organized collection of beliefs, cultural systems, and world views that relate humanity to an order of existence. You can think of religion as an individual's or community's values, beliefs, and practices which communities follow in an attempt to fulfill their spiritual needs.

Like culture, religion may provide practices to support dying and grief that can offer a sense of control by serving as a map for what to do next. Religion can create meaning and foster a sense of community, both of which can provide support for individuals on the end-of-life journey.

Spirituality influences all aspects of our lives, and it intensifies at the end of life. It involves identifying the feeling, sense, or belief that there is something greater than the self, something more to being human than simply a sensory experience. Spirituality suggests this greater whole we are part of is full of wonder or is divine in nature. Some refer to this as God, Krishna, life force, nature, spirit, universe, the Creator, or countless other titles representing a sacred presence. Some choose to call it nothing at all.

Spirituality arises from varied sources; it may come from membership with a religious or spiritual community, spending time in nature, sitting in silence, listening to music, or connecting with loved ones, each of which can open the heart, an essential aspect of spirituality. An individual's spiritual beliefs shape how they connect with the divine.

Faith plays a significant role at the end of life. If there is trust that everything is unfolding as it should, or if there is a strong conviction in a god, this belief will provide comfort during the dying process. Without faith, the dying may struggle to trust and give more weight to the negative. However, faith can come from many sources. A belief in oneself, others, or the universe can bring peace. In the face of death it isn't our specific religious beliefs that guide us, but our individual sense of spirituality.

CAMPP: CONNECTION, AWARENESS, MEANING, PLEASURE, PRESENCE

Being there as witness to a life in review

Offering spiritual support to the dying may feel overwhelming, but often the most profound way to help is simply by being a witness, allowing them space to reflect on their life experiences. Inner or spiritual work at the end of life centres on helping individuals make meaning of their experiences—offering the space to share what they have learned, revisiting regret and loss, and highlighting moments of gratitude and love as they arise naturally to be explored. Allowing the past to surface, and just loving it as is and gently letting go. With a little attention, allowing grief and regrets can lighten making the journey a little easier. As a companion, you can support a life review with gentle prompts about childhood, travels, people, and places. Offering a listening ear and soft heart can be deeply healing, as love always outweighs regret.

If your person is open to reflecting on the memories and moments that have made a mark on their heart, simply being there as they remember can offer a sense of connection, meaning, and completion. A life review includes reminiscing about the good times and the bad. Exploring relationships and experiences that caused hurt or resentment can create an opportunity for forgiveness; this letting go will support your person to travel with more ease. Grief will arise, asking to be shared and witnessed. Meet whatever arises with an open mind and an open heart. Remember that offering a grounded, steady, heart-centred presence is medicine. With the space for reflection comes the opportunity to integrate a lifetime of experiences, and perhaps reveal a little wonder and the sense of something more.

Beliefs

Beliefs, or ideas that one accepts to be true even without evidence, profoundly shape how we approach and experience death. The stories we gather over a lifetime are shaped by our direct personal experiences, and these beliefs guide us through the end-of-life journey. As mentioned, the different elements of our worldview often blur; the beliefs about death are also coloured by culture and spirituality.

Reflecting on personal myths and beliefs about dying help individuals to gain greater awareness about the stories they hold. Understanding where beliefs originate and questioning the validity of stories may lead to a more intimate relationship with death.

> *Certainty is the antidote to wonder. In order to access the mystery of wonder, we must be open to reconsider what we think we know. As a companion to the dying, the best way to prepare yourself to show up appropriately to support your person on the end-of-life journey is by unpacking your own "stuff." Exploring your personal myths and beliefs about death will enhance your ability to stay present with your person, be less reactive, and possibly even open up more space to meet death with curiosity and acceptance when your time comes.*

In the past 50 years there has been a growing tendancy to turn to science and medical professionals in the search for understanding death. With this shift has come the desire to "solve" death. Historically, cultures around the world have shared meaningful and supportive narratives around death shaped by cultural, spiritual, and personal beliefs. Regrettably, in today's science-driven world, many of the stories involving wonder are often dismissed. If they can't be proven, they are too easily labelled as pseudoscience and set aside. Pseudoscience suggests that the topic is lacking in truth, but this dismissal of information that can't be proven is limiting and not accurate. Science is inherently flawed and limited; as philosophy and history reminds us, science is a product of scientists. In this way it is a cultural product, influenced by people, place, and time. Science also extinguishes contemplation, the vast field of awareness in which all possibilities arise. In this way, science is not as objective as many of us believe it to be. We know a lot about death but there is a lot we don't know—there is so much that can't be tested scientifically, which leaves us a lot to wonder about.

When people share their personal stories with death to trusted others, they often weave in moment of wonder that transcends the ordinary. These accounts of unexplained happenings often evoke a sense of awe and curiosity. Stories of companioning the dying are woven with unexplained beauty and serendipity, highlighting the profound and mysterious nature of the journey. After years of hearing these stories and holding smany of my own from being with the dying, I have come to realize that experiencing wonder at end-of-life is almost always an inevitable part of the journey. It is heart-expanding to hear stories where acceptance of death blooms into awe, unfolding with tales of beauty, synchronicity, and love, and the profound realization that there is so much that we don't know and forces greater than ourselves at play.

Martha Atkins calls for the sharing of stories about wonder at end-of-life in her TED Talk titled "More to Dying Than Meets the Eye." Atkins explores the impact of the personal experiences of people who have accompanied the dying, proposing that normal dying is much less awful and more awe inspiring than most imagine. She encourages the audience to embrace narratives that offer less fear and more meaning and connection. Atkins shares about the deathbed phenomenon that has been recorded for over six centuries. She shares anecdotal accounts and research capturing sensory experiences of those nearing death, focusing on wonder—a quality, she notes, that eludes scientific proof.

These experiences include the dying reporting visits from deceased friends or family members, preparing to go on a trip, or feeling the urge to gather items together shortly before death occurs. Sometimes people experience visions about the phenomenal world, such as seeing landscapes or hearing music. According to Atkins, the purpose of these visions is to help the dying with the death experience by providing comfort, guidance, and reassurance.

Atkins explains that these experiences happen all over the world, regardless of age, or religious or cultural beliefs. Some skeptics believe that these visions are the result of the brain malfunctioning, while others believe these visions are proof of the soul's continuation after death, but neither hypothesis can be proven. Atkins says the debate is irrelevant, stating, "It doesn't matter why they happen; it matters that they do." These visions provide great comfort to the dying, and what is good for the dying is good for their people.

At the end of her talk, Atkins asks the audience, "Is any of this real? Yes! Because it is real to the people that it happens to. I am a researcher," she continues, "I don't know how to measure wonder; I know what it feels like."

Closing her speech, Atkins shares the last six words spoken by Steve Jobs, moments before his death in 2011: "Oh wow. Oh wow. Oh wow." Just imagine how the experience of dying would be changed if wonder-filled stories such as these were shared more frequently?

As a companion to the dying, it is important to connect rather than correct if your person experiences deathbed visions, as these visions often provide guidance and comfort during the final moments. With this understanding, it is important to support your person if they experience visions. Consider responding with open-ended comments and questions such as, "How did that make you feel?", "Did you see or hear anything else?", or "That sounds lovely." End-of-life visions are often filled with deep symbolism and as witnesses to these experiences, we are called to trust in the mystery they bring.

Responding to wonder in this way allows you to meet your person where they are, fostering connection. Regrettably, when well-meaning friends and family do misunderstand these visions—viewing them as hallucinations—they may resort to medication or reasoning, unintentionally creating disconnection. Recognizing that these visions are a natural and comforting part of the dying process increases the likelihood that they will be supported if they arise.

It is not uncommon for the dying to often seem preoccupied and this is understandable given the immense transition they are going through. Along with constant physical changes in the body, the gateway of wonder brings an added complexity of the overlapping layers of culture, spirituality, and personal beliefs to the experience. Let's continue to uncover opportunities related to wonder that can help you foster deeper connection, awareness, meaning, pleasure, and presence during this time.

> *"When we allow a sense of wonder to inhabit us, something magical and universal happens within us. We feel. Something 'of the spirit' flickers to life in us and we feel spiritual. Within that elevated spiritual feeling we begin to believe we can transcend our difficulties and old pain. We can. We seek out ceremony to help us rekindle that sense of awe and wonder and hope. We attend ceremonies in churches, mosques, temples, meeting houses, gurdwaras, jinjas, fire temples, and Kingdom Halls. We also attend them in yurts, igloos, teepees, kivas, and wigwams. No one way is the definitive one. Each way is merely a path toward the fulfillment of our common dream—communion.*
>
> *"When my people speak of communion they do not refer to religious ceremony. Instead they refer to the act of aligning personal energy with Earth energy, universal energy and, ultimately, eternal energy. All of our rituals, from prayer to smudging to the Pipe Ceremony to the Sun Dance and the sweat lodge, are about the act of aligning energy—of allowing our spirits to enter the flow of the great circle of spiritual energy that is everywhere around us. Always."*
>
> —Richard Wagamese, One Drum: Stories and Ceremonies for a Planet

EXPECTED CHANGES ON THE JOURNEY

Deathbed speech

As the dying approach the end of the journey, their language can reflect a shift in perspective. Linguist and researcher Lisa Smartt's work through the Final Words Project has identified reoccurring patterns in deathbed speech, offering a peek into the deathbed experience.

- Putting things in order for a trip
    - "I'm coming, I need to get my coat, they are ready for me."
    - "I'd better get dressed now, it's almost time to leave."
- Travelling
    - "The boat will be here soon."
    - "I need to find my passport before I can get on the plane."
- Movement up and out
    - "Help me get down from up here."
- Talking about birds, ladders, or high windows
- Reaching or looking up to the corners of the room
- Mixing up time and space
    - "You're in Tuesday but I am in Wednesday."
- Meeting unseen beings
- Talking to the dead
- Visions of crowds
- Visitations by guides
- Using the symbols of their life to talk about a big event
    - "I'm getting ready for the art opening on Saturday."
    - "They need a fourth person for the poker game."

If you hear this kind of speech, simply accept your person's experience for what it is. Don't try to make sense of it or ask too many questions. Your person may not be completely aware of what they're saying; rather, they are subconsciously integrating the transition from this life. Smartt recommends that companions respond with open-ended comments and questions:

- "How did that make you feel?"
- "Did you see or hear anything else?"
- "That sounds lovely."
- "If it bothers you, is there anything you can do to make it better?"
- "I'm happy you shared that with me."
- "I'm glad it made you feel safe."
- "It sounds like you are in good hands."

The veil is thinning, and the dying person is starting to transition from this world—it is almost as though they have a foot in each world. Their consciousness is being led to elsewhere. For this we are invited to trust the mystery.

Where Can You Find the Gateway of Wonder?

The gateway of wonder—the inseparable mix of culture, spirituality, and personal beliefs—is about how one makes meaning in life, including death. There are so many possibilities to transform our relationships if we are willing to stay curious together, admit how little we know, and be open to how much there is to wonder about. It is through the lens of respectful curiosity that we can learn from those we are supporting. Don't assume you understand the significance of culture, spirituality, or personal beliefs at the end of life, instead ask what it means to your person. The best practice is to actively listen and refrain from sharing your personal beliefs. If you do share about yourself, consider bringing the conversation back to your person with a question such as, "Is that similar to your experience?" The art of companioning the dying lies in following your person's lead, for they are the most important guide on this journey.

How can you help facilitate meaning-making for your person? As a companion, how can you support your person with feeling like their life has had significance? The first step is to simply listen, taking the time to understand where they find meaning. This requires your grounded presence, intuitive listening, and respectful curiousity. As a companion, you can help your person by encouraging them to share their story. As they do, you can listen with a non-judgemental ear, gently guiding them to revisit meaningful moments. By showing up in this way and holding space, you offer them the opportunity to reflect and find meaning. Let's explore how the gateway of wonder can enhance wellbeing at the end of life. What follows is evidence that shows that this process is not as complicated as it may seem.

Healing connections

Balfour Mount, a Canadian physician, surgeon, and academic, conducted a study called "Healing Connections: On Moving from Suffering to a Sense of Well-Being." This study explored the connection of the existential and spiritual domains to suffering, healing, and quality of life at the end of life. The participants were living in the final weeks or days of their lives. Surprisingly, Mount found that half of the participants were thriving and happy despite their prognosis, while the other half of participants were struggling. Through this qualitative study, Mount discovered that it was the presence or absence of a "healing connection" that accounted for this difference.

The study revealed that when individuals felt a healing connection to one or more of four key areas, they reported a good quality of life and considered their lives, including their dying process, to be meaningful. The four areas identified in the study were connection with self, connection with other people, connection with the phenomenal world (such as music or nature), and connection to an ultimate reality (such as a god or an ideal such as love). The study also revealed that finding a sense of meaning in the context of suffering and peace in the present moment directly increased the quality of life in the last days.

The study highlighted many simple interventions that can foster healing connections. Among the ways to offer comfort at the end of life, the act of simply being present stood out as particularily effective. This presence was measured by engaging in conversations, allowing the reality of the situation unfold, without minimizing, deflecting, or fixing. As a companion you can support your person by inviting presence by way of the senses and finding meaning and connection in everyday moments.

One participant observed, "There is that feeling of 'Presence'—such as when I go into the sunroom. I go, not because I have to talk to people [but]… to look at the snow, or a tree outside." Mount suggests ways to help bring your person into the present moment through meditation, music, or discussing their cherished interests. Asking a question such as, "What have you always been passionate about?" is likely to create connection. Exploring creative outlets such as art and music therapy may also deepen meaning.

Some participants shared how the unpredictability of their illness was difficult to navigate. One person mentioned how the familiar scent of roast beef on Sundays brought a sense of predictability and structure. "[I remember] the Sunday smell—always roast beef. It was always the same. That's why it was good."

As companions we can help foster healing connections by opening the space for meaningful moments. Whether it's simply being there to listen to life stories, reminiscing over old photos, or sharing memories of the past, a life review, whether written or spoken, can also be powerful.

Mount also discovered that people found benefit if they could identify current meanings of the illness for the person and for the family and friends. Exploring the sources of existential anguish—both before and during illness—can deepen these connections and support healing.

Furthermore, Mount and colleagues identified that legacy work supports healing connections. Legacy is simply how one is remembered, and it is deeply rooted in how one has lived. For some, the act of creating personalized photo albums for loved ones can bring comfort. If cooking holds special meaning, helping them create a cookbook to share with others could be a beautiful gesture. Or perhaps crafting a quilt with fabrics that carry personal significance might be the most healing gesture. If your person is open to it, explore ways to invite your person to explore what matters most to them.

Feeling an authentic sense of meaning about life provides great comfort at the end. The indicators of success that many cultures celebrate, such as titles and possessions, fade in the face of death. At the end of life, meaning is shaped by those who show up—they are evidence of a life well-lived—or it arises from reflecting on connections to self, nature, or the divine. A meaningful life is one in which connections such as these are nourished. In the end, it is almost always about love—expressing love and receiving love. Imagine if our dominant culture embraced this notion. What if we lived in a world that acknowledged and supported the notion that love is the only reality? This truth would guide us to live well and die well when the time comes.

Holding space

The gateway of wonder comes alive when we listen. If your person begins sharing about their culture, spirituality or personal beliefs, listen with curiosity and be fully present, seeking to understand what is being expressed and how it is impacting their journey. Your person may have clear spiritual goals that they pursue through prayer, reading, or being close to nature. They may wrestle with their faith, experiencing emotions like discontent, bitterness, or regret. It is not uncommon to feel angry. In all of these situations, your role is to be a companion, allowing your person to feel seen and heard, and offering empathy in times of struggle. A simple "You are going through a lot right now," may not seem like enough, but it is one of the most supportive things you can offer.

There are many ways to help someone in spiritual distress. Help can be offered one on one, or in small or large group settings. Support can be formal or informal and consist of prayer, worship services rituals, grief support, or celebrations. Don't forget that you need support too, perhaps someone to offer comfort with prayer or ritual, or someone to talk with about spiritual issues. Take care of yourself and lean out on others if you are in need of assistance with ethical dilemmas or support for your tender heart.

I have come to realize that holding space, or deeply listening, is love. When we listen with our hearts, offering our full attention without judgment, we can be truly present to what another is saying. So often we listen with our heads—judging, trying to fix things, or focusing on sharing our own experiences. This impaired listening, driven by the desire to change the situation, is usually more about easing our own discomfort than being fully present with what is being shared. True listening invites us to feel with another and truly understand what they are going through.

Your person may choose not to share their emotions or may have taboos about death and dying that don't align with the accepted notions of "dying well." It's important to hold space for their experience, respect the beliefs and practices they hold around dying, and honour the support they request. Showing up with intention and compassion offers great relief to those on the end of life journey. Sharing hopes, fears, and goals with another allows unresolved fears to be witnessed and in doing so, they become less burdensome.

The biggest gap in end-of-life care is simple compassionate support. This kind of care is often squeezed out of our overburdened healthcare system and further complicated by our discomfort with dying. Showing up as a grounded presence, normalizing, and validating what your person is going through is so supportive. The challenge lies in the fact that it is not about doing something, but it is about being something. It's easy to get caught up in tasks, and there are things that need to be done; but if we are not truly present with others, we can risk evoking feelings of abandonment.

> *"Technological society has forgotten what scholars call the 'dying role' and its importance to people as life approaches its end. People want to share memories, pass on wisdoms and keepsakes, settle relationships, establish their legacies, make peace with God, ensure that those who are left behind will be okay. They want to end their stories on their own terms. This role is, observers argue, among life's most important, for both the dying and those left behind."*
>
> —Dr. Atul Gawande, Being Mortal: Medicine and What Matters in the End

These words by Dr. Gawande reinforce the importance of a compassionate companion—someone who offers a grounded presence, is attuned to the person's needs, and creates space for them to express themselves while listening with a soft heart. It's easy to fall into busyness instead offering presence, especially because sitting with discomfort is not easy. The process of reconciling lives can be really uncomfortable. Keep in mind the closer you are to the dying person, the more challenging this beomes. Understanding that discomfort is normal can help, particularily when we realize the power of holding space for someone during times of distress. With this understanding we are more likely to step in and show up as a companion.

Your person can greatly benefit from having a companion who holds space for the wonderings that arise—there is a lot to process, and when you listen, be aware of what is being communicated in addition to the words. So much is shared through your person's tone of voice, mood, and body language—these are all clues as to how your person is really feeling. By listening with all your senses, allowing you to access your intuition and offer an unparalleled depth of presence.

You can support your person on the end-of-life journey by encouraging them to travel with ease, helping lighten the weight of regret and loss. This can be done by revisiting life's challenges and airing them out, while also celebrating the high notes of beauty, connection, and love. This is what wonder, or the blend of culture, spirituality, and personal beliefs is all about. It speaks to how people experience their connection to the moment, to themselves, to others, and to what is significant or sacred.

EXPECTED CHANGES ON THE JOURNEY

Common expressions signaling spiritual distress

Spiritual suffering or distress occurs when someone feels burdened by their past, is carrying the heavy load of unprocessed grief, has fear of the afterlife, or simply lacks a connection. You may notice one or more of the following in your person:

- Meaninglessness
- Despair and hopelessness
- Alienation and estrangement
- Abandonment and isolation
- Guilt and shame
- Anger

The most effective intervention for spiritual pain is acknowledging the presence of that pain and listening with empathy to your person's life story. This requires us to push beyond the natural tendency to try to avoid, push down, or fix difficult feelings, which only creates more disconnection.

CAMPP: CONNECTION, AWARENESS, MEANING, PLEASURE, PRESENCE

Spiritual invitations for end-of-life reflection

The following topics of conversation may offer spiritual support and encourage meaningful reflection during their end-of-life journey. These prompts can help open spaces for deep exploration. They may support your person to connect to what matters most to them, and find comfort through sharing their reflections.

- Understanding what gives their life meaning
- Exploring how they wish to be remembered
- Asking for forgiveness for themselves
- Asking what brings them joy
- Exploring regret and loss
- Offering forgiveness to others
- Sharing their life story
- Connecting with the faith and practices of their religion

Ritual and ceremony

> *"That, I think, is the power of ceremony: it marries the mundane to the sacred. The water turns to wine, the coffee to a prayer. The material and the spiritual mingle like grounds mingled with humus, transformed like steam rising from a mug into morning mist. A homemade ceremony, a ceremony that makes a home."*
>
> *—Robin Wall Kimmerer,* Braiding Sweetgrass

Ritual enhances wonder, inviting us to embrace all of life—the known and the unknown—to create meaning, and to express that which cannot be captured by language. The word ritual is evoking, sparking interest in some and skepticism in others, but the truth is, we are all ritual beings. In *Ritual: Power, Healing and Community*, author Malidoma Patrice Somé writes, "Ritual is called for because our soul communicates things to us that the body translates as need, or want, or absence. So we enter into ritual in order to respond to the call of the soul."

There is a pull at our collective knowing, and many of us are yearning to reconnect with our ritual selves. Rituals and ceremonies remind us that we are part of something larger than ourselves. To engage in or create a ritual, we are called to slow down and listen. Moving more slowly on the end-of-life journey allows us to travel with more ease. Somé suggests that "speed is a way to prevent ourselves from having to deal with something we do not want to face." There are so many external changes that evoke internal responses, and there are so many losses and transitions to keep up with, all compounded by fears of the unknown. To keep up with these changes and address fears, we need time to integrate. Ritual is supportive on the end-of-life journey because it encourages us to slow down and reflect.

A ritual is defined as simply an action performed with intention, and when done in succession, these rituals form a ceremony. Rituals and ceremonies can be cultural, religious, spiritual, or social, and different traditions around the world approach them in unique ways. Each tradition offers distinct knowledge and practices passed down by ancestors, helping people navigate the end-of-life journey, find connection, make meaning, and anchor themselves in an ever-changing reality. There are rituals for birth, marriage, rites of passage, coming of age, festivals honouring seasons, death, grief, and more. Regrettably, in dominant Western culture, much of this knowledge has been lost, making both living and dying a lot more challenging. This creates an enormous gap in spiritual and emotional support at the end of life, offering us a great opportunity to re-establish ritual healing for those living, those dying, and even the deceased.

As a companion, rituals can help you to feel more grounded, deepen your presence, and support emotional regulation in the role. Ritual brings us into the present moment, anchoring participants in the here and now. Rituals don't have to be complex; sometimes a simple act such as pausing to light a candle with intention can be a powerful ritual. When we act with reverence, we create a space that feels suspended, allowing what's being held inside to be expressed, experienced, and acknowledged. These soul-affirming acts enable us to honour the unspeakable parts of ourselves that might otherwise remain hidden.

> *"Ritual can offer a bit of ground in the groundlessness, not necessarily to return to the dilution of safety but to be able to recognize what is changing and to attempt to make sense of it."*
>
> *—Day Schildkret,* Hello, Goodbye: 75 Rituals for Times of Loss, Celebration, and Change

Schildkret explains that rituals have been mistakenly claimed by the realm of religion; in fact, they existed long before. He believes that rituals belong to the people and more precisely, to the people's imaginations. As we create a new paradigm for death and dying, we can look to ancient practices of the faith traditions that offered connection and meaning making for guidance, but we now have the option of creating new personal rites that speak profoundly to our needs and the needs of the dying.

Think about the rituals that your family practices. Singing "Happy Birthday" and blowing out candles to commemorate the day of someone's birth is a common example. You might also have your own personal rituals, created with intention to support yourself or to honour transition. Prayer is a universal ritual that connects us to to the present moment, allowing us to express ourselves from our intuitive heart rather than our linear brain. Children are naturally drawn to ritual, and its creative and symbolic language seems to come effortlessly to young people. There is a good chance that you have participated in simple intentional actions throughout your life without even realizing it.

We lack cultural or religious rituals for many of our modern-day circumstances for dying, calling us to create rituals to offer support in complex times such as during a medical assistance in dying provision (MAID), or the impossible moment of turning off a ventilator. Due to a trend toward the personalization of end-of-life care, more and more people are creating their own rituals to support the end-of-life journey. We are all qualified to perform rituals and we are invited to use our imaginations to improvise—bringing in new rituals with familiar items like objects from nature, personal belongings, or meaningful music to create connection and usher in acceptance and healing.

STORIES FROM THE TRAIL

Seven days of light: A MAID ritual in practice

With love and reverence for Deirdre, and gratitude to Dr. Sarah Kerr

The need for support for individuals and families who choose a medically assisted death is swiftly increasing. In my practice, over half of the people who reach out for doula support around medical assistance in dying (MAID) are seeking more education, understanding, and preparation—for both the head and the heart. For this reason, I am grateful to Dr. Kerr for generously sharing a MAID ritual, one that she refers to as an advent calendar ritual. I have invited several clients to explore different variations of this countdown ritual, and it has been deeply moving to witness the support that comes from this intentional action. The story of Deirdre touched my heart in unforgettable ways.

A while back I was contacted by a man seeking doula support for his mother who was living in anticipation of a MAID provision. She lived a short drive away and I agreed to visit her the following day to better understand her needs around her end-of-life decision. I met with Deirdre in her back garden. We sipped tea, noted the birds at the feeder, and spoke about where she was on her end-of-life journey and how she hoped to be supported moving forward. Her heart and mind were open and she welcomed the companionship.

She expressed that she was feeling quite anxious about her upcoming MAID provision. She lived alone. Her dedicated adult children came by often to spend time with her, but during their visits Deirdre found it challenging to discuss the complexities of MAID with the people she loved the most. She was carrying so many emotions and she felt grateful for the chance to have a neutral companion with whom she could share her hopes, fears, and goals with in the week leading up to her provision.

I offered to support Deirdre with a MAID countdown ritual, and she was receptive and excited about the support. I learned of this idea from the wise, vibrant, and generous Dr. Sarah Kerr, sacred deathcare practitioner and founder of Sacred Deathcare. Dr. Kerr truly is a Canadian treasure—she has been in practice since 2012, and she is a wellspring of soul-based wisdom. Her focus is on contemporary ritual healing, and she is fuelled by helping her clients and students find the healing gifts that can accompany death and loss.

Dr. Kerr acknowledges that something intense happens when the date for a MAID provision is made. She says that things in the field coalesce and snap into reality in a way that they haven't before, and they don't until that happens. She believes that the client needs a way to catch up to this new reality so they can ready their soul to be prepared for the day, recognizing that physical time and soul time don't always align. Ritual is physical; it uses our bodies and allows us to get real in a different way. Here are the steps involved in Dr. Kerr's MAID countdown ritual:

1. Before proceeding, ask your person if they are interested in participating in this ritual. Consent is key.
2. Allow your person to choose a dedicated place to have the altar for this ritual. This may be a fireplace mantle, a dresser, or a shelf.
3. Place candles or tea lights on the altar to represent the number of days remaining before the provision.
4. Invite your person to light a candle each morning and state the number of days remaining before the MAID provision—"There are ten days remaining." Saying the number of days out loud makes it a reality.
5. Ask your person to set and share an intention for how they want to spend that day. Take a moment to be with that intention, then ask your person to blow out the candle.
6. In the evening, go back to altar with your person to light the candle dedicated to that day again.
7. Invite your person to express gratitude for the day, take a moment to be with their praise, and guide them to blow out the candle. Remove the candle from the altar to mark the day as complete.
8. Clearly acknowledge how many days left—"There are now nine days remaining."
9. Repeat daily until the day of the provision.

This ritual can be done solo, with a family member or friend, with another end-of-life companion such as a doula, or with a group of people.

Dr. Kerr believes that counting down the candles, living with intention, and acknowledging the number of days remaining creates a profound energetic gesture, helping the internal—or soul—timing align with the external timing of an upcoming provision. "When you see ten candles, nine, eight, seven, it gets real in a different way." She suggests that this ritual supports people to "arrive there, body and soul together, so that on no level you are surprised about what is happening; so that you get there complete and in one piece."

I offered to return to Deirdre's home each day leading up to her MAID provision date to support her with this countdown ritual and to hold space for her experience—offering her the opportunity to live out her dying role. My intention was to allow her to share memories, regrets, wisdoms, as well as to celebrate the moments, guiding her to gratitude and love. After seeking her permission, I offered to send her adult children a daily email summarizing our visits and the candle ritual so they too could arrive at that day feeling a little more prepared.

We sat together a while longer and she asked about the medications used for MAID and what to expect. I reassured her that MAID is a very peaceful process, that it is just like going to sleep. She seemed relieved to hear that it was unlikely that she would fall off the chair or choke. She shared that for her, MAID has been a very complicated choice. I left her home with the promise to return the following afternoon.

7 days

It was early fall and the dahlias were still in full bloom. As I left my house the next day I passed a bunch of enormous brightly coloured flowers and I decided to snip off a bloom and offer it to Deirdre as a reminder of beauty. Deirdre met me at her door with a light-hearted smile, welcomed me inside, and offered me a tea. After a short visit we started the ritual. We lined up seven glass tea-light holders on her fireplace mantle and dropped a candle in each one.

I encouraged her to make the most of her moments—to find beauty where she could. I reminded her that her children loved her so much, and that they supported her wishes. I acknowledged that saying goodbye is never easy and that her upcoming MAID provision date was deeply felt by everybody who cared for her. We lit the candle for the day, and she set an intention. We shared a moment of silence, and I guided her to blow out the candle. I put the tealight in my bag and said, "There are now six days remaining." I placed the bright orange dahlia on the mantle next to the six remaining candles.

6 days

The next day I returned with a sprig of rosemary from my front garden. Rosemary symbolizes remembrance and memory. Before lighting the candle we sat and talked about the natural desire that arises in people facing death, to look back and remember a lifetime of memories. We sat in silence sipping our tea and after a while she opened up. She told me all about her family, pointing out people in the framed photos around her living room. She talked about her love of tennis, the lazy summers at the family cabin, and hosting lively themed dinner parties. She lit up as she recalled her career as a teacher and told stories of a few of her most memorable students. She went on and on with contagious enthusiasm. After a while she asked if we could light the candle. We approached the mantle and performed the daily ritual. "There are now five days remaining," I announced.

Deirdre shook her head. "The waiting is hard."

I met her eyes and placed a hand on her shoulder. As she saw me to the door, she stopped and thanked me for coming. We shared a hug, and I set off down her walkway to my car.

5 days

The next day I brought a rock to symbolize the heaviness of regret. We talked about how none of us escapes life without regrets—these heavy emotions of sadness, disappointment, or remorse about an action, decision, or circumstance from the past haunt us all. Regrets often linger, consuming us with the desire to undo choices or take a different path. They can arise from perceived mistakes, missed opportunities, or life circumstances that did not meet our expectations.

We wondered together about how to lighten these heavy emotions so we don't have to lug them around. We talked about how exploring regrets and sharing these deep feelings with others helped to lighten the burden. As the conversation continued, Deirdre shared some of her life regrets. I sat and listened, feeling with her as she picked up these heavy memories, felt the weight, explored them from different angles, and put them down. We stood and performed the candle ritual, leaving four remaining tea lights on the altar. In the doorway she offered a cheery bye—my sense was she was travelling a little lighter.

4 days

Four days before her scheduled provision I brought Deirdre a mushroom. During my morning walk in the forest, I noticed so many mushrooms emerging from the ground in various shapes, sizes, and colours, all bursting to life after a weekend of steady rain. I was inspired by the mushrooms and mycelial networks—the underground web that connects plants and trees, providing nutrients and communication. I chose to bring a mushroom to remind Deirdre of how many people care for her—how many people are holding her during this challenging time.

Before I left for my visit with Deirdre, I found a message from her son in my inbox. How serendipitous! The email was filled with heartfelt messages from Deirdre's network! He sent it along to me to share with Deirdre during our visit. Old friends, family members, and neighbours had offered messages—love notes filled with treasured memories and well wishes. I tucked my computer in my bag and hopped in my car.

I passed Deirdre the mushroom as I entered her home. She gave me a little smile and raised her eyebrows. She went into the kitchen and returned with two cups of tea. We sat in the living room and had a conversation about the significance of mycelial networks the unifying force of nature—life-giving networks. I pulled my laptop from my purse and began reading the notes to Deirdre as she listened closely. Some of the messages made her laugh, while others brought a quiet, reflective stillness. She asked me to read a couple of the notes twice. It was deeply moving to witness. When it was time to go, we said our goodbyes and I headed down the walkway. I glanced back over my shoulder to see her dancing in the doorway.

3 days

I visited Deirdre just before noon, three days before her MAID date. I asked her to hold her hands out in front of her, then placed a few drops of sweet orange essential oil in her palm and asked her to rub her hands together. I guided her to cup her hands over her nose and mouth and inhale. She was enlivened by the bright smell of citrus and flashed a wide smile. I placed a small orange on the mantle, and we talked about the heaviness of grief that accumulates from all the change that is a natural part of the end-of-life journey. The orange oil was offered to brighten any darkness she might be feeling and to help invigorate her when she is feeling low. We lit the candle in honour of brightness, and she set an intention for the day. After sharing some silence she blew the candle out. I tucked it into my bag and glanced at the growing altar of meaning—there was a dahlia, a sprig of rosemary, a rock, a mushroom, an orange, and two tea lights remaining.

2 days

The next day I arrived at Deirdre's home and passed her an owl's feather at the door. Over tea I shared that on the end-of-life journey it is best to travel light. We talked about how sharing regrets and grief with trusted others is one way to travel lighter. She gazed out her living room window as we sat in silence for a while. She talked a lot about her hometown. She spoke about her childhood and sang a little song that her father used to sing to her when she was young. She shared about motherhood, being a wife, and being a friend. We performed our little ritual and I reminded her that there was one day remaining.

1 day

When I arrived at Deirdre's home on the day of her MAID provision I was greeted by her three adult children. The living room was thick with emotion. We exchanged hugs and care. I acknowledged the enormity of the day and shared my wish that they take the time to tune into their hearts and say whatever is asking to be said, be it forgiveness, gratitude, love, or anything else. I was there to complete the countdown ritual, so Deirdre and I walked up to the mantlepiece. We stood there for a while, then Deirdre picked up the one remaining tea light and I struck a match. We lit the last candle. She silently set her intention for the day and blew out the flame. I put the candle in my bag and placed a maple leaf with hints of red, burnt orange, and yellow on the mantle. We talked about impermanence and change, about the nature of life, about cycles and seasons. She opened her arms and we had a long embrace.

After an emotional goodbye, I walked out the door, and down the walkway, I turned to look over my shoulder to see Deirdre in the doorway surrounded by her three children waving goodbye.

Later that evening I received an email from Deirdre's son. He said that when the physician who came to administer the MAID provision asked her if she was ready, she answered calmly and unequivocally, "Yes." She passed away peacefully in her living room, with her three children at her side. He shared that his mom would have been quite pleased that, as I had assured her, she did not choke. He felt that she would also be pleased with everybody's efforts to ensure that she did not fall off the chair, a fear she had shared with all. He expressed heartfelt gratitude for the support and guidance I offered Deirdre to prepare her and their family in the days leading up to the big day.

Her daughter reached out too, grateful for the support offered to the family as they all navigated the very difficult end-of-life decision she was facing. She felt that the connection created in the week leading up to the provision allowed her mom to speak more freely about her wishes and fears. She shared that despite the intensely emotional journey, she felt at peace with her decision in the end. This sense of peace gave her children comfort, as they believed she was finally ready. Shortly before the provision she spoke to her kids about the wonderful life she had lived. Her daughter mentioned that it felt as though a weight had lifted, allowing them to fully embrace their final moments together as a family.

This ritual supported Deirdre by inviting connection, awareness, meaning, pleasure, and presence right up until the final moments.

Rituals can guide people to what to do next. In this way, ceremonies can help us find our way. For example, creating rituals for the vigil time, those last few days of life, can be deeply supportive. This is typically a swirling time when the people present are charged with emotion but don't often know what to do next. During this time the dying person is unable to communicate verbally, so the symbolic language of ritual is fitting. Engaging in simple actions with intention such as holding hands around the bed or playing a favourite song can create connection, awareness, meaning, pleasure, and presence. This can help people fully embrace what is happening, guiding them into the next moment with more ease. Whether practicing cultural or secular rituals, or co-creating universal, nature-inspired ceremonies, this practice offers a powerful way to honour times of transition.

> *"A diagnosis can leave us breathless, grasping, undone. It can also be an opportunity to breathe into all that is changing—relenting, rather than relentlessly trying to fix, resist, or run away. Ritualizing their time can offer ground to stand on where you can touch the fleeting, messy, uncertainty of life with reflection, with beauty, with grief, with rage, with community, with courage, and with love."*
>
> —Day Schildkret, Hello, Goodbye: 75 Rituals for Times of Loss, Celebration, and Change

With ritual demystified, you may feel inspired to experiment with this symbolic language and create personalized practices of your own. As a companion to the dying, you can consider creating rituals to support yourself in your role as caregiver. The trail notes in this book offer a variety of suggestions for personal rituals, each designed with the intention of helping you stay grounded, calm, present, and connected to your heart.

You may also consider creating and practicing personal rituals to help you to travel light, supporting you to put down that which is not yours to carry. Rituals for purification or release—such as taking an epsom salt bath, or symbolically choosing a stone to represent what you would like to release, then returning the stone to nature—may allow you to let go of the heavy energy that can accumulate from caring for others so that you can sustain your role as companion.

So how do we co-create ritual? Personalized ritual should be aligned with one's values and beliefs, be it religious, spiritual, or atheist. It can be inspiring to look into your family lineages and cultural traditions to identify and find inspiration in ritual practices used by ancestors.

The first step to creating a meaningful ritual is simply to pause and listen—tune into the feelings and needs in the moment. Pay attention with all the senses—allow your intuition to guide you. Consider using the breath and the body as a compass—your natural wisdom will lead you. Decide if the ceremony is best suited to be held solo, in a pair, or in a group. The senses can be a source of inspiration when creating rituals, so consider meaningful sights, sounds, tastes, feels, and smells. Perhaps it is fitting to include a favourite song, food or activity, or all three. Perhaps it's a poem, a blessing, the laying of flowers, lighting a candle, or gifting a treasured item. With ritual, less is more.

It is essential that you set your intention, know your desired outcome, and then let go. Rituals are organic, so the goal is not to direct every moment. Sometimes the most meaningful and profound elements are happenstance. I remember a time when I was facilitating a memorial ceremony to honour a young father who died. I led a few simple rituals in the backyard gazebo, such as inviting people to recall and share favourite sayings that the man used to say. We then we stood and walked over to a palm tree that had been planted in his memory. The family members were holding rocks that had just been infused with favourite memories, and they were preparing to place the stones at the base of the tree when suddenly a huge gush of water washed over our feet. The wall of the inflatable pool beside us gave way, causing water to cover the grass, our feet, and the palm tree! The heavy silence was disrupted by an eruption of laughter. The family members had a sense that the unexpected event was a practical joke from the other side, which was very much in keeping with the spirit of the man we were honouring. This spontaneous happening created so much connection and meaning—it was definitely the highlight of the ceremony.

Ritual begins when you start planning, and ends when you stop reflecting on the event—this is another reason why this symbolic expression is so potent. Once you have decided on a ritual or ceremony, gather your supplies, and reach out to others if it is not a solo ceremony. Before the event, ground your energy and connect with your heart. Focus on your intention, begin, and trust.

How wonderful it is that so many are looking to ritual to feel supported by creating new personal rites that speak to the specific needs of the dying and their people. May we become ritual beings ourselves so that we can normalize, inspire, and encourage others to practice ritual and create community—yet another benefit of ritual. We are relational beings who are designed to live authentically connected to others and support each other during times of transition with rites of passage. When we honour our deepest needs and vulnerably come together to practice ritual, the byproduct is the creation of community which is exactly what we desire and need, now more than ever.

When one lacks cultural, spiritual, or religious beliefs to offer comfort and guidance on the end-of-life journey, it is common to turn to the phenomenal world to find meaning. The phenomenal world is the world as it appears to us through the lens of human understanding—the world as experienced, as opposed to the actual world. As identified in Balfour Mount's study "Healing Connections," two examples of the phenomenal world that commonly offer comfort to the dying are nature and music, but it can really be anything cognizable by the senses that one inspires the sense of wonder.

GROUNDING PRACTICES

Tips for creating personalized ritual and ceremony

Rituals can be as elaborate as a celebration of life or as simple as an intentional moment alone with a candle. Unless you are following specific religious or cultural rituals, there are no hard and fast rules. Inspiration for your ritual may come from religion, spirituality, or culture. If you draw from cultural practices different from your own, it's important to approach them with cultural appreciation rather than appropriation.

Exploring your ancestral lineage can be nourishing, allowing you to connect with the ritual practices your ancestors. Rituals can also be created from scratch, drawing on events, hobbies, or a meaningful song. The most powerful rituals are those that best reflect your personal beliefs and values.

Some people find comfort in small, spontaneous rituals, while others prefer more structure. You may choose to create a ritual as a one-time event, or you may decide to practice it daily or on special occasions such as birthdays, anniversaries, holidays, or other significant moments. Here are some questions to guide ritual creation:

1. What is the need; what is the meaning you wish to create?
2. When and where will the ritual take place?
3. Who should be present?
4. What will be done?

Notes on Ritual

- Perfection is the enemy of ritual, creativity, and love. Personal ritual is about letting go, asking us to trust that it will take you where you need to go. Invite your rational mind to take a break.
- It is important to understand that ritual may open you up to a deeper level of feeling—that is precisely what it is designed to do. Rituals are meant to evoke emotions because emotions contain the energy required for change.

- Consider a structure that offers an opening, acknowledgment of what was, what is, and what will be, followed by a closing.
- Mark the opening and closing of with practices that signal entry into and exit from this liminal space. For instance, you might begin with a song that signals to your body and deeper self that the ritual is starting. For group rituals, welcoming participants could involve lighting a candle, reading or reciting a poem, or ringing a chime. There are countless ways to cue your deep self to emerge; the key is creating an intentional space.

Nature

Let's take a moment to look at the role of the natural world in supporting the dying and their people. Many consider being in nature a spiritual experience. Being in nature or contemplating nature reminds us that change is inevitable. Being in nature reminds us that we too are nature, governed by cycles and forces beyond our control. The spring of our infancy, the summer of our young adulthood, the fall of middle age, and the winter of old age. These cycles rule all living things. The question we are asked to consider is where does our own autonomy stop and at what point are we best served to resign to forces greater than ourselves?

Over the years of supporting the dying and their people, I have noticed that the natural world consistently brings great comfort and peace at the end of life. In the final days, people often want their beds positioned so they can look out a window and see the trees, birds, sunrises, sunsets, or stars. Folks often request nature soundtracks for guided meditations almost always involve vivid descriptions of sensorial pleasures from the natural world. This makes sense because as humans we have evolved in nature. The natural world is our home, the creatures are our kin. The human species has lived outside for 99.99 percent of its evolutionary history and we have adapted to thrive in the natural world.

Regardless of the chaos, nature is still held together by a beauty and intelligence that is vast, connective, and kind. The sun and the moon reliably journey through the sky. The seasons come and go playing out the cycle of birth, life, death, and rebirth. Just to see a flower in bloom, hear a songbird, or spot a busy squirrel scurrying around can help us remember our true nature, one that hasn't been influenced by culture. This wild knowing will always understand the cyclical nature of life and seek connection and health. Remembering that we are nature can serve to remind us that we are complete, and kind, that we live, we die, and we are whole. This knowing can offer a sense of acceptance.

After noticing the comfort that nature brings, I became curious as to how I could collaborate with the natural world to support people on the end-of-life journey. I trained in to become a Forest Therapy Guide with the Association of Nature and Forest Therapy, an influence that greatly informs the work I do in supporting the dying and their people. This exploration has led me to understand why nature can offer so much comfort on the end-of-life journey.

We evolved in nature; our senses and body rhythms are best suited for that environment. The sounds, smells, sights are our evolutionary home where we can rest and rejuvenate. Nature invites us to slow down and honour our internal timing, for some it offers a sense of timelessness that connects us to our natural wisdom. It invites us into a depth of presence with a potency of moments that are not so easy to find elsewhere. These moments can serve as portals to wonder through sensorial delight.

Research confirms that being in nature has a profoundly positive impact on our mental and physical health by making us feel more connected to ourselves, our environment, and others. Nature immersion for the dying and grieving can increase meaning, wellbeing, and presence. Many find that just being outside changes things, be it the wildness, the vastness, the good-enough-ness, or the wonder. The natural world offers healing to our bodies and souls.

As human beings we are not separate from nature; rather, we are part of it. When we attune to nature, we connect with our most authentic selves. This deep sense of belonging overrides cultural, spiritual, religious, and personal differences. The friction between nature and culture brings into question old forms, allowing us to see the world with fresh eyes. Finding and following a new vision asks for an open heart and an open mind. We are deeply tied to a world from which we have become distant. In our recent past we have rapidly shifted toward urban and digital environments that do not support the body's need for the biological stimulation of nature that enhances health and wellbeing. When we are in nature, we are invited to a state of inter-being. This involves the mending of damaged relationships humans have with themselves, with the concept of time, with their communities, and with other living beings in the natural world. Just being in a forest challenges the dominant cultural ideas such as being obsessed with youth and living forever. It reveals the absurdity of the resistance to change and impermanence and the disdain of uncertainty. In nature we are called to remember an older and deeper wisdom that we often resist at the personal and cultural level. We are inspired to practice non-attachment and be reminded of the ever-changing nature of reality.

Nature is accessible to everyone. One can take a break at quiet cabin, take a short walk, care for houseplants, or simply gaze out the window at a tree. If all else fails, there are endless nature shows to watch, which have been shown to have equally positive effects on the body, mind, and spirit. Every experience outside is an opportunity to access the healing power of nature. Trees are incredible living beings, shorelines, even neighborhood parks can serve as sacred sites for connecting with the natural world. Imagining nature through guided meditation is also a powerful practice. Consider a favourite natural setting and invite the imagination to explore, experiencing that place through the senses, including as much detail as possible.

The vastness of the natural world and the epic sense of time reflected in the seasons, the decades captured in an old tree, or the canyons carved out by glaciers tens of thousands of years ago, some how support us in framing our own existence. It can both minimize our suffering and enhance our belonging when we understand ourselves within the context of the natural world. Nature invites us to love all of life—its beginnings, its middles, and its endings too. This is the natural order of things which is so often overlooked in a clinical medical setting, and the lack of presence of this story in our dominant culture makes dying more challenging than necessary.

Nature is good for us. It reduces symptoms of psychological and physiological stress, regulates our nervous system, improves respiratory and cardiovascular functions, boosts our immune system, enhances cognitive abilities, and increases alertness. Our bodies were designed to be in relationship with trees, water, and the sky. Being in nature activates the self-healing potential of our own nature. The natural world can be supportive as a potent adjunctive therapy. The beauty of this design is that nature benefits from our attention and gratitude in this reciprocal relationship. It also motivates us to protect the planet—we care for what we love.

In natural settings we are invited to be present through our senses. Consider the sounds of birds, waves, or wind through the trees; the smell of a forest, fragrant flowers or salty ocean air; the taste of a crisp cold breeze, the feel of sun or rain on our exposed skin, and the sight of forests, plains, mountains, or oceans. We can be inspired by beauty and pleasure when we take notice of the natural world. This brings us to presence, which can help shift our focus and redirect attention away from unwanted thoughts and toward sensations of the body. When we get out of our minds and into our bodies, we can decrease rumination, and we are given the mental space to rest. Wonder is the feeling we get from encountering something vast that challenges our limited knowledge and inspires us to consider that there are forces greater than ourselves at play. When we sense wonder, our bodies respond.

> *"Keep some room in your heart for the unimaginable."*
>
> *—Mary Oliver*

When There Are Gaps in the Gateway of Wonder

If your person is struggling to connect to the gateway of wonder, if they are lacking cultural, spiritual or personal beliefs to support meaning-making on the end-of-life journey, dying can be challenging. Remember, the goal as a companion is to walk alongside, taking your person's lead, and serving as a witness for whatever arises. Don't forget to support yourself and seek answers to any questions that come up for you. Trust that simply being present with your person makes a meaningful difference.

People live as they die, so if your person is struggling to find meaning perhaps it is not out of character. For some, the proximity to death can bring clarity about the meaning of life, yet for others, it can cause anxiety and fear. It is not easy to be a companion for someone who struggles to connect with wonder. In such cases it might be helpful to call in others for support. Remember, simply being present and sharing in their experience creates connection, even if it is companioning them in their disconnection. Just letting them know they're not alone is often all it takes to bring comfort.

STORIES FROM THE TRAIL

Softening the hurt: Giving anger a little space

I once accompanied a very private man who had a reputation for snapping at his caregivers at the care home where he lived and was now dying. One afternoon I quietly tidied up around his bed. The man, unwilling to acknowledge my presence, turned away from me with a furrowed brow, and stared out the window. As I watched him, a mantra that my mom has shared many times over my lifetime came to mind: "Love the unlovable."

"Excuse me," I said. He turned and met my eyes, and I offered a little kindness. "Can I bring you anything? A coffee perhaps?" There was a long pause. I was offering him more than a coffee. I sensed he was holding a lot, something unspoken. I could feel it. I had yet to see a visitor come by and he had no photos of friends and family. On his table lay a copy of the newspaper, his cell phone, and a plastic glass of ice water. He had a gritty demeanour, but beneath it I sensed a lot of fear.

He broke the silence with a question. "So, you are here to help me?"

"Yes." I waited. His pace, his lead.

"Why are you doing this?" he asked, searching. I shared a bit about my journey and how I was drawn to the deep sense of peace and authenticity I often found in the rooms of the dying. There, things were usually distilled to what mattered most—people and relationships. Those rooms were almost always filled with love.

"Yes," he said. "I have been thinking about that a lot. About how I have treated others. A lot of regrets have come up but I am trying not to be too hard on myself."

I just listened into the silence. "Regrets," I repeated. "We all have them!" With respectful curiosity, I asked, "Is there a person you feel like you have something to say to?"

"Yes," he answered. I sensed he was ready to open up just enough. I didn't need the name, the details, or the plan. In that moment, it felt like enough. I reminded him that in the end, it is usually about valuing the people in our lives. His face lit up as he mentioned his sister and a brother-in-law who were coming to visit soon.

We discussed how our dominant culture often prioritizes other things and in this way, pulls us away from what matters most. The conversation meandered to gratitude for the great care he was receiving, his teaching career, and world events.

For over a month I had been wearing a large, round, bright pink button with the word LOVE in black capitalized letters. It was part of a project encouraging more love to be expressed into the world. The instructions on the back of the button said that it should be worn to absorb good vibes, and then passed on to someone who could use some love. This man inspired me to pass it on.

Just before I left for the day, I gently knocked on the door, button in hand. "I would like you to have this," I said. I thanked him for reminding me of why I do the work I do, for reminding me about love. I handed him the shocking bright pink button. With discomfort, he admitted that he likely wouldn't be wearing it on his hospital gown. "Oh no, there is no need to," I said. I placed it on his bedside table and explained the initiative to him. "You are just supposed to feel love, infuse it into the button and pass it on, maybe to someone like your sister…"

His eyes sparkled. "Yes. Thank you," he said.

"Thank you!" I felt love beaming out from between the words. I held his gaze and we met in silence.

STORIES FROM THE TRAIL

A simple ceremony: How a handful of rituals holds so much

I had the privledge of companioning Bev as she navigated her end-of-life journey. Living alone in a one-bedroom apartment, and without children or a spouse, Bev faced this journey with intention and clarity. In the weeks leading up to her medically assisted death, we spent time together as she naturally played out the dying role, sharing her life story. Bev leaned out on me for companionship and support with planning the day of her MAID provision. Bev was clear, she knew who she wanted there and it was important to her that everyone was supported by ritual.

Together we planned a simple ceremony of sorts for the day of her provision. She wished for an old friend, her nephew, and me to be present in her apartment. For the occasion she wanted new underwear, a candle to be lit, nature sounds playing softly, and a photo of her European ancestors within view. She also chose affirmations to be read to her once the provision began—"We will keep you warm," "It is okay to let go," "You are not alone," "You are so dignified," "You are so grateful," "Wild horse," "New beginnings," "It's a wonderful world," and "I'll be looking at the moon but I'll be seeing you." Her final wish included those present to join hands around her bed after her death and sing her "Happy Birthday" to celebrate her death as an act of rebirth.

That morning around 11, the doctor and two nurses arrived at the door of her apartment. She sprang out of bed in her nightie and welcomed them joyfully. I offered tea and homemade cookies as a gesture of hospitality. Being there, in her cozy apartment, as the medical team quietly prepared, was strangely normal and deeply profound at the same time.

As she had wished, the provision began in candlelight, gentle sounds of birds softly chirping in the background, and meaningful photos surrounding her bed. Her dear friend quietly spoke Bev's chosen affirmations.

At the moment of her death a small bird landed on the balcony—we all noticed. After the MAID team had left the three of us gathered around her in the bedroom, just off the front door in her apartment. Less than half an hour earlier she had opened that door to welcome in the doctor and nurse practitioner with radical hospitality. It was a challenge to catch up to the swift ending of a life, to integrate such an enormous transition.

We clasped hands around her, and began to sing. It was a song that I have sung my whole life. The only ceremonial song that my culture has handed me. I had sung it for over 50 years but this time it came from a different source. It was more than a celebration of birth—it was a hymn, a lullaby, an anthem, a ditty, a fight song, a torch song, a serenade, a requiem. It came from deep within my bones and it travelled beyond this world.

The Gifts of the Gateway

> *"I sat with my anger long enough until she told me her real name was grief."*
>
> *—Unknown*

When navigating the end-of-life journey, there are many signposts to guide us. We can look to the anticipated signs that signal the dying person's transition, as there are physical, emotional, psychologica, social, and spiritual landmarks to help us along the way. But there is also a lot of wandering and wondering which reveals the depth of one's worldview and may generously open an inquiry into the very nature of self. The dying may roam off trail, and as a companion you are called to feel your way, with all of your senses.

Wonder asks us to drop from our heads into our hearts, allowing ourselves to be led by the dying. Honouring this heart wisdom can be challenging as we are so often focused on directions and getting somewhere. But wandering and wondering doesn't mean being lost; it's an invitation to listen attentively and respond to the unique situation unfolding before us.

It is through this curiosity and questioning, this need to look again and again, that the dying are drawn into an intimacy with death. Questions that arise are not necessarily meant to be answered; rather, they serve to draw folks more deeply into the unknown, into the miracle of it all. Sitting with this wonder and embracing what we don't know with humility changes things. Fear will likely arise in the company of the unknown, but wonder is also ripe with endless possibilities for those who choose to embrace the mystery. By staying open to what is unknown, an intimacy with death—which is also an engagement with life right up until the last moments—is revealed.

It is normal to feel overwhelmed about how to show up for your person. This is the nature of the journey. Dying is full of mystery which can be uncomfortable, especially in this age where answers are just a click away. We know so much about dying—there are many signposts to guide us through the expected changes.There is also comfort in knowing that the body is designed to die. This book shares many of these trail markers but invites you to turn toward what we simply can't yet understand. There is so much wonder in this world, so much that we are blinded by it—it is often only in times of intense crisis that wonder becomes startlingly apparent.

GROUNDING PRACTICES

The medicine of gratitude

Gratitude is an action, and when we act, we are less debilitated. There is always something to be grateful for—a sunset, a pet, good health, cherished memories, friends, trees, or a kind smile.

Praise opens us to the fullness of life, holding both the pain of loss and the blessings that are delivered by way of small wonders. It widens our perspective, helping us to see goodness even amid suffering. In times of struggle, we often fixate on what is wrong, but gratitude softens this tendency, allowing our hearts to rest. It reminds us that the good in the world is just as true as the pain.

What are three things that you are grateful for?

Placing Attention
By Rosemerry Wathola Trommer

As the weather is changing
and the light is changing
and the birds at the feeder
in the yard are changing,
as the leaders are changing
and the feelings are changing
and the way that we see
each other is changing,
I notice the invitation to turn
toward the truth
of what does not change—
something so vast, so unnamable,
so unable to be grasped and held,
something so present
there is no life without it,
that knows itself
through you, through me,
through clover and tree and cloud
and goes on and on and on forever.
That. I turn again and again
toward that.

Chapter 10

The Gateway of Wisdom

> *"I have found that among its other benefits, giving liberates the soul of the giver."*
>
> —Maya Angelou

Wisdom is an Old English word for knowledge, learning, and experience, and is accumulated over a lifetime. It is action-oriented and centers around doing the right thing. In the context of end-of-life care, wisdom guides us to lean out on others. It is understanding that living and dying is about both giving and receiving.

Regrettably, community care, rooted in the generous principles of mutal aid and the kind of support that was once commonly offered to dying, has become less common. Today, much of the support for living, including dying, is outsourced to systems shaped by settler colonialism and extractive capitalism, pushing mutual care into the margins. While some cultures continue to be supported by an Indigenous worldview, seeing death as a natural part of life that is best supported in community, for most of us, the experience is different.

This book aims to guide us back to community care, a more generous approach for relationships and creativity lead the way. Imagine a world where everyone is tended to by community from birth to death. It is written in the spirit of care that embraces all, regardless of their status or wealth. In such a world, domination, isolation, and control cannot thrive when we meet each other with open hearts. The concepts praised in this culture—linear, binary, fast, and productivity-focused—often make living and dying difficult. But these ideas fade away when we meet one another human to human and moment to moment.

I often think of a man whose care team I was once a part of. In his mid-seventies, he was living with glioblastoma. When we first met, he laughed and said, "I am such a Boomer. Not only am I supported by my kids, my wife, my brothers, my friends, and my colleagues, but I also have a doctor, an oncologist, a neurosurgeon, a therapist, a psychiatrist, and now a doula!" He looked at me from across the kitchen table and flashed a big smile.

Dying is inherently a social event. While there are medical aspects to dying—more today than ever before—death remains emotional and communal by nature. Not long ago in North America, dying was honoured as such—a social event. People died in their homes, surrounded by family, friends, neighbours, and community members who provided care. This care wasn't always perfect and interventions were simpler, but people came together and did their best. Dying often involved intimate care, where spontaneous moments of connection and laughter were organic parts of day-to-day care. These moments are rare in institutionalized settings where most people in the West die today. In this overculture we live under the spell of autonomy and those who are cared for in such places often feel like a burden, a common fear among the dying.

Some cultures today place a greater value on social connection, relying less on outsourced care and more on mutual support. We can look to these cultures for inspiration, helping us envision how we might approach death more collectively as we move forward.

I am constantly inspired when I pass by a mysterious living stump in a local park on my morning walks. This lumpy broken tree is branchless, yet it continues to grow a covering of bark despite losing its life-giving foliage long ago. The surrounding trees offer support, providing nourishment through grafted roots and a vast network of fungal connections. Through these connections many beings interact and care for each other. There is a large Douglas fir that stands beside the stump; this great tree, along with the other trees and plants in the forest, keep this stump alive.

When it comes to living and dying, we can take inspiration from the natural world. All ecosystems involve species that depend on each other for health. Wellbeing does not exist in isolation;

it is nurtured by relationships. In the global North, we live in a culture that values individualism, leading to loneliness for many. Many of us struggle to truly connect with others, and lack a sense of belonging. Passivity and neediness—qualities associated with dependency—have negative connotations in this culture. As a result, we have become more isolated and independent, which makes dying harder than it needs to be. The living stump serves as a reminder of the importance of inter-being.

In the deeply nourishing book *The Wild Edge of Sorrow: Rituals of Renewal and the Sacred Work of Grief*, Francis Weller writes about the five gates of grief that most modern-day humans walk through. One of these gates is the loss we feel about what we expected when we arrived here, but didn't receive. Weller notes that as humans, we are wired for the rich tribal experience that our deep time ancestors had—we are wired for village life, to be in community with others. He suggests that we are designed to wake up in the morning to forty pairs of eyes greeting us and asking us what we dreamt about. Weller believes that the lack of this tribal experience has caused an aching that echoes in our bodies; we are haunted by what we didn't know to name but isn't there. Weller insists we have always been communal, and that we need each other to live fully.

We are social beings who come into this world dependent on others, and we are called to soften into the idea of leaving the same way. When people die slowly, there is a gradual loss of control over the body—it becomes weaker and weaker, and stops its many functions. In the end, most people are unable to feed themselves or use the bathroom independently. It is uncomfortable to confront this reality, so we often avoid it. Most people don't plan for dependency or the vulnerabilities that come with it. Dying is a time when we are called to lean on others—accepting support and connection from those around us.

The gateway of wisdom reminds you to honour your own needs as a caregiver. Without attending to yourself, you won't be able to care for your person effectively. Wisdom nudges you to slow down and listen to what you need to be well. This is the golden thread woven throughout this book—that listening is love. It is only when you tend to your own needs, an act of self-love, can you offer a depth of care and true presence to others.

Studies have shown that accepting help from others through social connection leads to a significantly increased chance of longevity. Leaning out on others strengthens the immune system and speeds up recovery from disease faster. People who feel more connected to others also have lower levels of depression and anxiety, they feel more empathy, report higher levels of self-esteem, and are shown to be more connected to others. Because of these positive traits, people are more inclined to want to connect with individuals who are socially robust, so in this way social bonding works as a positive feedback loop.

Accepting support from others may feel edgy. If your person is private by nature, independent, or strongly identifies with the role of helper, it may be challenging for them to lean out for support when it is needed. People typically die as they have lived, and we must always meet individuals where they are and adjust care appropriately.

Keep in mind that having a web of support in place for your person does not negate responsibility. Dependance on others can be difficult, as it often brings up a sense of lost control and helplessness, feelings that most of us in this culture have spent our lifetime turning away from. Encourage your person to maintain as much independance as possible, allowing them to do as much for themselves as they are able. Autonomy is paramount—follow your person's lead and involve them in decision making when possible. When self-determination is honoured, the sense of helplessness is diminished.

> *ME: Sometimes, when things are hardest, it feels like Creator's not listening.*
>
> *OLD WOMAN: Creator can do whatever Creator chooses. When we are in doubt or confusion or fear, She could send us thunderbolts or lightning or a huge pile of unexpected cash. But most of the time, she sends people. People are the miracles that emerge from the ripped and worn pattern of your life and help you stitch it back together. You learn to see the pattern better then.*
>
> —Richard Wagamese, Embers

STORIES FROM THE TRAIL

Accepting support: When it feels easier to say no

Accepting help is not always easy. Often, the reasons we give—though completely valid—can also serve as barriers that keep us from receiving the care we need. Do you relate to the sentiments in this email I received from a client? He had been caring for his wife at home for over a year and he was frayed. Leaning out for the support he needed was challenging.

Hi Tracy,

I've been thinking about you lately and wondering why I haven't reached out. Here are the reasons (or maybe excuses?) I've come up with:

1. *I never seem to have time to myself.*
2. *It's too overwhelming to talk about.*
3. *I don't like how I'm feeling about this situation.*
4. *I'm angry that she might live forever, and as a result, my life is ruined (not thoughts I'm proud of).*
5. *When I do get time to myself, I just want quiet.*

Possible solution: I could call during my morning dog walk one day… (at least I'm looking for a solution!).

Have to run to physio, but I'm grateful for the chance to put this out there. And thank you for your patience. I do find some time for myself—at the gym, the pool, or tennis but I always have to come home…

—Stan

It may take a little courage to receive relief. Consider leaning out on others—you don't have to journey alone.

Where Can You Find the Gateway of Wisdom?

Often when we ask for help, we may feel selfish or as though we are asking too much of others. However, there are many people eager to lend a hand, though they often go unnoticed. They may hesitate to offer assistance, fearing they'll come across as too pushy. Perhaps there is the assumption that the person in need may value privacy, or already has enough support.

Most of the time, help is given only after a direct request, a reminder that people need explicit information about what is required. A direct request removes any uncertainties. Asking for support gives others to the chance to show kindness and it nourishes social connections. You might find it helpful to ask for support around the home, running errands, or simply for companionship. When we allow ourselves to soften and be vulnerable, it creates a connection. Both the giver and the receiver benefit from interdependency. Letting someone help is a gift.

Strong social connections tend to be more common in rural areas. People may also benefit from membership of spiritual groups, interest groups, and sports teams. These communities often come alongside to assist when a crisis occurs. The strength of a person's web of social support is a reliable indicator of how well they navigate stressful life experiences.

It can be helpful to think ahead about who you can lean out on for support. Think of those around you and the strengths and skills they have. The goal is to bolster the web of support for you and your person, doing what you can to ensure that it is balanced and strong.

I WONDER . . .

Sustaining your role as caregiver

As the caregiver, it is protective to be introspective, taking time to reflect on your personality and support sytem. Below are some questions to guide this reflection:

- What is your coping style?
- What are your support systems?
- Who or what can you lean out on?
- Who or what do you want to avoid?
- It can be helpful to consider how you have responded to challenges in the past. Are you resilient, or do you require more support in challenging situations?
- What are your boundaries?
- How do you see your boundaries affecting your role as care provider to your person?
- It can be helpful to take some time to listen in and tune in to your body as well. What is it telling you?

Go slow and listen—your innate wisdom will guide you to the most supportive ways to care for yourself along the journey.

GROUNDING PRACTICES

Weaving a resilient web of support for your person

Consider following your person's lead in gathering support where it's needed. You might find it helpful to guide them through an inventory of the qualities in those around them, helping to identify who can offer the right kind of support at different times.

- Who is the most rational?
- Who can watch the kids?
- Who is the best listener?
- Who will sleep on the couch?
- Who will help to navigate the healthcare system?
- Who will respond swiftly in an emergency?
- Who can sort through belongings?
- Who will help with the cleaning?
- Who can crack a joke?
- Who can drive the kids to school and activities?
- Who will be honest?
- Who will notice when you are struggling?
- Who will join you for a walk?
- Who will answer the phone at 3 a.m.?
- Who can offer a prayer?
- Who is likely to share a poem?

For some people on the end-of-life journey it can be easier to accept the unconditional support of animals. I have witnessed firsthand the comfort offered by the companionship of pets and it is powerful medicine for the dying and their people. In addition to bringing joy, the presence of animals has been found to reduce blood pressure, decrease physical pain, ease mental suffering, increase social interaction, decrease boredom, and reduce anxiety. Animals are also masters of holding space.

Peer support groups can also be a great support by normalizing and validating the experience of both those living with a life-limiting illness and their caregivers. These groups create connections with others who are going through similar challenges and allow individuals to share experiences, providing an opportunity to be completely honest about what is going on. Caregiver support groups can be a lifeline. These groups are usually centred around creating space for sharing as opposed to fixing or counseling. They are often offered on a drop-in basis with no obligation to attend. You can investigate what is available where you live or search for a group online. There is solace in knowing you are not alone.

Keep in mind that there is such a thing as too much help—your person may feel overwhelmed if too many well-meaning people participate in providing care. This seems to be more common as people journey closer to death. People seem to cocoon inward and desire less and less company. Usually at the very end, there is a small intimate group of individuals at the bedside.

If you sense that your person is becoming overwhelmed by the number of people offering care, it may be appropriate to advocate for them by limiting contact. Perhaps there is a friend or family member who excels in management skills? You can consider appointing such a person to coordinate care and serve as a gatekeeper, someone to advocate for the dying by honouring their need for privacy, and waning energy levels.

With this team-based approach it is helpful to understand that each individual will respond to the challenges of caregiving in their own unique way. This will be influenced by their intimacy to your person as well as how they have handled crisis in the past. Personalities intensify when situations become challenging, so do what you can to keep communication open and listen. There is no need for everyone to be in agreement—simply feeling seen and heard will help everyone involved, diffusing most heated situations. Whatever you and your family and friends are going through on the end-of-life journey is completely normal. Knowing that there are resources to lean out on, and being open to accepting help, will support everyone involved.

Becoming a companion is not a role that most people imagine, dream of, or prepare for. Yet eventually, nearly everyone is drafted into this role, and through the journey is deeply changed by it. The role of companion is all encompassing and touches all aspects of our lives. Caregivers are often not trained for the practical tasks that are asked of them such as administering medication, inserting catheters, and tending to bed sores. These tasks are expected to be done while carrying the big feelings that come with grief for all that has been lost, and all that is about to be lost. Leaning out on others will support you to sustain your role as companion. Consider outsourcing tasks where possible by accepting help with cleaning, groceries, and other errands required for daily living.

End-of-life doulas offer personalized, non-medical support to the dying and their people, serving as a companion along the end-of-life journey, seeking to fill the gaps in care. The end-of-life doula movement is rooted in building greater understanding, skills, and competency around death within communities. A supportive doula understands that friends and family are the most important members of the palliative care team, and they do what they can to empower those closest to the dying to step in and provide supportive care. There is often a steep learning curve after a life-limiting diagnosis, and caregivers can benefit from the guidance of those who have walked the path before. Doulas are familiar with the signs of normal dying and share information to prepare people for what to expect.

Doulas can offer education about end-of-life options, support decision making, co-create rituals, advocate for wishes, and model care. They help normalize the experience and encourage people to be gentle with themselves, and to be honest about what they need to be well.

The word doula is of Greek origin, meaning female servant. Today, the word often refers to those who provide physical, emotional, and spiritual guidance through a significant experience. Service is imbued with humility, it is about trusting that the dying intuitively know how to play out the dying role. Service is built on a relationship between equals, fostering a sense of gratitude for the opportunity to serve and be served. Showing up this way is not draining; it is generative. Approaching care with the doula heart, rooted in service, is available to all.

Each doula has a unique community of practice made up of a variety of individuals and organizations that offer a variety of services. Doulas work alongside friends and family, medical professionals, homecare organizations, hospice outreach programs, massage therapists, energy healers, support groups, naturopaths, estate lawyers, counsellors, other doulas, care aides, spiritual advisors, funeral directors, and more. If you hire a doula, ensure that their personal values are aligned with yours and are reflected in the services that they offer.

If you are considering working with an end-of-life doula, start by asking trusted acquaintances, or browse a local or national directory. Most doulas offer a free 30-minute intake interview to assess needs and compatibility. If both parties agree to move forward, there is a conversation about hopes, fears, and goals, and a personalized plan is created. Once the support begins the plan remains flexible—the journey is unpredictable and needs can often change. Doulas walk alongside and companion the dying and their people as the end-of-life journey progresses. The role takes inspiration from the archetype of the wise guide, or sage, offering wisdom or counsel and support; with the understanding that the central person is capable and ultimately completes their journey on their own.

Consider reaching out to a doula before the feelings of overwhelm and exhaustion set in. It is easier for people to consider end-of-life wishes and plan while they have clarity and energy. It always seems too early until it is too late.

It is important that caring for your person doesn't take priority over listening to yourself and recognizing your own needs. You can't offer sustained support to others if you are not properly resourced and taking care of yourself. A holistic approach to self-care is essential in supporting you. Most of us will agree that it is healthy practice to eat more fruits and vegetables and less processed sugar. We are familiar with the importance of a restful sleep, staying hydrated, and moving the body. It may be news to some that social connection is just as critical for our wellbeing.

Healthy boundaries are an important consideration as well. Clearly communicating your boundaries to others isn't always easy but this practice will support you to remain open-hearted and generous. Boundaries are defined by what's okay with you and what is not okay with you. Simply state your boundary by communicating your needs as opposed to directing the behavior of others. Perhaps you need a change of scenery or a break from mundane burdens such as doing the dishes or weeding the garden. Honouring yourself will allow you to sustain supportive care.

Nourishing self-care requires you to slow down and listen to your needs. It is as simple as asking what it would look like to be kind to yourself today. Engage in activities that bring you joy, pleasure, presence, comfort, or rest. Acknowledge all that you do and make time to connect with and express your emotions.

GROUNDING PRACTICES

No-self self-care

Take some time to consider the deep connection practices that support you—places, people, and activities that invite you into an experience where self becomes fluid and interconnected. These practices shift feelings of isolation to a sense of interbeing.

- How can you care for yourself in ways that honor your interconnectedness?
- What makes you feel most awake, alive, and connected?
- What brings you into gratitude?
- What brings you into a sense of deep belonging?
- What awakens in you a longing to care for all beings

I WONDER . . .

Essential questions to ask when choosing an end-of-life doula

Doulas are either hired by the friends and family, or by the dying person directly. Here are some questions to guide you in finding the doula that is just right for you:

- What inspired you to become an end of life doula?
- What services to you offer?
- How do you approach emotional, spiritual, and physical support for those who are dying and their families?
- How do you collaborate with other care providers, such as family members and hospice teams?
- What is your availability, and how do you handle emergencies or unexpected changes in schedule?
- What is your fee structure?
- Do you provide ongoing support for families after the death has occurred?

These questions are a helpful starting point for choosing a doula who aligns with your person's values, needs, and vision.

As disease progresses, there are always unanswered questions. Doulas serve to find answers or hold space for wondering; the goal is to be like water and flow to where the need is. Doulas walk alongside clients through whole journey, not just on the worn path—what we know and can predict—but also through the wilderness, the off-trail parts of the end-of-life journey where there is no clear path and no trail markers in sight.

Doulas have a unique split focus advantage. While their primary focus is on the dying person, who is the most important, they also observe and support friends and family. There is great value to having the support of a neutral presence to normalize the journey and gently guide the dying and their people along the way.

CAMPP: CONNECTION, AWARENESS, MEANING, PLEASURE, PRESENCE

Doula support: Ongoing and holistic

Doulas can companion people before, during, and after a death. Here is a snapshot of the scope of practice:

- Offering holistic end-of-life planning
- Facilitating conversations that invite reflection on beliefs, values, and wishes
- Providing referrals and raising awareness of therapeutic supports within communities
- Offering emotional, practical, and spiritual support
- Advocating to help realize the end-of-life goals
- Supporting the strengthening and completion of relationships
- Assisting with legacy projects
- Sitting vigil at the bedside
- Facilitating home funerals
- Offering respite to family and friends
- Community care through conversations that familiarize people with death and normalize this inevitable experience

GROUNDING PRACTICES

Anchored in stillness

Consider a contemplative practice. This can be as simple as intentionally slowing down. Perhaps you choose to start your day by sitting and just noticing the morning. Don't bring a book, don't bring your phone, don't try to be or do anything, simply notice where you are—the birds, the sky, your mood. Just let thoughts come and go.

The grief storms of the end-of-life journey ask for a slower pace—space for you to keep up with the many losses as they arise. From this place of presence, you are invited into a deeper intimacy with life. As you cultivate a closer connection with yourself, you become able to offer a deeper intimacy to others. There can be a lot to do on the end-of-life journey. As a companion, you will likely find yourself advocating, learning, filling out forms, checking boxes, and planning. However, the pace and space through which you offer and guidance, even in the more pragmatic aspects of the journey, will be supported by a contemplative practice helping you to show up steadier, less reactive, and more intentional

EXPECTED CHANGES ON THE JOURNEY

Ring theory

Psychologist Susan Silk and her friend Barry Goldman provide valuable insights into how to give and receive support in a crisis. In an article published in the Los Angeles Times, Silk and Goldman propose the Ring Theory. The idea is represented by a set of concentric rings, like the pattern that is created when you toss a stone into water. Your person who is living with a life-limiting illness is in the very centre of the circles. Closest family and friends are in the next ring out—these are the people who are in the trenches and impacted day-to-day by the crisis. The next ring out represents other friends and family. In rings radiating further out represent extended community, more distant friends, and work colleagues.

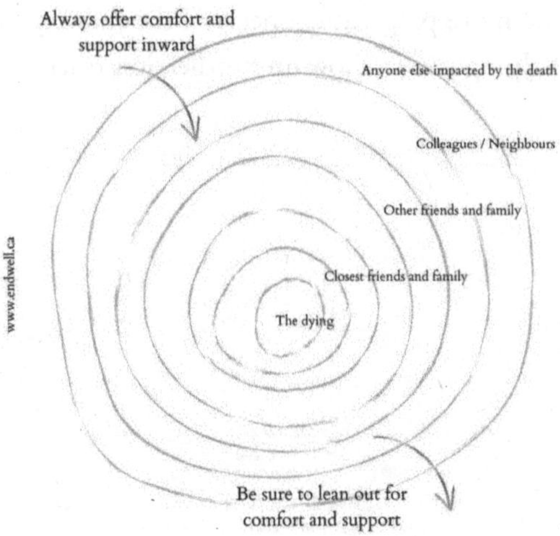

The theory guides people to direct support inward, taking cues from those in need. Support and comfort can be practical acts such as picking up children from school, dropping off meals, or walking the dog. Appropriate emotional support is almost always simply listening. If you do speak, do so with the intention to offer comfort. Keep in mind that giving advice is not comforting unless it is requested. The goal of offering support is to let others know they are understood and not alone.

If you feel the need to cry or vent or express your emotions, that's perfectly okay, just make sure to lean on someone in a larger ring than your own. Silk and Goldman stress the importance of comforting in, and dumping out—offering support to others while ensuring you have a safe space to release your own feelings. According to this theory, your person in the center is to be completely protected, and exclusively receive comfort. In their dying, they are the most important person, and they are to be guarded from the troubles of others.

The Ring Theory can be applied to any crisis, offering valuable insight into how to give and receive support. It emphasizes that caregiving can only be sustained through reciprocity, where both the caregiver and the one receiving care are nourished and supported in return. We will all find ourselves in the centre of the rings at different times throughout our lives. We can prepare to do this well by softening to receiving support now. We can begin by asking for help when needed it and leaning out on others with grace.

GROUNDING PRACTICES

Weaving a web of support

As a companion to the dying, you can draw a series of concentric rings and begin to write down the names of all of the people who are supporting you as a caregiver. Are you feeling supported enough? Does your web reflect the reality that dying is a social event? Are your needs being met? Is there anyone you could bring in to bolster your web of support, who can offer help for specific things so that you can sustain your role by caring for yourself?

At the end of life, a web of support can include friends and family as well as members of the palliative care team that provide parallel care. Palliative care is holistic care that includes anyone who offers support including, nurses, care aides, doctors, doulas, music therapists, physiotherapists, dieticians, energy medicine healers, plant medicine practitioners, social workers, counselors, and many others. Varied spiritual guidance is available as many houses of worship offer programs and counseling. Secular practices such as meditation and yoga both in the community or online can also bring peace and perspective.

Your person's web of support depends on the amount of care needed and the desire for help. This is determined by personality and level of comfort with receiving assistance. It is also dependent on the care available in the community. Your person may need a bit of encouragement to reach out; you can encourage your person to receive support by sharing that most people want to help.

Dr. Kristen Neff is a pioneer in the field of self-compassion, teaching skills for daily life, skills that are rooted in being gentle and kind to yourself. Neff believes that having compassion for yourself means that you honour and accept your humanness and acknowledge that things will not always go your way. You will encounter frustrations, losses will occur, you will make mistakes, bump up against your limitations, and fall short of your ideals. This is the human condition, a reality shared by everyone. Neff encourages folks to open their hearts to these truths. This compassionate approach will enable you to feel more compassion, not only for yourself, but for your fellow humans as well.

The gateway of wisdom reminds you to attune to your inner wisdom, and your intuition will guide you to ask yourself questions about how you can find support in your role as companion. This requires listening to your heart as opposed to your head.

In Western culture we are not often guided to seek out this inner wisdom. Answers from the heart are simple and direct and yet there is a deep knowing that comes when this wisdom presents itself. The heart is not just an organ of emotion, but the most important sense we have—a muscle of perception that can be awakened. Indigenous cultures have long understood the wisdom the heart offers. By tuning into the present moment and feeling it through the heart, we allow ourselves to truly sense what's around us. In awakening our heart sense, we open to the flow of wisdom that connects us to all things. You will not be able to control the trajectory of your person's disease but you can control your experience of the journey as a companion, and your heart will be your most reliable compass.

As you consider people and activities that nourish you, honour how companioning the dying affects your whole self, your body, mind, and spirit. Hold a deep reverence for the sacredness of dying and the intensity involved in caring for the dying; consider what you can do to intentionally shift the focus away from the realm of death and back into the wonder of living. Simply participating in ordinary life can be supportive. Spend time with your favourite people, eat the foods you love, and participate in activities that fill you up. Loving touch can often bring comfort. Ordinary life can remind you that the wonder of life is here, now.

I WONDER . . .

Engaging intentionally in ordinary life as an act of self-care

What people, pets, places, or activities bring you comfort? Why not pick up the phone and make a date to spend time with your favourite people? Maybe take a trip to the grocery store or your favourite cafe so you can enjoy the foods you love? What activities truly fill you up? Can you make arrangements to do what you love to do?

You likely already engage in activities that support and sustain you—you can make a list and start there. Attuning to your needs will guide you to refresh yourself when you need a break.

Cicero called gratitude the parent of all other virtues. The simple yet profound act of gratitude can offer hope, support, and protection when experiencing loss. Consider keeping a gratitude journal to remind yourself of what brings you joy—a smile, a joke, the light filtering through the trees, a bird singing, a hot cup of tea. Grateful people are happier, healthier, and experience less stress. As a caregiver, it is best practice to find balance by holding grief and gratitude simultaneously.

When There are Gaps in the Gateway of Wisdom

Culture and individual personality will determine the degree of social connection that is supportive in life, including death. If your person is independent and values privacy, be sure to support them appropriately by honouring these traits and taking the time to consider how this will impact their final days. Due to the lack of community, end-of-life care in dominant culture today and the predominance of the outsourcing of care, people often lean out on hired help, or distant family or acquaintances. This may feel uncomfortable for you or your person if they are introverted or independent.

We know that social connection is necessary for health and survival, yet social connectedness is at an all-time low. This increase in isolation is serious as loneliness represents one of the leading reasons people seek psychological counseling. According to Health Canada's fifth annual report on medical assistance in dying, nearly half of non-terminally ill Canadians who chose euthanasia cited loneliness as a reason.

Interestingly, social connection has more to do with one's felt sense of belonging rather than their actual number of friends. A person could have 200 friends and still feel disconnected, yet another could have no close acquaintances and still feel very connected from within. This sense of connection creates belonging which is protective.

As mentioned earlier, people generally die the way they live; gentle-natured people usually become quieter, while private people in life will likely seek a discreet death; deeply caring people show increased concern for those around them; busy people get busier; controlling people often attempt to stay in charge, trying even harder as their bodies fail them; and angry people may become more intense and difficult. It is normal to progress through life using our behaviour patterns and coping mechanisms that we have turned to in times of stress in the past.

I WONDER . . .

Self-reflection questions about preparing for the journey

Not knowing what lies ahead can be unsettling and worrisome. You may have questions about practical things, like how to acquire equipment for the home such as hospital beds or wheelchairs, how to administer medications, or how to best make arrangements with a funeral home. You may wonder how the disease will progress, how long your person may live, and what you can expect to see. You may wonder whether you are able to continue care at home, or whether you need to consider inpatient palliative care or hospice care. Contact your local community support to seek information and resources. It can be helpful to have a roadmap for the disease—understanding the big picture view will likely offer you some sure footing. Like all journeys, it is wise to plan for both the expected and the unexpected.

Think about what you are hoping for in the coming weeks and months. What information would be most helpful to you at this time? Are there things you will want to know in the future? Would you be supported by seeking legal support, or the help of a local funeral director, or… ?

STORIES FROM THE TRAIL

Continuity of care in a siloed system: The quiet strength of doula support

I had the privilege of supporting a young man dying of a brain tumour. He sought every treatment available to him—radiation, surgeries, chemotherapy—and in doing so, became surrounded by a remarkable and vast team of healthcare providers.

He received care at home, where a number of different nurses and care aides would arrive each day. He travelled multiple times a week to the Cancer Agency. There, a radiation specialist, oncologist, and a team of compassionate professionals supported him alongside his local oncologist, family doctor, and therapist.

Eventually, when it became clear that the treatments were no longer helping, he was referred to hospice for comfort-focused care. The hospice was extraordinary and filled with caring people: social workers, counsellors, spiritual care providers, a music therapist, and even a pet therapist. Volunteers came in daily. A private physiotherapist and palliative massage therapist was brought into the web of support as well. Nurses and care aides rotated through, and the palliative physicians worked in one-week shifts, returning every five weeks. This man was held by so many hands and so many hearts.

This is what we hope for: a full, well-resourced community surrounding someone at the end of life. But even in this privileged scenario, with such deep and broad support, there were cracks.

Each new caregiver required an emotional investment. Each shift brought someone new who needed to learn the story, build trust, and understand the family's values and goals. The system, though abundant in services, was still fragmented and siloed.

And through it all, I was there. From the moment I was invited in, three months before his death, until the moment he took his last breath—and beyond, as grief enveloped his friends and family—I remained a constant. I was available in person, by phone, by text. I did my best to hold space and create a container for both him and his family. I offered information and options. I witnessed, validated, and normalized the experience and offered a steadiness through my grounded presence.

In a sea of changing faces and shifting schedules, it was my goal to be a calm, neutral presence. One who walks alongside. One who listens deeply. One who remembers the whole story when others may only hold a piece.

Continuity of care doesn't always come from the system. Sometimes, it comes from a single person showing up with their whole heart—again and again.

We are born into the arms of many, and we deserve to be held by many as we leave. In a system where care often shifts and fragments, doulas help weave the through-line—a presence who gently remembers and bears witness. Not to fix, but to companion. To remind the dying and their people that they are not alone, even in the most uncertain moments.

STORIES FROM THE TRAIL

Facilitating a home death

Jane was completely preoccupied with worry. She was experiencing some changes in her health that her doctor couldn't explain. She had cancer a decade before, and she was worried that it had returned. I sensed her anxiety and fear when we first spoke over the phone.

She explained that her family lived on the other side of the country—she had never married, never had children; she was new to her community and had only a handful of acquaintances.

Jane was very clear about what mattered most. She loved spending time in nature.

Due to her quiet and reserved nature, she was terrified of getting sick and being cared for by strangers who were not aware of her preferences. The thought of dying unsupported left her sleepless. On our first visit I reassured her that we could plan with her current situation and bolster her web of support to do our best to ensure her end-of-life wishes would be upheld.

A big focus of her end-of-life planning was creating a web of support. With the understanding that it would take many to help her to die in her home, we worked together to build a web of support. I introduced Jane to another end-of-life doula, a palliative care physician who lived nearby offered home visits, and a homecare nursing support company. She wanted her care circle to be intimate, and to have a clear understanding of her wishes.

We spent hours together planning for her journey—by the end, all the boxes were checked. She had considered her beliefs, values, and wishes; appointed a representative; engaged in conversations with those closest to her about her plan; and had the appropriate legal paperwork in place. "You have no idea what this means to me," she said. "I can't even tell you how relieved I am to have this planning done. I can now sleep at night."

Jane understood that end-of-life plans are like birth plans—they do not come with guarantees. Nonetheless, contemplating her eventual end-of-life journey and feeling held by those in her web of support brought her comfort. She was relieved knowing that when her health status eventually changed, she was likely to get the care she hoped to receive from the people she had chosen to support her.

STORIES FROM THE TRAIL

Community care

When Andrew received a life-limiting diagnosis his web of support was already in place. He had close connections with his family, work colleagues, neighbours, and had an extended community made up of relationships he had established through living and raising his kids in a close-knit town. A robust web joined together to support him and his closest people.

This group was especially well organized as one close family friend had a passion for service and exceptional planning skills. She got things done! Throughout his treatment, which involved surgery, radiation, and chemotherapy, the kids were shuttled to and from school and activities, and meals were dropped off five nights a week. The dog was walked, and some folks stepped up to drive Andrew across town to his various doctors' appointments. A couple of neighbours who enjoyed gardening stopped by unannounced and tidied up the yard. It was a beautiful example of a village stepping up and stepping in at a time of need.

All this help wasn't easy for Andrew's wife to receive in the beginning. She was an independent, hard-working, family-centred woman. But with caring for her two young boys, managing Andrew's appointments, and adjusting to good days and bad days, she began to feel frayed. As time passed, Andrew became increasingly more dependent on her, nudging her to lean out for support from others. Gradually, she accepted more and more help and was held by the web of support surrounding her and her family.

Witnessing this little community rallying around Andrew was a heart-expanding example of people coming together to help when help was needed most. Andrew died just after Christmas that year. We organized a beautiful candlelight ceremony to honour his life and death and the community that supported him. It was apparent that everyone in Andrew's web of care was changed by showing up for Andrew and his family. The community connections were deepened by the call of service. Andrew's story is a testament to the idea that death can be community-building when we open ourselves to compassionate action. There is such a yearning for this village-like way of living and dying, and service is an opportunity to create these connections.

Dying asks for collectivism. This can be a challenge for many since almost everything in this culture is framed for the individual. Dying asks us to consider a new way of being, based on the values of connection and community. This involves relearning for many, and remembering how to lean out on each other.

To die well, we must practice receiving from others—a vulnerability that is often undervalued in our dominant culture. You can begin this practice today by making a simple, direct request, like asking someone to help you open a door or fasten a necklace clasp. These small acts of receiving care will serve you when the time comes for you to be in the centre of those concentric rings, held by others.

Human beings have an inherent need for one another. We are being called to rethink our understanding of community, shifting from closed protectionism to an openness and an embrace of others. In nature, communities of diverse organisms live together in ways that support both the individual and the entire system. As these systems form, new capabilities and strengths emerge from the interconnectedness. They remind us of our innate desire for community. Writer and teacher Stephen Jenkinson agrees; he believes the essence of a good death is that it be a village-making event. "That is what dying asks of us. To construct a village where none has been before."

GROUNDING PRACTICES

Caring for yourself by leaning out on others

- How can you care for yourself while caring for another?
- What three things would be most helpful to you at this time?
- Think about ways your family, friends, or neighbours could support you; for example, doing errands and practical chores, or offering respite.
- What would a mini-rest or break look like to you right now?

GROUNDING PRACTICES

Connect with your heart's wisdom

If you slow down and listen, your heart will guide you to what you need to be well. Take a moment to settle in. Feel your feet on the floor and your body making contact with the seat of your chair. Look around wherever you are, right, left, up, down—and notice your surroundings.

Become aware of your breathing, just normal breathing. When you feel settled, tune in to your heart space. It may be helpful to place your hand over your heart. What is arising from your heart? Is your heart calling you to care for yourself in a certain way in this moment? Your body is so wise, and your heart will never lead you astray. Your heart is wise, kind, and clear.

Is your heart guiding you to spend time in nature? Light a candle? Call a friend? Have a good cry?

Can you find ways to talk about your experience of being a caregiver? Are there caregiver support organizations in your community? Are you feeling lonely or isolated? Can you think of a friend, a neighbour, or another community member that you can talk to?

I WONDER . . .

The realities of a home death

Many people hope to die at home, yet only a small percentage of deaths actually occur there. Most people die in hospitals, hospices, and nursing homes, which can be a mixed blessing; dying at home is possible but it is much more complicated than many people think.

It is important that we watch our biases. It is not uncommon to associate good deaths with home deaths, but you can have a really good death in a hospital and a bad death at home.

Most of us today do not live in big houses with extended families like we used to when home deaths were commonplace. Back in the days when death happened in the home by default, folks were more equipped to facilitate a death. The way we live has changed so much in the last hundred years. Take a moment to consider what a home death would look like in an apartment with nobody around at night.

If you are companioning someone who is planning on dying at home, here are some important questions to consider:

- Do you have access to the required equipment, such as a hospital bed, wheelchair, and commode?
- Who can order the equipment?
- Will the equipment fit in the home?
- Will your person be able to access the bathroom?
- What are your person's wishes around privacy?
- Who can be there to help, and what is each person on the care team prepared to do?
- How will your person access medications?
- Who will support your person with buying and preparing food?
- Who will help with laundry?

Dying is an intimate affair. Modesty tends to go out the window. Relatives and close friends may be doing most of the personal care. This requires emotional stability and physical strength.

Consider what it would look like if you were providing care to your person at home and your person became:

- confused
- emotionally distressed
- agitated
- restless
- at risk of bleeding
- at risk of having a fall
- incontinent of urine and stool.

If homecare is offered, it is important to get clear on how many hours of care can be provided. As your person becomes more reliant on care, every other hour of care required must be coordinated by friends and family.

Dying in care is in no way a failure. There are so many needs on the end-of-life journey. Your person will be supported in being kept clean, with pain control, and possibly in other holistic comfort measures depending on the facility. This team-based approach will allow you and others to be present to companion and support unmet needs. Being there—in the role of friend, child, sibling, or partner—to offer your presence is such a generous offering. It is what matters most.

Cohesive family care starts with communication, and good communication requires time, honest discussion, respect, and agreements about ways to make decisions. While it may seem easier to deal with this situation on your own, to hide your thoughts and feelings, or to protect other family members from the worry, this will likely not serve you well.

Resentment can build when people are excluded or ill-informed, making it more challenging to work together. Finding nourishing ways to communicate with one another will support everyone involved. Sharing thoughts and feelings can ease one's sorrow and lighten the sense of being isolated and alone. However, these are not always easy conversations.

Involving others in tasks, sharing information, and making decisions together can ease the burden and lead to more supportive planning. Don't forget to relate to each other naturally. Be how you have always been—continue to reminisce about the past, do the things you like to do together, and talk about upcoming events—and this will serve to nurture and normalize family life.

Chapter 11

Approaching the End of the Journey

> *"We must look deeply in order to see and understand the needs, aspirations and suffering of the person we love. This is the ground of real love."*
>
> *—Thich Nhat Hanh*

Meeting Your Person Where They Are

The heart-first role of companion is rooted in stillness, curiosity, and following the lead of others. It's about honouring silence, witnessing struggle, offering presence, and accepting the unpredictable nature of the journey. In essesence it is about recognizing the value of your true presence and acknowledging that you are enough.

This approach deepens connection and cohesion not just with ourselves, but also with friends, family, and within larger systems—whether organizations, corporations, congregations, nations, or the world at large. It also strengthens our bond to the more-than-human world, linking us to past beings, present beings, and future beings. When we tend to our own wellbeing and consider how to be well in an unwell culture—by slowing down, tuning in, and remembering—we naturally find ourselves called to service. This leads to gratitude and with it, a lightness of being. This is exactly what the world is asking for—and has always needed—now more than ever.

In this guide we have considered some complicated questions to reveal some simple answers. As a companion, having an open mind and an open heart will serve you well. We explored the importance of this topic and considered why dying has become complicated. Our distancing from death in this culture makes dying harder than it needs to be. This guide aims to help shift this reality a bit.

System-wide change is complicated, and it happens very slowly; however, as individuals, we can make a difference now. Cultural regeneration is possible when enough people hold new narratives, but this requires buy-in from people of all ages. It is reassuring to see the ways in which we meet death shifting—the upcoming generations are listening and acquainting themselves with death. More and more, people are getting curious about this natural human experience; they are taking courses, reading, and attending death cafes—gatherings where people come together to talk openly about death and dying, usually over coffee, tea, and cake, to normalize conversations about death and to reflect on their mortality. Change happens one person at a time until there is a tipping point. These small acts, what I refer to as "ripples,"can create great change.

Showing up for your person and offering meaningful personalized support is an act of community care that that can bloom alongside the healthcare system. In this book, we have considered that the senses are a good place to start. The gateways of the senses—seeing, hearing, smelling, tasting, touching, as well as wonder and wisdom—can be considered as openings to moments of connection, awareness, meaning, pleasure, and presence.

The End of the Journey

When it became clear that my friend Linda was at the end of her journey, I was so grateful to have this book project on the go to guide me. It served to anchor me when I was grieving and slammed with disbelief. This book reminded me how to show up. I supported Linda's people to seek opportunities to find life in the time she had left. The waypoints of the expected physical, emotional, social, and spiritual changes were like the little coloured markers nailed to the trees on hiking trails, reassuring us that we weren't lost. Just like the coordinates that she charted for us a few months before as we hiked the West Coast Trail, these waypoints supported us to stay present and keep walking forward with her.

We helped Linda keep up with the many losses that accumulated along the way. She took the lead and expressed many of her needs and we did our best to fulfill her requests. Tears and anger were sometimes all she could muster up. Her dying role was honoured and she was able to share her experience and express her emotions to the people around her—her wife, her friends, her family, doctors, nurses, a spiritual care advisor, a social worker, and volunteers. I did my best to support those in the rings closest to Linda by normalizing the journey, modelling care, all the while allowing my soft heart be my compass. The senses served as a starting point, as a way to care for Linda.

Linda resisted being at the centre—right up until her last moments Linda was fixated on how to make the journey as easeful as possible for her loving partner. She wanted her to be okay more than anything else. Linda went as far as to create a binder labelled "When the Shit Gets Real." She hired someone to help her wife navigate the business side of death after she was gone, and she asked me to help her write a letter for her wife, one that would offer support when she was struggling with grief. The note contained the names of people and suggestions for activities to offer comfort after her death.

Near the end of her journey, Linda's disease progressed to the point where simply speaking was exhausting. One day, she urgently put her finger up in the air. Our eyes met, and she looked at me desperately. She struggled to speak, yet forced out the words, "There is something that we forgot to mention in the book." Being a tech expert, it was, ironically, technology. Linda shared that when she was admitted to the hospital for what would be the last time, she realized that the most important item she grabbed from home was her cell phone. This little device held her treasured photos—a life review of sorts, it represented connection to her people by way of messaging and phone calls. It connected her to the entire world, offering her answers to the questions that would arise, and it played music that offered comfort and joy. For her, it provided the perfect distraction when the reality of her situation became too much to bear.

In her last days, Linda's heart of service led her to design a washable cloth phone pouch that could be attached to the rails of hospital beds. This simple and thoughtful invention allowed people to keep their phones close and prevent them from sliding off the bed. I have initiated this project at the hospice where I volunteer, and where Linda died. Even in her final days Linda was thinking of others and driven to find solutions and make a difference, just as she always had.

The day she was admitted to hospice, I spent time preparing her room for her arrival. Drawing on the guidance shared in this book, I turned to the the senses as a starting point, offering intentional invitations designed to create connection, awareness, meaning, pleasure, and presence—I wanted to direct her focus to life.

It was December when Linda was admitted to hospice, and she had always loved Christmas. I hung a string of warm white lights around her room and placed a bowl of shiny mandarin oranges on her bedside table. I turned on the nature-sound channel and birdsong gently filled the room. I bought a cuddly caramel-coloured teddy bear with a removable pouch inside that can be warmed up in the microwave and placed back in the bear. When Linda arrived at hospice that evening, she was in a liminal state, almost as though she had one foot in this world and one foot in the next. She looked around the room and smiled gently, remarking that she felt as though she had just checked into a luxury hotel.

In the end, Linda was surrounded by her inner circle—her wife, her brother, and her best friend. Her wife decorated the room with items of meaning that she brought from home. There were photos of her most memorable experiences, favourite people, and her beloved pets. Her dog, Ryder, even came to visit. A few days after her arrival, on her fifty-sixth birthday, hours before her death, there was a a huge whiteboard propped up at the foot of her bed. It was covered in colourful sticky-notes expressing birthday wishes that had been sent in by family, friends, and co-workers. Words of praise, well wishes, and love. What a legacy, evidence of a life well-lived. The board was a display of Linda's unbounded generosity, integrity, and love for the world.

In her last days she continued to be how she always was—thoughtful and generous. The day before she died, I came into her room with my computer in hand. Weeks earlier she had expressed great worry that I didn't have my name and phone number on my computer. Linda's last words to me were "Get a label."

I saw Linda the night she died. Sacred is the most fitting word to describe the feeling of the room. The lighting was dim, her wife sat in a chair beside the bed gently holding her hand and offering words of comfort. The bed was bathed in the soft glow from a lamp that sat on the bedside table. Soothing instrumental music was playing softly. The whiteboard legacy of love was still displayed at the foot of her bed. I could sense that Linda was barely there.

I sat down in a chair beside the bed, touched her hand and gently said, "I couldn't miss the chance to come by and see the birthday girl." Her eyes barely opened but for a moment her gaze met mine. She didn't speak, but she communicated so much before she drifted off. I sat there quietly, telling her how grateful I was to know her, how much I cared for her, and how her partner would be okay. I told her it was okay for her to let go. It was wondrous to me that every few seconds she would break into an enormous smile. I narrated her expression, saying "that's amazing" and "oh wow" as she smiled again, again, and again.

As you walk alongside your person, the path will be unpredictable. It can be steep, gnarly, and wild, and can even completely disappear. Then it can transition into a flat clearly marked route, with no need to watch your step or search for trail markers, only to become rugged and disorienting again. If you look ahead, you will see that there are waypoints in this wilderness to offer reassurance. This path has been traveled countless times before and you are not lost. The best way to ensure that you arrive at the destination in good shape is to slow down, listen deeply to yourself and your person, and use your heart as a compass.

In each moment there is a choice—love or fear. The unknown nature of the end-of-life journey naturally evokes fear, which is truer today more than ever, due to the distancing we have from death. We fear what we do not know. We can tame fear by welcoming it in; fear asks to be acknowledged. It and it shows up right in our face. If we don't do what fear tells us to do—if we can just be with it—it will retreat. While this seems simple, it is an ongoing practice. If we begin this practice now in our day to day lives, it will serve us well in the end.

Love is the capacity to become changed through being in relationships. It is through our senses that we engage with others, using our bodies as a medium for connection. Bodyfulness is the awareness of your body's response to a situation. It is the space where heart wisdom arises —listening with all of our senses. This bodyfulness is similar to mindfulness, but offers a more fluid, dynamic, and relational experience. When we embrace bodyfulness, being present becomes effortless—it simply happens.

By nature, we are loving beings, designed to form connections with others in many ways. Can you feel love working through you?

By showing up with compassionate action, we reconnect with humanity. In a world full of complexity we often search outward for answers, yet everything we need to serve others is already within us.

> *We just need to slow down and tune in. To take a beat. Take a breath.*

Say what is asking to be said and welcome in silence when the conversation moves beyond words. Remind yourself that there is no right or wrong, and that we are only human. Life is wild so death is wild and the journey will unfold. The path becomes more visible the slower you go and the more presence you bring. Follow the lead of your person and remember that the senses are a good starting point; they can serve as a portal to the present moment, to life. It's as simple as grabbing an orange out of the fruit bowl or gathering pieces of the forest on your next walk. Perhaps a song or a soft blanket would bring comfort. Keep listening. The little things matter; let the senses lead to connection, awareness, meaning, pleasure, and presence.

Be normal and show up in the relationship in the way you always have, don't make it weird. This is still your person; this is still life. Welcome in humour. You do not have to say everything is going to be okay. This is not about fixing or tidying up, it is about respecting the wildness of this journey. Seek pleasure, whenever possible, just because.

Slow Down. Allow your person to determine the appropriate direction, the most suitable pace, and when it is time to take a break. Listen. Remember, what you hear depends on what you listen with! You can listen through your mind to understand, you can listen through your heart to feel, or you can access an even deeper level of listening when you listen with all your senses. This will grant you access to the emerging field of the future, a place of grace. Listening with your senses changes you because it connects you to a deeper source—your authentic self responding to the moment.

It takes courage to turn toward beginnings and endings, but these are the moments that make us. There are heaps of sorrow, regret, anger, fear, and loneliness on the end-of-life journey. It takes courage to be present to death. But if you choose to step in, you will also find vivid moments of beauty, joy, healing, and love. We are designed to be with each other through the whole experience of life.

As a culture, our failure to know or embrace death is deeply connected to how estranged we've become from nature, more so than at any other time in human history. If we can turn to the natural world, we can see the cycles and rhythms of all life unfolding uninterrupted. Nature offers inspiration to reconnect with more authentic ways of being. When people face death, everything we thought mattered but doesn't is stripped away. Nature shows us that we can bear death, that the stories that this culture has given us about what is true and valuable are debatable. Go for a walk, look up at the sky. The more-than-human world guides us to what truly matters most which is almost always people, relationships, and love.

At her celebration of life Linda was praised repeatedly for her talents as an engineer, tech executive, mentor, author, and speaker. However, what really is indicative of a life steeped with meaning, is who is around you in the end. Linda was surrounded.

There are aspects of the journey you can control—make a list and take action, just as Linda did. There are also things beyond your control, and for these, you are asked to practice acceptance, stay curious, and be present.

Companioning your person offers a precious opportunity for you to get acquainted with dying. Befriending death helps to reduce fear. I wonder what is being revealed to you by being respectfully curious about death. By staying present with your person on this journey you may gain insight into how to do it well, so that when your own time comes, you can meet your own dying with more understanding and peace.

Show up

The goal here is not perfection. It is not about making everything neat and tidy, or wrapping the experience in a shiny bow. It's about honouring our humanness and showing up with self-compassion.

In the end death will come as it will, just as things are. It's not for us to try to choreograph. However, through companioning you can create a shift—helping your person feel understood and reassuring them that everything they are experiencing is normal. Set your expectations realistically by accepting the imperfect nature of this role. Let go of the idea of a "good death." It's about honouring the messiness of life and death and creating the space to allow for everything to unfold.

It's about love

Companioning is about listening. It's about love. Death is the great reckoning; in its presence all that doesn't matter—the layers and layers of titles, possessions, and sources of identity acquired over a lifetime, the veneer that separates us from who we are and what's important—falls away. When our egos begin to fade away and the to-do list is no longer relevant, what is left? Who are we?

I love the idea that only three things remain after a person dies: what they have taught others, what they have created with their hands, and how much love they have offered the world. So much of your person will remain—in the memories you share and in the grief you carry. Grief is love for what we have lost. By all accounts, this is a book of love.

Maybe loving life to its fullest comes when you understand that you are going to lose everything you care about, and because of this, love it all even more. Death reminds us to invest in what matters most. It guides us to soften to ourselves and others.

I wish you grace, courage, and love as you step in to show up as a companion. May this guide offer comfort and support as you companion, helping to shift the focus from diminishment of death toward what cannot be taken—the connection and love that we have for one another. Love is a bond that is unbreakable in death.

After death

In the moments after death, do your best to stay in grounded your body and present in the moment. Breathe. The shock of the finality of the last breath is disorienting. Take it slow—there's no rush. This is not an emergency. If it feels right, stay with your person and continue to offer companionship. Let your heart wisdom lead the way through this new terrain. Consider simple rituals: speak from the heart, listen to a favourite song, hold hands around the bed, sit in silence, read a prayer, or simply allow yourself to cry, laugh, or carry on. Taking time immediately after death will allow you arrive in this new reality a little more whole. If you are at home, settle in. If you are in a hospital, hospice, or care home, let the staff know you need time and that you will inform them when you are ready to leave.

People who choose to remain with the body often describe the experience as life changing. While it's natural to feel scared or uncertain about how to care for the body, gentle guidance from a doula who is trained in home funerals or other community members, can turn this into a sacred opportunity to offer loving care to your person one last time.

This vigil space after alleviates the sense of helplessness that often arises when a body is taken away too soon. It provides a container where mourning can begin naturally, in community. It allows people to make informed choices that align with their hearts, beliefs, and values, reaffirming that it's natural and healing to be with the dead.

CAMPP: CONNECTION, AWARENESS, MEANING, PLEASURE, PRESENCE

After-death care: You can do it your way

There are many options for after-death care—you can do it your way. It is important to research your provincial or state laws around after-death care. In many areas, it is entirely legal to:

- sew a shroud or build you own coffin
- transport the body with a permit
- keep the body at home for a certain period of time
- wash and dress the body (with someone who is trained)
- use a cardboard coffin or biodegradable shroud for burial or cremation.

After your person dies, your grief response will be unique to you and this loss. In the beginning, lean into anything that offers you rest, comfort, or joy, and keep breathing. Listen to your body, letting it guide you with its wisdom. Surround yourself with people who understand and will support you by letting you know that you are not alone. Know that love continues after death. There is a German word to describe the concept—*Nachliebe*, which combines *nach* (after) and *liebe* (love)—that refers to a love that not only continues but one that can grow, even though your person is not here in the way they were before.

Know that you will be forever changed and integrating this loss will take as long as it needs and be unique to you. Companion yourself in this time of grief, tenderly, give your soft body and broken heart what it is asking for from moment to moment. Honour your own timeline, which may differ greatly from the expectations of those around you.

You may choose to meet the grief-filled days ahead with intention—birthdays, Mother's Day, the death anniversary, and Christmas may be a little easier if met with supportive rituals. Even small acts such as visiting special place, lighting a candle, or wearing a meaningful piece of jewellery will support you through connection. Trust that in time your life will grow around your grief. Your grief won't shrink—how can it? It is love. And with this growing and this passing of time you won't bump up against the jagged edges of your loss as often. New connections will be formed. There is no guarantee this new reality will be better than reality with your person—it will just be different. Grief isn't met well with striving, expectations, or "shoulds." It is wild, so let its feral nature unfold. Let your grief guide you.

We need each other in times of grief. If you have one person who listens, who feels deeply with you, lets you know that you are not alone, consider yourself lucky. Grief can be isolating and often people are often shocked at how many friends and acquaintances turn away after a death. Grief is uncomfortable and sometimes the people you thought would be there for you quietly turn away and sneak off.

You may be surprised by who shows up for you—perhaps a colleague, neighbour, teammate, or distant friend will recognize something in you. They have been there too, in the lonely caverns of loss, and they understand the need of companionship in times of grief. Stay with your broken heart the best that you can and know that it is okay to take a break when you need to. Stay with your grief. Give it all the space it needs to express itself.

Chapter 12

As Your Person Journeys Ahead

I wish you grace, courage, and love as you companion. May this guide offer support as you walk alongside, shifting the focus from diminishment of death toward what cannot be taken; that is, the connection and love that we have for one another.

Birth and death, like an inhale and an exhale, are so intimately connected. When I was pregnant with my first child, I became startlingly aware of the influence our busy minds have over our wise bodies. I was filled with fear at the thought of giving birth. When I saw a pregnant woman—belly protruding, maybe a hand resting on top—I would become overwhelmed with empathy. How horrible. The idea of excruciating contractions forcing a baby out of a body—cursing, writhing, gnashing as labour plays out—what a nightmare.

The fear of giving birth consumed me until I changed my mind. In time, the story I held began to shift, and through the experience of giving birth to three babies, I came to trust that the body is designed to give birth. Pain was not an indication that something was wrong, it became a powerful signal from my body to bring my baby to me. No births are the same, and the same holds true for death. Just as with birth, we don't often see accurate images or hear stories that capture "normal" dying. Soap operas, movies, and news headlines offer sensationalized narratives embedded with fear. No wonder we are a death-phobic bunch; our dominant culture consistently perpetuates fear of death.

It's natural to cultivate our survival instinct, but the fear that many of us feel about dying is often irrational. It's shaped by cultural perspectives and the human mind. This fear can be harmful because it spreads through words and imagined futures that have no factual basis in the present moment.

The intention of this book is to prune the dead branches of limiting ideas, reduce fear, and plant seeds of inspiration, inviting people to meet death feeling more resourced and supported, allowing their curious and imaginative minds to remember and envision a different story. Setting out on the end-of-life journey can feel like an overwhelming place to be; my hope is that you find reassurance in knowing where to start. Take a breath and begin. Offer a hand on the back, a cup of tea, or sit in silence. With your presence and the intention of creating connection, awareness, meaning, pleasure, and presence—the little things aren't so little. Go slow as slow as you can, finding moments of stillness along the way, being in each moment as it unfolds.

I WONDER . . .

Death as part of life

What if we practiced loving all of life, its beginnings, its middle, and its ending too?

In my work of companioning the dying I am constantly reminded.

I am reminded that listening, offering our truest attention by witnessing, is love for ourselves and all beings—it is the salve for everything. I see you. I hear you. I feel you.

I am reminded of the lusciousness of slowing right down, of listening to the rhythm of the moment.

I am reminded that life is wild, we are wild, love is wild, grief is wild, death is wild.

I am reminded that we don't always need to be fixed or cleaned up or added to.

I am reminded of the importance of humility—to follow the lead of others especially when others are only whispering; to trust that I am worthy to step in and take the lead when it benefits others.

I am reminded to seek pleasure—just because and whenever possible.

I am reminded of our need for each other and how we ourselves are asked to soften our hearts, so that we can truly connect with others.

I am reminded of the importance of boundaries, calmly honouring the self with every action by simply asking, "Is this okay for me?"

I am reminded of the importance of being in my body, and entering through the gateways of the senses.

I am reminded of the importance of sitting with discomfort, making space for ourselves, and giving the same generous space to others—to our family, our friends, our communities, all humans—to all beings.

May we seek to nourish all relationships, understanding that being of service is as simple as listening deeply.

In the End

> *"When life feels too big to handle, go outside. Everything looks smaller when you're standing under the sky."*
>
> —L. R. Knost

Imagine death as part of an ecosystem. As we walk through a forest, the life cycles of the more-than-human beings are on display. Ancient trees lie fallen on the forest floor, providing sustenance for saplings, while other trees stand by as silent witnesses. This is evidence of the great cycle of birth, life, death, and rebirth, each stage perfectly designed to sustain one another. This cycle unfolds with the seasons: leaves fall in autumn, winter brings death and decay, and spring offers new life, coming to full bloom in summer. Yet much of human dying today has been strangely separated from these natural cycles. Death is often hidden away, behind closed doors. When a person dies, funeral home attendants typically whisk bodies away through back doors into cars in alleyways and our dead are returned to us as ash in sealed containers. Few realize the huge environmental cost of this process. But the tides are shifting, and we are exploring more life-affirming and generative forms of deathcare. In some places natural organic reduction allows for the legal disposition of a body through composting—returning our atoms to the earth to create and sustain future life. How beautiful it is to reclaim these life-giving narratives. This Indigenous worldview invites us to remember that we are no different from the more-than-human beings we share this planet with. It invites us to remember that we are nature.

Acknowledgements

It is a morning in late August. I am sitting on my back porch. A hummingbird is chattering, a black squirrel just ran under the deck, and chickadees are flitting about. The sky is slightly overcast and the touch of coolness of fall is making itself known to my bare feet. I hear crows in the distance. There is so much wonder on our doorstep if we choose to slow down and tune in. Being in nature is a homecoming; the natural world holds us so effortlessly. Connecting to our senses and simply being part of this world is enough.

I am grateful for the land and the more-than-human beings of this place where I live. The mountains, forests, and shores of the Salish Sea hold me completely and support me in so many ways, allowing me to return to myself; allowing me to offer all of who I am to my friends and family, and to those I serve. The land constantly reminds me of impermanence—the natural cycle of birth, life, death, and rebirth, leading me towards acceptance. While writing this book, it was the time spent on the trails deep in the forest behind my home that helped to reveal many of the insights shared in this guide. The beauty of this place continues to bring me pleasure daily.

I am grateful for my ancestors: my spiritual ancestors, my many guides, my blood and chosen-family ancestors, and the people who have trusted me to companion them in my role of end-of-life doula. Your lives and deaths continue to support me on this path.

I am grateful for my parents. I grew up in a medical family where it is was commonplace to talk about death and dying at the dinner table. My parents practiced frontier medicine in the late 1960s after graduating from university. Dad trained in medicine, and Mom in nursing. They lived in Haida Gwaii, an archipelago located off the northern Pacific coast of Canada, for many years, falling in love with the land and the people of the Haida Nation.

I am grateful for my late father, George. He was a deeply sensitive soul, modelling humility, service, and deep-rooted community care in his role as a general practitioner. My parents later moved to the North Shore of Vancouver where he served for decades in an old-school family practice, offering house calls and delivering babies. Near the end of his life, he was delivering the babies of babies he delivered. His humility was apparent by how he greeted his patients, offering a humble "How can I serve you today?" On the North Shore he cared for many of the Coast Salish Communities, holding a deep regard for their knowledge, wisdom, kindness, and generosity.

I am deeply grateful for my mom, Norma, who has an extraordinary capacity for unconditional love. She has held space for me always with her patience and incredible depth of presence. My mom continues to be my guide in this heart work. Her nursing knowledge and experience has also inspired me; I loved hearing her and Dad discuss cases at the dinner table, challenging each other with predictions of prognosis and outcomes.

I am so grateful for my husband, Don, who has led me to know love so completely. He inspires me daily to embrace joy and live life with passion. He has supported me completely on my journey to pursue end-of-life care; a path that isn't always easy in a culture where death and grief are considered taboo.

I am grateful for my three boys for guiding me to what is truly important and giving me so many opportunities to grow. My oldest son, Nicholas, consistently stirs me to seek truth, be kind, and find the fun. My middle son, Zander, who evokes my beginner's mind and inspires me to slow down and notice the wonder in details—he is curious about everything. My youngest, Christopher, has always seemed like the oldest of us all; he holds a grounded, calm presence, and a soulful wisdom, and serves as my anchor.

I am grateful for my stepsons, Hunter and Jack, who have expanded my understanding of love.

I am grateful for my dear friends Alex, Emily, Kat, Sheona, Steph, Tiffany, and Willow (listed in alphabetical order!). You have anchored me through life's ups and downs, and I am so grateful for the wisdom, laughter, and love that each of you offer.

I am grateful for the people who have guided me on this book project that wouldn't have been possible without your knowledge, expertise, and cheerleading. Thank you Alison, Charlie, Elizabeth, Sheona, Willow, and Tempo.

I am grateful for my friend Linda, my self-appointed coach and mentor.

I am grateful for Genevieve and Mo and their team at Pownal Street Press. How wonderful to be supported by these two who strike the perfect balance between head and heart. How wonderful to be supported by a women-led, grassroots, boutique Canadian publishing house.

About the Author

End-of-Life Doula Tracy Chalmers is the founder of Endwell and a facilitator at Douglas College, co-founder and grief educator and tender at The Grief Well, Certified Forest Therapy Guide, and Hospice Volunteer. She is grateful and humbled to be living on Coast Salish land known as the North Shore of Vancouver, in British Columbia. A friend to grief and death and servant to many, Tracy also considers herself a perpetual student. She is of Norwegian, Swedish, Scottish, and English ancestry, and values her roles as mother, daughter, wife, sister, friend, listener, and lover of the natural world and all of life. The work that Tracy does honors and is supported by countless ancestors.

About Endwell

Heart Center for Community End-of-Life Care

Since 2017, end-of life doula Tracy Chalmers has co-founded the End-of-Life Doula Association of Canada, founded Endwell, co-founded The Grief Well, served as a hospice volunteer and mentor, trained as a Forest Therapy guide, facilitated various training and community workshops through Endwell, written her first book, *The Nature of the Journey*, and facilitated the End-of-Life Doula Care program at Douglas College. The thousands of hours of facilitation with folks from all over the world has served as confirmation that more and more people are seeking an increased understanding of death and grief. Over the years, Tracy has won the hearts of many and earned loyal followers, partnerships, and clients who value her heart-centred and practical approach. She continues to create accessible and enriching offerings for all community members, the dying and their people, and end-of-life care practitioners. She is doing what she can to change the narrative around dying from one of avoidance and fear, to acceptance and love.

References and Works Cited

Angelou, M. (1994). *Wouldn't Take Nothing for My Journey Now*. Bantam.

Ardiel, E. L., & Rankin, C. H. (2010). The importance of touch in development. *Paediatrics & child health, 15*(3), 153–156. https://doi.org/10.1093/pch/15.3.153

Blundon, E.G., Gallagher, R.E. & Ward, L.M. (2020). Electrophysiological evidence of preserved hearing at the end of life. *Sci Rep* 10, 10336. https://doi.org/10.1038/s41598-020-67234-9

Boston, P. H., Cohen, S. R. & Mount, B. M. (2007). Healing Connections: On Moving from Suffering to a Sense of Well-Being. *Journal of Pain and Symptom Management, 33*(4), 372-388. https://doi.org/10.1016/j.jpainsymman.2006.09.014

Butler Bass, D. (2018). *Grateful: The Transformative Power of Giving Thanks*. HarperOne.

Cameron, J. (2021). *The Listening Path: The Creative Art of Attention*. Souvenir Press.

Cassell, E. J. (2012). *The Nature of Healing: The Modern Practice of Medicine*. Oxford University Press.

Causton, E. (2003). The Dance. In M. Cairns; M. Thompson; W. Wainwright (Eds.), *Transitions in Dying and Bereavement: A Psychosocial Guide for Hospice and Palliative Care*. Health Professions Press.

*Reproduced with permission from the author.

Chalmers, T. L. (2024). *Guided Meditations*. Endwell. https://www.endwell.ca/guidance

Clare, E. (n.d.). *What is death competency?* Center for Death Competency Development. Retrieved from https://deathcompetency.co.uk/what-is-death-competency%3F

Dass, R. & Bush, M. (2018). *Walking Each Other Home: Conversations on Loving and Dying*. Sounds True.

Doughty, C. (2017). *From Here to Eternity: Travelling the World to Find the Good Death*. WW Norton.

Ellison, K. P., & Weingast, M. (Eds.). (2016). *Awake at the Bedside: Contemplative Teachings on Palliative and End-of-Life Care*. Wisdom Publications.

Field, T. (2019). Social touch, CT touch and massage therapy: A narrative review. *Developmental Review. 51*. 123-145. 10.1016/j.dr.2019.01.002.

Field, T., Poling, S., Mines, S., Bendell, D., & Veazey, C. (2020). Touch Deprivation and Exercise During the COVID-19 Lockdown April 2020. *Medical Research Archives, 8*(8). doi:10.18103/mra.v8i8.2204

Gawande, A. (2017). *Being Mortal: Medicine and What Matters in the End*. Anchor Canada.

*Excerpts reproduced with permission from the publisher

Goldman, B. & Silk, S. (2013, April 7). How to not say the wrong thing. *Los Angeles Times*. Retrieved from https://www.latimes.com/opinion/story/la-timeless/how-not-to-say-the-wrong-thing

Grimes, R. L. (2002). *Deeply into the Bone: Re-Inventing Rites of Passage*. University of California Press.

Grollman, E. A. (2011). *Talking About Death: A Dialogue Between Parents and Children.* Beacon Press.

Jenkinson, S. (2015). *Die Wise: A Manifesto for Sanity and Soul.* North Atlantic Books.

Keppel, A. M. (2019, March 23). Get the psychopomp. *Medium.* https://annemariekeppel.medium.com/get-the-psychopomp-2b69abda22c9

Kim, H.-J., & Lee, K.-Y. (2016). Effects of Hand Massage on Depression, Self-esteem and Vitality of the Elderly Patients in Convalescent Hospital. *The Journal of Korean Academic Society of Nursing Education.* The Korean Academic Society of Nursing Education. https://doi.org/10.5977/jkasne.2016.22.2.202

Kuhl, D. (2003). *What Dying People Want: Practical Wisdom for the End of Life.* Anchor Canada.

Levine, S. (1998). *A Year to Live: How to Live This Year As If It Were Your Last.* Harmony.

Liu, F., Shen, C., Yao, L., & Li, Z. (2018). Acupoint Massage for Managing Cognitive Alterations in Older Adults: A Systematic Review and Meta-Analysis. *Journal of alternative and complementary medicine (New York, N.Y.), 24*(6), 532–540. https://doi.org/10.1089/acm.2017.0142

Miller, B.J. (2015, March). *What really matters at the end of life* [Video]. TED Conferences. https://www.ted.com/talks/bj_miller_what_really_matters_at_the_end_of_life

Morhenn, V., Beavin, L. E., & Zak, P. J. (2012). Massage increases oxytocin and reduces adrenocorticotropin hormone in humans. *Alternative therapies in health and medicine, 18*(6), 11–18.

Mount, B. M., Boston, P. H., & Cohen, S. R. (2007). Healing Connections: On Moving from Suffering to a Sense of Well-being. *Journal of Pain and Symptom Management, 33*(4), 372–388. https://doi.org/10.1016/j.jpainsymman.2006.09.014

Neff, K. (2025). *Self-compassion.* Retrieved from https://self-compassion.org/

Nepo, M. (2013). *Seven Thousand Ways to Listen: Staying Close to What is Sacred.* Atria Books.

Nhat Hanh, T. (1992). *Peace Is Every Step: The Path of Mindfulness in Everyday Life.* Random House Publishing Group.

Nowinski, J., & Okun, B. (2012). *Saying Goodbye: A Guide to Coping with a Loved One's Terminal Illness.* Berkley.

Orange, T. (2019). *There There.* McClelland & Stewart.

Patterson, O. (1982). *Slavery and Social Death: A Comparative Study.* Harvard University Press.

Pearson, J., Naselaris, T., Holmes, E. A., & Kosslyn, S. M. (2015). Mental Imagery: Functional Mechanisms and Clinical Applications. *Trends in cognitive sciences, 19*(10), 590–602. https://doi.org/10.1016/j.tics.2015.08.003

Richmond, C. (2005, July 23). Dame Cicely Saunders. *BMJ, 331*(7510), 238. https://doi.org/10.1136/bmj.331.7510.238

Saunders, C. (1983). *Living with Dying: The Management of Terminal Disease.* Oxford University Press.

Schildkret, D. (2022). *Hello, Goodbye: 75 Rituals for Times of Loss, Celebration, and Change.* Simon & Schuster.

Sen, Y. [End Well]. (2020, January 7). *Resonant Beauty | Yoko Sen* [Video]. Youtube. https://www.youtube.com/watch?v=x1M09p2mr18

Somé, M. P. (1997). *Ritual: Power, Healing and Community*. Penguin Publishing Group.

Stein, G. (2008). *The Art of Racing in the Rain*. Harper Collins.

Stein, S. B. (1983). *About Dying: An Open Family Book for Parents and Children Together*. Walker & Co.

Stroebe, M. (2018). The Poetry of Grief: Beyond Scientific Portrayal. *OMEGA - Journal of Death and Dying*, *78*(1), 67-96. https://doi.org/10.1177/0030222818792706

*Excerpt reprinted by permission of Sage Publications.

Suzuki, S. (1970). *Zen Mind, Beginner's Mind*. Weatherhill.

Tisdale, S. (2018). *Advice to Future Corpses (and Those Who Love Them): A Practical Perspective on Death and Dying*. Gallery Books.

*Fears of the Dying list was compiled through a variety of sources such as surveys, memoirs, academic work, and input from participants in the workshops that Sallie Tisdale teaches.

Van Hedger, S. C., Nusbaum, H. C., Clohisy, L., Jaeggi, S. M., Buschkuehl, M., & Berman, M. G. (2019). Of cricket chirps and car horns: The effect of nature sounds on cognitive performance. *Psychonomic bulletin & review*, *26*(2), 522–530. https://doi.org/10.3758/s13423-018-1539-1

Wagamese, R. (2016). *Embers: One Ojibway's Meditations*. Douglas & McIntyre.

Wall Kimmerer, R. (2013). *Braiding Sweetgrass: Indigenous Wisdom, Scientific Knowledge and the Teachings of Plants*. Milkweed Editions.

Wathola Trommer, R. (2024). "One Way She's Shaped Me". *A Hundred Falling Veils*.

https://ahundredfallingveils.com/2024/03/01/one-way-shes-shaped-me/

*Used with permission from the author.

Wathola Trommer, R. (2024). "Placing Attention". *A Hundred Falling Veils*. https://ahundredfallingveils.com/2024/11/13/placing-attention/

*Used with permission from the author.

Weller, F. (2015). *The Wild Edge of Sorrow: Rituals of Renewal and the Sacred Work of Grief*. North Atlantic Books.

Whyte, D. (2014). *Consolations: The Solace, Nourishment, and Underlying Meaning of Everyday Words*. Many Rivers Press.

*Reprinted with permission from David Whyte and Many Rivers Company, LLC, Langley, WA www.davidwhyte.com

Wolfelt, A. (2009). *The Handbook for Companioning the Mourner: Eleven Essential Principles*. Companion Press.

